FINALLY

·········· A <u>LOCALLY</u> PRODUCED ··········

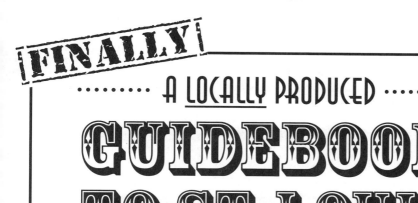

GUIDEBOOK TO ST. LOUIS

BY AND FOR ST. LOUISANS

NEIGHBORHOOD BY NEIGHBORHOOD

AMANDA E. DOYLE -WITH- KERRI BONASCH

REEDY PRESS
St. Louis, Missouri

Reedy Press
PO Box 5131
St. Louis, MO 63139, USA

Library of Congress Control Number: 2011938245

ISBN: 978-1-935806-07-3

Please note that websites, phone numbers, addresses, and company names are subject to change or cancellation. We did our best to relay the most accurate information available, but due to circumstances beyond our control, please do not hold us liable for misinformation. When exploring new neighborhoods or suburbs, please do your homework before you go.

Design by Jill Halpin
Map by Jill Halpin

Photography in the book provided by Kerri Bonasch, Samantha Couchoud, Amanda Doyle, Jill Halpin, Matt Heidenry, Don Korte, Library of Congress (110, 111), Brian Marston, Kris Rattini, and individual companies and institutions listed in the book. Thank you to everyone who assisted with the book's illustrations.

Please visit our website at www.reedypress.com.

For more information, upcoming author events and booksignings, and even more insider stuff from St. Louis neighborhoods, please visit www.STLGuidebook.com, and find us on Facebook and Twitter.

Printed in the United States of America
11 12 13 14 15   5 4 3 2 1

CONTENTS

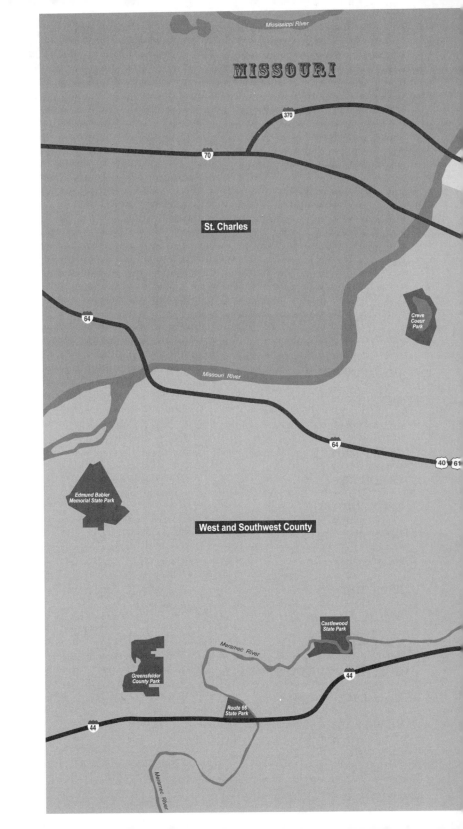

FOREWORD

Beer! Baseball! Blues! Bricks! St. Louis may be renowned for many things, but its heart is in its neighborhoods. The dynamic history and current vitality of the region are reflected in these colorful enclaves, and perhaps no better example of this exists than in my home neighborhood of the Delmar Loop.

In 1972 I opened Blueberry Hill, a restaurant and music club, in the Delmar Loop. For decades, The Loop had been a high fashion shopping district built up around a streetcar system, but the trolleys stopped running in the 1960s and the area was in decline like many areas of its kind around the country. I hoped that by programming the jukebox with an ever-changing selection of great tunes and displaying my collections of pop-culture memorabilia that visitors would feel comfortable and enjoy the atmosphere as much as the food and drinks. What started out as two storefronts is now a St. Louis landmark that electrifies the whole block.

The groundwork for the gradual turnaround of The Loop was laid in the early 1970s with legislation that limited occupancy of first-floor storefronts to retail shops, galleries, and restaurants to attract more pedestrians. Sidewalks were widened to encourage outside cafes. Blueberry Hill became the first of a new era of unique owner-operated businesses.

In 1980 several businesses formed a committee to address challenges regarding lighting and cleanliness, and to create special events. In 1988 I founded the not-for-profit St. Louis Walk of Fame as a unifying educational attraction for the area. Now more than 130 stars and informative plaques are embedded in the sidewalks providing an illuminating and engaging self-tour to pedestrians.

During the 1990s the Delmar Loop MetroLink stop opened, allowing visitors to take a clean, quick light-rail train right to The Loop and begin their visit by walking west. The once-elegant Tivoli movie theatre was beautifully restored, and many new gift shops, clothing boutiques, and restaurants with a wide variety of cuisines opened. Expansion continued in the 2000s with the grand opening of The Pageant, a 2000+ capacity concert nightclub that has featured a myriad of artists such as Bob Dylan, Green Day, Dolly Parton, and Nelly. The Loop now has ten stages on which visitors can enjoy music of all genres.

Exciting new attractions include The Loop Planet Walk (along which one can take a three-billion-mile walk across a scale model of the solar system), an eight-foot bronze statue of Rock & Roll Hall of Fame legend Chuck Berry, and the Centennial Greenway Bicycle Path. In 2013, streetcars will return to the area: As new fixed-track historic trolley system will connect The Loop with two MetroLink stations and Forest Park attractions.

This capsulized history of The Loop shows some of the involvement I've had in helping revitalize an historic street along with the intense dedication of countless other people, culminating in the Delmar Loop being designated "One of the 10 Great Streets in America" by the American Planning Association. The importance of such unique neighborhoods in St. Louis cannot be overstated. Other local areas are also experiencing rebirth as each community builds on its distinct characteristics.

Some of our wonderfully novel or ethnic areas are located downtown, others in Midtown, South City, North City, and the county. All of these elements are critical because they add to the quality of life for those who live across the metropolitan area, and they add to the quality of the travel experience for visitors as they discover various neighborhoods' warmth and charm. I hope you enjoy these pockets of culture, the corner bars, churches, parks, arts centers, universities, confectionaries, antique stores, historic buildings, boutiques, and more.

In this guidebook, you'll find many must-see places that make our city like no other. Amanda Doyle has taken the insider approach in the pages of this book by digging up the hidden treasures in dozens of neighborhoods across the area and providing the kind of tour recommendations you'd hope to get from a good friend. When I have friends visit St. Louis, or touring musicians perform at Blueberry Hill or The Pageant, I often recommend they check out the Museum of Transportation, get engrossed in the ever-changing exhibits at the Missouri History Museum, or make a day of exploring Washington Avenue by having lunch at Mosaic, crawling all over the City Museum, and then ending up at Flamingo Bowl for cocktails and a few frames. Of course, we have an excellent live music scene: Two of my favorite venues are Off Broadway and, for live local music almost every night, BB's Jazz, Blues & Soups. And I always remind them as they visit different neighborhoods to marvel at the distinctive architecture.

The more you get into our local scene, the more I think you'll see what I see—St. Louis is a wonderful patchwork of old and new, of classical styles and whimsical styles. It's a city with a rich heritage of music and arts in general. It's a city of exciting sports and entertainment. It's as good a restaurant city as any in the United States. It's a fascinating city to explore, whether you've lived here since birth or made it your home last week. Maybe I'll run into you soon, checking out some of the spots in these pages.

—Joe Edwards

PREFACE

This is a love letter to St. Louis, one I've been working on now for more than a decade.

When I moved here in 1997, newly married to an almost-native, I remember distinctly that we drove from our apartment in Lafayette Square to Creve Coeur (where my husband grew up) to buy batteries, because we didn't know any better and were unsure of our local options. My, how the times have changed . . . I didn't know then what I know now, that we live in one of America's great cities, that neighborhoods from west to east are teeming with activity, hotspots, and hidden gems. A year later, my horizons had been broadened to the point that, when a tall, thin gentleman wearing nothing but briefs, boots, and a cowboy hat loped across the street at Spring and Juniata while we were house-hunting, I turned to my husband and said, "Oh, yeah, now this is what I'm talking about!" That, and the proximity of MoKaBe's coffeehouse and Tower Grove Park, were deal-closers. That may not be your particular cup of tea, but luckily, there's probably a pocket of town that's perfectly aligned with your vibe, too.

What you'll find in these pages is a unique take on the elements that make many of the pockets of this metropolitan area such an appealing one in which to live. If you came to my house on a Saturday morning, I'd want to take you to the farmers' market, then hit the coffeeshop, walk the shops and restaurants of South Grand and Morgan Ford, and maybe get in the car to go check out an art show on Cherokee. What would you want to show off in your neck of the woods? This book began as that conversation, and I hope you'll find some of your favorites in its pages, but even more, I hope you'll find places you didn't even know were here. Neighborhoods and municipalities are grouped (and named) here in ways that may be a bit different than you're used to seeing, in the hope of reflecting how we actually talk about them. Information in each chapter may be arranged slightly differently, according to the most important features in each area. National chains have been largely avoided, because they usually have less influence on the character of a place than the one-offs and the independents. And good gracious, this book is by no means an attempt to be comprehensive in its scope. How could it be? Instead, take our suggestions as a starting point for your own further explorations.

The good and the bad of living in a thriving metropolis is the constant of change. Let's just assume up front that something in these pages (perhaps several somethings!) will have opened, closed, or otherwise morphed in the time since I wrote; while we've done our best to make sure all information is current and accurate, *Things Change*, and it's always worth a phone call to make sure you know what you're getting into. Have fun, and viva St. Louis!

—Amanda E. Doyle, August 2011

x

ACKNOWLEDGMENTS

The powers-that-be at Reedy Press—a.k.a. Matt and Josh—had a vision for this book that made it easy to sign on enthusiastically, and their support, suggestions, and tolerance of a sliding editorial schedule is here, gratefully, acknowledged by me. Their wisdom in pairing me with Kerri Bonasch, who did Herculean work on the neighborhood histories and several chapters, will become evident as you read. Thanks also to Don Korte for his attention to the details!

For a special recognition, I'd like to acknowledge the role in my life in St. Louis of two organizations, Metropolis St. Louis and The Commonspace, that provided me an introduction to many of the spots I still love, and some of this town's most interesting folks, whom I am still proud to call friends. My day job, at *Where Magazine*, has given me a unique perspective on our city, and a soapbox from which to propagandize it shamelessly; my colleagues there, past and present, make it fun to go to work. Thanks to Joe Edwards for agreeing to write a foreword—his work, and the tireless efforts of like-minded folks, is inspiring to me.

Finally, my thanks and affection go out to so many family members and friends, both here in St. Louis and points farther afield, who showed me to get out and get involved in a place. My mom and dad taught me to bloom where I was planted (even if they wish my roots had taken hold in a less-northerly spot!); my maternal grandmother and godmother taught me to always be looking forward to the next adventure; and my aunts and two dear cousins have been my lifelong companions in exploration. Friends far and near remind me daily that it's just geography, that the essential bonds we share take no heed of ZIP code or time zone. But the joys and rhythm of daily discoveries, with my husband Brian Marston and our son Milo, couldn't be better met by any place than here.

TOP SEVEN THINGS THAT AREN'T IN THIS BOOK

Before we get to the Neighborhoods You Should Know, a roundup of a different sort: St. Louis Stuff I Love That's Not Confined to a Single Neighborhood. Sounds like my next book project...but in the meantime, briefly and in no special order:

1. Eyez. We're blessed with many talented and visible artists in all media in St. Louis, but Peat Wolleager and his ubiquitous Eyez are among my favorites. Eyez on the street, isn't that something every city needs? Keep your eyes open for his. (Fun fact: My son learned at age two to ID these, and say Peat's name, on our morning daycare commute.)

2. The Happy Lady. She smiles broadly, she waves, she dances and sings loudly along with whatever's pumping through her headphones, and you just can't help but smile back. Formerly a regular at the corner of Chouteau and

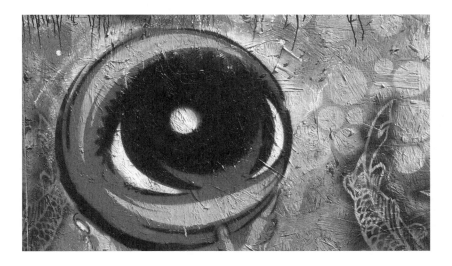

Grand (pre-construction), The Lady Also Known As Erica McElrath can be spotted at Forest Park and Vandeventer and plenty of other intersections.

3. Citywide Open Studios. A free, weeklong celebration of the working artists of our town, with more than 150 creators in all kinds of media and genres throwing open the doors of their workspaces for the public to come in, experience art, ask questions about the creative process, artistic life in St. Louis, and more. Contemporary Art Museum-St. Louis sponsors the event.

4. Kick Ass Awards. In its eighth year of celebrating St. Louis's "unsung heroes, muses and gadflies," a scrappy, ad-hoc meeting of the minds serves as a kind of MacArthur genius committee, writ small: no formal application, as such; no required letters of recommendation; no public comment period. There's no way to ensure you'll get the coveted Kick Ass trophy, other than just to keep on doing your thing to the best of your ability. The free awards ceremony, held each fall, is a hoot and a half.

5. KDHX. They say it often during pledge drives, but it bears repeating here: Not every city has a diverse, independent, non-commercial community radio station like KDHX-88.1 on the FM dial. (Full disclosure: I have been a programmer there in a past life.) When everything from funk to swamp rock to Mongolian yodeling to indie rock, with an extra helping of several local talk shows on topics from the environment to theatre, pours into your ears, you are bound to learn something new whenever you tune in. If you have or know or were once a child, may I offer a special nod to Saturday morning's "Musical Merry-Go-Round" program? It's smart, soulful music that kids and their grownups will enjoy together, and a civic treasure.

6. Driving Broadway. OK, this one is totally stolen from my husband, but it's so good I couldn't resist. He's convinced that by starting out at one endpoint of Broadway, and making a leisurely drive down (or up) to the other, you can experience a microcosm of St. Louis. The river, light industry, countless corner bars, churches, abandonment, homes, commerce, tattoo parlors, and really, life's rich pageant are yours, all along one single St. Louis street. (Hint: doesn't have to be Broadway: metro-straddlers like Gravois, Olive, and many others are good for this kind of hometown tourism, too.)

7. Limitless Potential. St. Louis is a place where it's relatively easy to make a big splash, for doing even a small thing. Enjoy the benefits of the (sometimes)-sleepy midwestern milieu and do something! Seriously. You'll probably make the news. You might make a million bucks. You will for sure make people who like to write about St. Louis Awesomeness quite happy.

DOWNTOWN & NEAR NORTH

DOWNTOWN ★ HYDE PARK ★ OLD NORTH ST. LOUIS ★ ST. LOUIS PLACE

HISTORY

The portal to past and present St. Louis begins at the world-famous St. Louis Gateway Arch and its underground Museum of Westward Expansion. In 1764, Laclede's Village, which would become St. Louis, was established on the Arch Grounds. Two more legacies of the past are nearby: the Old Cathedral and the Old Courthouse, site of the Dred Scott case. Revel in the present at Busch Stadium—a.k.a. Baseball Heaven—and don't miss the City Museum and its MonstroCity, a monumental montage of monkey bars masquerading as airplane fuselages, a fire truck, and a castle turret. Vintage architectural gems have found a place in the present as urban lofts and condominiums, trendy boutiques, restaurants, and clubs. Downtown living offers a walkable quality of life which has brought an influx of residents into the neighborhood.

OLD NORTH ST. LOUIS

Crown Candy Kitchen has been serving St. Louisans in Old North St. Louis since 1913. Lines form out the door for the handcrafted Christmas and Easter candy. Their ice cream is created and blended on site in an antique copper candy kettle. Try a World's Fair sundae or make it a Newport with whipped cream and pecans.

North City experienced population and ethnic changes beginning in the 1950s. After a period of disinvestment, revitalization returned. Today you will see rehabilitated historic homes in harmony with newer homes built in keeping with the neighborhood's character. The Old North Coop and the 13th Street Community Garden next door promote sustainable farming practices. You'll find straight-from-the-garden produce in season between April and November at the Old North Coop. Crown Square, the revitalized and reopened 14th Street

Mall, joins its neighbor, Crown Candy, as a classic example of melding old and new. Affectionately dubbed "Old North" by residents, this urban village is truly one to watch as an up-and-coming area.

HYDE PARK

The German-speaking enclave of New Bremen joined the city of St. Louis in 1855 and became known as Hyde Park. Designated as a local historic district, Hyde Park is architecturally rich. The Bissell Mansion, built in 1823, is one of the oldest homes in St. Louis. Nearby, both the Grand and Bissell Point Water Towers, along with Holy Trinity Catholic Church, continue to withstand the tests and challenges of time.

ST. LOUIS PLACE

Also designated an historic district, St. Louis Place is finally beginning to receive some well-deserved TLC. Columbia Brewery, former producer of once-local favorite Alpenbrau, has found new life as the Brewery Apartments. There are other historically significant buildings, such as Zion Lutheran and St. Liborius, still waiting for redemption. Plans are underway for the rehabilitation of the 140-year-old Clemens House, once owned by a close relative of Samuel Clemens (Mark Twain). The famed author spent time here in his early days. The Clemens home has become the poster child of decay of St. Louis's North Side region.

DOWNTOWN

There's more than just the Gateway Arch in Downtown. There is a wealth of history, hipness, and fun that awaits visitors. City Hall was architecturally inspired by Hotel de Ville, Paris's City Hall; the Civil Courts Building was inspired by the Mausoleum of Maussollos; and the fortress-like Old Post Office is a must-see. These are just a few of the dozens of Downtown's historic landmarks. For cyclists there's the Riverfront Trail, which takes bikers on an eleven-mile trek along the Mississippi. Citygarden is a recent and successful Downtown addition. Hailed as a national design model, Citygarden is a favorite spot for workers and tourists alike, with its lush landscape and internationally renowned sculpture. Washington Avenue is filled with street cafes, nightlife, and cool lofts. Holidays like Thanksgiving, St. Patrick's, and the Fourth of July bring some of the best parades around—marching bands, floats, and balloons, which rival anything you'll see at the Macy's Parade. St. Louis Rams football plays at the Edward Jones Dome. St. Louis Blues hockey fans "bleed blue" in season, at the Scottrade Center. One word that definitely describes the energy in Downtown is *progress*.

FOOD AND DRINK

From haute cuisine to tourist traps, you'll find it all Downtown; some spots cater to office workers (read here: roll up the sidewalks at 5 and on weekends), but a burgeoning full-time population has brought more and better restaurants than ever back to the core. Up North, a handful of favorites draw from their immediate neighborhoods and way beyond.

A BITE TO EAT

400 OLIVE
400 Olive St.
314-554-7098
400olive.com
Contemporary American
in historic room

AL'S
1200 N. 1st St.
314-421-6399
alsrestaurant.net
Old-school steakhouse

BROADWAY OYSTER BAR
736 S. Broadway
314-621-8811
broadwayoysterbar.com
N'awlins come north,
crawfish, gumbo, and all

CARMINE'S
20 S. 4th St.
314-241-1631
lombardosrestaurants.
com
Contemporary Italian
steakhouse

CHARLIE GITTO'S
207 N. 6th St.
314-436-2828
charliegittosdowntown.com
Classic Italian stalwart

CLARK STREET GRILL
811 Spruce St.
314-552-5850
clarkstreetgrill.com
Contemporary
American cuisine

{ HIGHER POWER LUNCH }

Rub shoulders with politicos and parishoners, plus hungry downtowners, at **St. Raymond's Maronite Cathedral**'s regular Wednesday cafeteria-line lunch of homemade Lebanese food. Kibbe, spinach pies, chicken and dumplings, and lentils and rice are on the menu; baklava and, for the hard-boiled, Lebanese coffee (think motor oil) for dessert. Mayor Slay is among the regulars here (931 Lebanon Dr., 314-621-0056, straymonds.net).

{ KIDZONE }

Crown Candy Kitchen (1401 St. Louis Ave., 314-621-9650, crowncandykitchen.net) will charm every generation in your party, but kids especially will enjoy the throwback soda fountain that packs 'em in for egg salad sandwiches, heart-stoppingly large BLTs, chili dogs, and oh, yes, handmade chocolates, candies, and ice cream concoctions. Small booths mean families are gonna get squished together, but that makes sharing a chocolate malt that much easier! Bring change for the jukebox to pass the time if there's a wait.

THE DRUNKEN FISH
612 N. 2nd St.
314-241-9595
drunkenfish.com
Sushi and Japanese
cuisine

EAT RITE DINER
622 Chouteau Ave.
314-621-9621
Greasy menu, semi-
greasy ambience, the
slinger is king

GELATERIA TAVOLINI
1327 Washington Ave.
314-621-8838
gelateriatavolini.com
Gelato and coffee drinks

**LOMBARDO'S
TRATTORIA**
201 S. 20th
(in the Drury Inn)
314-621-0666
lombardosrestaurants.com
Fancy Italian standards;
great homemade toasted
ravioli

LONDON TEA ROOM
1520 Washington Ave.
314-241-6556
thelondontearoom.com
Brit-tastic pastries, teas,
quiche, sandwiches,
and high tea

LUCAS PARK GRILLE
1234 Washington Ave.
314-241-7770
lucasparkgrille.com
Modern American cuisine,
great patio

MANGO
1101 Lucas Ave.
314-621-9993
mangoperu.com
Peruvian cuisine with an
elegant touch

MARSHA'S, LTD.
3501 Kossuth Ave.
314-371-0188
Soul food upstairs
(bar downstairs)

MAURIZIO'S PIZZA & PASTA BOWL
1107 Olive St.
314-621-1997
maurizios.com
Pizza, pasta, and a buffet til 3 a.m.

MOSAIC
1001 Washington Ave.
314-621-6001
mosaictapas.com
Multi-culti tapas

ROOSTER
1104 Locust St.
314-241-8118
roosterstl.com
Crepes, sandwiches, breakfast

SEN THAI
1221 Locust St., #104
314-436-3456
senthaibistro.com
Thai cuisine

SMOKING JOE'S
1901 Washington Ave.
314-436-3876
smokingjoesbbq.com
BBQ pulled pork, brisket, ribs, & sides

THE TAP ROOM
2100 Locust St.
314-241-BEER
schlafly.com
Microbrewery for Schlafly beer, pub grub with loca-vore leanings

TONY'S
410 Market St.
314-231-7007
saucecafe.com/tonys
Bucket-list gourmet Italian

WASABI
1228 Washington Ave.
314-421-3500
wasabistl.com
Sushi and Japanese cuisine

WASHINGTON AVENUE POST
1315 Washington Ave.
314-588-0545
washingtonavepost.com
Deli and coffee, smoothie bar

1982 WORLD SERIES
St. Louis Cardinals
GO RED BIRDS!
WORLD SERIES FEVER

{SPORT SET}

Soak in Cardinals team spirit in memorabilia-laden dining rooms **Mike Shannon's** (fancy, glassed-in steak and seafood house; 620 Market St., 314-421-1540, shannonsteak.com) and **Joe Buck's** (casually hip spot great for pre-game eats, 1000 Clark Ave., 314-436-0394, jbucks.com).

{ HOLY GROUND }

The spotlight (and news camera) has been trained often on the parish of **St. Stanislaus Kostka** (1413 N. 20th St., 314-421-5948, www. stanislauskostka.com), just below Cass Ave. in North St. Louis. Much of the recent attention has focused on the church's separation from the archdiocese (due to disputes over property rights, finances, lay control, and especially the controversial leadership and vision of its pastor, Marek Bozek), but the church has soldiered on, with an influx of new congregants replacing some of the disgruntled who've departed. Historically designated the city's Polish parish, the church continues to offer a weekly Polish mass (Su at 11 a.m.) and annual Polka Mass/Fall Festival.

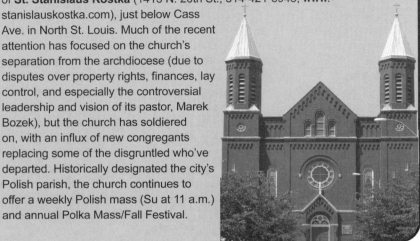

{ ROOMS WITH A VIEW }

Need to be inspired by the skyline or cultural amenities of our fair city? Book a table, sit back, and enjoy the panorama before you at **Top of the Riverfront** (revolving restaurant atop 200 S. 4th St., 314-241-3191, millenniumhotels.com/millenniumstlouis); **Harry's** (popular patio facing downtown, 2144 Market St., 314-421-6969, harrysrestaurantandbar.com); **Point of View** (atop Laclede Gas Building, 720 Olive, 314-421-5941); **Cielo** (Archside on the 8th floor of the **Four Seasons Hotel**; 999 North 2nd Street, 314-881-5800); **Kemoll's** (40th floor of Met Square, kemolls. com, 314-421-0555); and **Terrace View** (perched astride Citygarden, 808 Chestnut St., 314-436-8855, fialafood.com); and **Three Sixty** (just named one of the top new hotel rooftop bars in the world by Frommer's, atop Hilton at the Ballpark, One S. Broadway, 314-241-8439, 360-stl.com).

{ FOODIE FINDS }

Several spots, ranging from haute to homely, deal in gourmet goodies for your next dinner party. **Culinaria** (a fancy name for a boutique Schnucks grocery) has grocery staples plus their own line of pastas & sauces, and a nicely stocked upstairs wine department (315 N. 9th St., 314-436-7694, culinariaschnucks.com); **Bussone's** (1011 Olive St., 314-241-1083) keeps a decent selection of beer, wine, and spirits on-hand in its grungy digs. **Grande Petite Market**'s (2017 Chouteau Ave., 314-241-7799, grandpetitemarket.com) inventory is a bit more expansive, covering spices, wines, olives, vinegars, rubs and dips, plus fine cookware, kitchen linens, and gadgetry. Hit **Piekutowski's** (4100 N. Florissant Ave., 314-534-6256) for an old-school butcher shop experience, where the fresh Polish sausage, kielbasa, brats, and pickles were sought out by Pope John Paul II on his 1999 visit to the city.

SOMETHING TO DRINK

BEALE ON BROADWAY
701 S. Broadway
314-621-7880
bealonbroadway.com
Live blues nightly from local & national
luminaries, til 3 a.m.

BIG DADDY'S - LANDING
118 Morgan St.
314-621-6700
bigdaddystl.com
Hot-girl bartenders & drinking games

BRIDGE TAP HOUSE & WINE BAR
1004 Locust St.
314-241-8141
thebridgestl.com
Vast and worldly selection by tap,
bottle, and glass

COPIA URBAN WINERY & MARKET
1122 Washington Ave.
314-241-9463
copiaurbanwinery.com
Pretty patio, pretty people

DUBLINER PUB
1025 Washington Ave.
314-421-4300
dublinerstl.com
Pints and pub ambiance

LOLA
500 N. 14th St.
314-621-7277
welovelola.com
Ambitious cocktails and absinthe bar

MANDINA'S SPORTS BAR
1319 St. Louis Ave.
314-588-7149
mandinasbar.com
Low-key neighborhood spot

MISSOURI BAR & GRILLE
701 N. Tucker
314-231-2234
Basic beer & mixed drinks with
the non-hipster crowd; former hangout
for newspapermen

MORGAN STREET BREWERY
721 N. 2nd St.
314-231-9970
morganstreetbrewery.com
Microbrewer of award-winning varieties

OVERUNDER BAR & GRILL
911 Washington Ave.
314-621-8881
overunderstl.com
Upscale sports bar

THE PEPPER LOUNGE
2005 Locust St.
314-241-2005
thepepperlounge.com
Tiki and 'tinis in true loungey atmosphere

THE POUR HOUSE
1933 Washington Ave.
314-241-5999
stlpourhouse.com
Games, karaoke, drinks, grub

RUE 13
1311 Washington Ave.
314-588-7070
rue13stl.com
Sushi, dancing, mixed drinks

SHIVER
1130 Washington Ave.
314-241-3900
shivervodkabar.com
Ice-themed vodka bar

SIDEBAR
1317 Washington Ave.
314-621-7376
Handsome wooden bar,
good basics (food & drink)

THAXTON SPEAKEASY
1009 Olive St.
314-241-3279
thaxtonspeakeasy.com
F & Sa only, utter the password
(found on the website) and gain
access to "Art Deco meets the DJ"

TIN CAN TAVERN
1909 Locust Ave.
314-241-9330
tincantavern.com
Canned beers you forgot existed

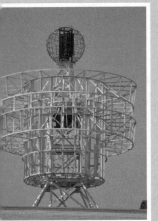

{ ARCHITECTURAL ODDITY }

What is that odd ball atop the glazed white **Terra Cotta Lofts** (at 15th & Locust streets)? Take off your tinfoil hat and relax: the Weather Ball started its life as a clever advertising gimmick. The General American Life Insurance Company that called the building home in the early decades of the 1900s built the eight-foot-diameter ball in 1956 and installed it on a 50-foot rotating tower, utilizing a color-coded lighting system to alert folks as far as 10 miles away as to the weather forecast for the immediate future. Didn't hurt, of course, that when the meteorologically curious took an upward glance, the company's logo, in 20-foot neon letters, was in the line of sight, too.

RECREATION

Downtown St. Louis serves, naturally, as the public face of our town, both to ourselves and to the larger world. It's only fitting, then, that many of the longest-running parades, festivals, and civic celebrations have their home here. Additionally, the influx of residents in recent years has significantly increased feet on the streets, and both attention and investment in amenities (witness the newest, Citygarden) have followed. Former mayor Clarence Harmon used to say that he would know that Downtown had turned a corner when he saw "people walking their dogs on Downtown streets at any hour of day or night"; his dream has come true, and thanks to the law of unintended consequences, copious canine companions recently required a campaign to remind downtowners to pick up the resulting poop.

The near North Side neighborhoods, within sight of the Gateway Arch, have to some extent fallen prey to decades of disinvestment and disintegration of social capital—they don't house the same density of population or businesses as many of their South Side counterparts. Still, for those willing to look beyond the surface, the architecture and community resources (like parks, elite residential streets, and churches) are worth discovering, and pockets of interesting neighborhoods, restaurants, bars, and shops hold some treasures.

FESTIVITIES

ANNIE MALONE MAY DAY PARADE
Mid-May
Marching bands, floats, drill teams, and tricked-out cars compete in this annual fundraiser for a longstanding children's charity founded by a female African-American entrepreneur from the early 1900s

BIG MUDDY BLUES FESTIVAL
Labor Day weekend
Free, family-friendly outdoor music festival attracts big-name and up-and-coming blues, soul, and R&B acts.

CARDINALS OPENING DAY
Early April
A street party attended by hooky-playing office workers and schoolkids alike, with music, contests, and a lot of red

CELEBRATE ST. LOUIS CONCERTS
Fridays and Saturdays throughout the summer
Big national musical acts (often with homegrown openers) play for free at the Soldiers Memorial.

DR. MARTIN LUTHER KING JR., HOLIDAY CELEBRATION

On the Monday holiday
A program at the Old Courthouse and a chilly but uplifting march through Downtown to Powell Hall

FAIR ST. LOUIS VEILED PROPHET PARADE

Weekend prior to July 4
Free lineup of concerts, airshows, and fireworks under the Gateway Arch; VP Parade is among the nation's oldest continuous parades, at 130+ years, and has the distinction of having been dreamt up by a group of businessmen in 1878 who imagined that the appearance of a mysterious "Veiled Prophet" could capture the public's imagination.

FAT TUESDAY PARADE

Saturday prior to Ash Wendesday
Official end of Mardi Gras season lights up the night streets of Downtown

HOLIDAY MAGIC

December
In the dead of winter, this gathering of shopping, carnival rides, ice-skating, and holiday music (plus indoor beer/wine garden!) promises families a reprieve from cabin fever. Inside the confines of America's Center, at 8th & Washington.

LABOR DAY PARADE

On the Monday holiday
Need a reminder of the role of union organizing in our Midwestern burg? Workingmen and women march, wave, and ride in comically small cars to show strength in numbers.

MOONLIGHT RAMBLE

August
Leisurely nighttime bicycle ride draws cyclists of all ages for fun & games, then a midnight kickoff for cruising the streets of Downtown and beyond with tens of thousands of compatriots, all to raise money for the Gateway Chapter of Hostelling International.

POLISH FESTIVAL

September
Polish pride (and food, beer, music, and polka dancing!) abounds at this annual celebration, with newcomers welcome among those who've attended for generations; inside and on grounds of the Polish Falcons Nest 45, 2013 St. Louis Ave.

RIB AMERICA

Memorial Day weekend
An unholy alliance of meat and music that only the USA could conceive; award-winning BBQ is prime, the performing artists often are just past

ST. PATRICK'S DAY PARADE

Saturday prior to St. Patrick's Day
When all of St. Louis is Irish and green

SAINT LOUIS BLUES WEEK

End of August, beginning of September
A newcomer event promising annual concerts, workshops, parties, awards, also inaugurating a Blues Hall of Fame and Blues Trail markers throughout the city.

THANKSGIVING DAY PARADE

November
Giant balloons, floats, and holiday cheer—plus the arrival of the Man in Red himself.

A civic success story, **Citygarden** (801 Market St., citygardenstl.org) has garnered international attention and acclaim since it opened in 2009; national art publications fawn over the world-class sculptures amassed on the two-square-block site, and locals love the unprecedented access—the public's thus far been allowed to touch, climb on, swim in, and generally interact with the art, landscaping, and water features. St. Louisans' propensity to treat it as their own backyard swimming pool can lead to some odd encounters between well-heeled patrons of the restaurant and bikini-clad tweens, but isn't that what urban spaces are supposed to foster?

{ GET LOW }

Underneath a curved, silver riverfront landmark, the **Museum of Westward Expansion** (200 Washington Ave., 314-655-1700, gatewayarch.com/Arch/info/act.museum.aspx) often gets treated as just "the place you have to kill time while you wait for your Arch ride," but its meticulous documentation of the history, from geologic to cultural, of our region deserves a thorough look. Kids love the shaggy stuffed buffalo and an authentic native tipi, and the photo-illustrated excerpts from the journals of the Lewis & Clark expedition are riveting.

EXERCISE

FLAMINGO BOWL
1117 Washington Ave.
314-436-6666
flamingobowl.net
Roll a few frames & toss back a
Mai Tai on 12 lanes

RIVERFRONT TRAIL
Eleven paved miles for your cycling/
running/walking/equestrian pleasure,
along the Mississippi River, including
some amazing juxtapositions of the wild
and the urban; easily accessed from the
Laclede Power Center from the south
or the Old Chain of Rocks Bridge to
the north

UPPER LIMITS
ROCK CLIMBING GYM
326 S. 21st St.
314-241-7625
upperlimits.com
Quit bitching about our lack of an ocean
or mountains, and instead take out your
frustrations on the 10,000 square feet
of climbable sculpted surface in this
downtown gym. Equipment rentals and
lessons make it easy to get started

ARTS, ENTERTAINMENT, & EDUCATION

ART ST. LOUIS
555 Washington Ave., #150
314-241-4810
artstlouis.org
Regional promoter of visual arts
mounts great group shows at its
downtown gallery space

BB'S JAZZ, BLUES, AND SOUPS
700 S. Broadway
314-436-5222
bbsjazzbluessoups.com
Sip and sup to live music

CITY MUSEUM
701 N. 15th Street St.
314-231-CITY
citymuseum.org
If Willie Wonka dropped acid, inherited a
former factory building, and designed a
fantastical playscape for kids and adults,
well...it couldn't compare to this. Highlights
include the architectural museum, resident
circus, and everything on the building's roof

{ PEDALS OF STEEL }

Wander into the lower level of the Millennium Hotel during Labor Day weekend
and you'll find yourself in the middle of a worldwide tourist attraction that few
locals have heard of or seen. The **International Steel Guitar Convention**
(200 S. 4th St., scottysmusic.com) draws thousands for workshops and
performances, while its flagship **Hall of Fame** project honors the greats of
the instrument from the first inductee, Jerry Byrd (1978), to country superstar
Barbara Mandrell (2009), with relief-cast biographical plaques.

GRIOT MUSEUM
2505 St. Louis Ave.
314-241-7057
thegriotmuseum.com
Small but serious collection of artifacts
and wax figurines of important African-
American historical figures, all with ties to
St. Louis, make for an eye-opening afternoon of racial and social history lessons

PHILIP SLEIN GALLERY
1319 Washington Ave.
314-621-4634
philipsleingallery.com
Contemporary gallery has a soft spot for
edgy underground art, à la Art Chantry,
R. Crumb, and Tom Huck

SHOPPORTUNITIES

AIA BOOKSTORE
911 Washington Ave. #100
314-231-4252
aia-stlouis.org
Architecture-themed books, toys, and gifts

CITY PET SUPPLY
210 N. 9th St.
314-436-9581
citypetsupply.net
Toys, food, and gear for Fido & Fluffy,
Fin & Ferret

ENGLISH LIVING
1520 Washington Ave.
314-241-6226
englishliving.com
Big, gorgeous furniture and homegoods
for classicists

LEFT BANK BOOKS
321 N. 10th St.
314-436-3049
left-bank.com
Second location for indy
full-service bookstore

{ WEAR IT WELL }

No longer a working garment district, Downtown's nonetheless still got a few tricks
up its stylish sleeves. A must-stop is **Levine Hats** (1416 Washington Ave., 314-
231-3359, levinehat.com), making heads dapper for more than a century: stellar
service and advice, and some of the most fun you can have in a store, with a wide
range (race, age, and hat preference) of customers. Inside City Museum at the
Shoelace Factory (701 N. 15th St., 314-621-9633, shoelacefactory.com), they're
cranking out colorful shoelaces in homage to the building's former life as a shoe
factory; upstairs (4th Floor), **The Bale Out** (701 N. 15th St., 314-258-3644, theba-
leout.com) has cheap and browse-worth vintage for men and women. And beneath
it all, make sure you're looking good, with undies and lingerie for guys and gals,
from **Beverly's Hill** (1309 Washington Ave., 314-621-1633, 123underwear.com)
and **Boxers** (1305 Washington Ave., 314-454-0209, mensunderwearstore.com).

{ BIG-TIME BUILDINGS }

Among the scores of significant structures, some of the more noteworthy include **City Hall** (1200 Market St., 314-622-4000; completed in 1904, constructed of Missouri pink granite and brick, and based on a design inspired by the City Hall of Paris); **Soldier's Memorial Military Museum** (1315 Chestnut St., 314-622-4550, stlsoldiersmemorial.org; completed in 1938, to honor World War I veterans and dedicated by President Franklin D. Roosevelt); **Central Library** (1301 Olive St., 314-241-2288, slpl.org; completed 1912, closed for major renovation but scheduled to reopen in late 2012, designed by architect Cass Gilbert); **Union Station** (1820 Market St., 314-421-6655, stlouisunionstation.com; opened 1894; once the largest and busiest train station in the world, it ended rail service in 1978); **Peabody Opera House** (1400 Market St., peabodyoperahouse.com; completed 1934; former Kiel Opera House reopened as the Peabody in fall 2011, after extensive renovation); **Old Post Office** (9th & Locust; completed 1884, in French Second Empire style, and now home to a library branch, campus of Webster University and offices); **Wainwright Building** (705 Chestnut St., completed 1891, internationally known as the "first skyscraper" at ten stories high, and designed by architect Louis Sullivan); and **Mullanphy Emigrant Home** (built in 1867 as a welcoming haven for the immigrants arriving to settle in St. Louis or points westward, currently partially collapsed).

{ NORTHERN RENAISSANCE }

Downtown's neighbor to the north, Old North St. Louis, is rising, phoenix-like, from decades of physical and social disarray. The most noticeable turnaround? The complete rehabilitation, renovation, and rebirth of an attractive, viable neighborhood business district along the former 14th Street Mall (a 1970s urban-planning fiasco). Now known as **Crown Square**, the mixed-use storefront and apartment buildings houses a clothing boutique, the neighborhood association, law offices, and other retail and service options. It's also the site of a thriving weekly farmers' market, and adjacent to Crown Candy Kitchen, an innovative grocery coop and **La Mancha Coffeehouse** (2815 N. 14th St., 314-932-5581), a community gathering spot that serves a tasty gazpacho.

Missouri's first documented site on the Underground Railroad lies along the Riverfront Trail. **The Mary Meachum Freedom Crossing** (on the riverfront, just north of the Merchants Bridge) was named for the free woman of color who accompanied a group of would-be runaway slaves as they embarked from the point in 1855, seeking an escape through Illinois. A colorful mural and historical marker tell the story.

MACROSUN INTERNATIONAL
1310 Washington Ave.
314-421-6400
macrosun.com
Asian textiles, clothing, art, jewelry

MAKABOO
609 N. 13th St.
314-553-9555
makaboo.com
Personalizable, coo-coo cute baby blankets, kid clothes

MARX HARDWARE
2501 N. 14th St.
314-231-8435
135 years selling hardware and paint to North Siders

NICHE
300 N. Broadway
314-621-8131
nichestl.com
Retail arm of interior design shop sells Knoll, Herman Miller, & other modern stuff

SPA AT FOUR SEASONS
999 North 2nd St.
314-881-5800
fourseasons.com/stlouis/spa
Decadent spa experience overlooking Mississippi River

{ HISTORIC HOMES }

Two historic home museums merit a visit, for a refresher on your Missouri history. **The Eugene Field House** (634 S. Broadway, 314-421-4689, eugenefieldhouse.org) was the boyhood home of the popular "children's poet" (home also to his father Roswell, the local lawyer who took the Dred Scott Case to federal court). Along with various early Victoriana, it boasts an impressive Toy Museum with collectibles dating back to the 1700s. Further west, **Campbell House** (1508 Locust St., 314-421-0325, campbellhousemuseum.org) has reopened after a significant restoration and is now among the best high-Victorian-era mansions in the country: Campbell family possessions populate the rooms, and the tales of fur trader Robert Campbell (who underwent a remarkable transformation from rough-and-tumble to domesticated pillar of society, and along the way acquired a strong-minded wife who challenged conventions of her era) brings local history to colorful life.

MIDTOWN

GRAND CENTER ★ MIDTOWN ALLEY ★ SAINT LOUIS UNIVERSITY

HISTORY

The Jesuit-founded Saint Louis University, at almost two centuries old, is partially located on the site of Camp Jackson, a Civil War Confederate encampment that was quickly seized by a Union force. Future Union generals Grant and Sherman were on hand as civilians. The eastern half of SLU is known as Frost Campus, in honor of a Confederate general at Camp Jackson. A statue of General Nathaniel Lyon—leader of Union forces at the affair—was quietly relocated from this part of campus to Soulard. SLU's Pius XII Memorial Library holds the only reliquary of Vatican documents outside of Vatican City in their entirety. SLU gives its part of Midtown a Gothic flair, with the recognizable Gothic arches and stylized fleur de lis—as well as the extraordinary St. Francis Xavier Church. SLU has played a major role in the renovation of Midtown, purchasing more than 40 acres and 30 buildings.

St. Louis's theatre district—Grand Center—rests just north of SLU. The long-gone Princess, the first vaudeville theatre in St. Louis, opened Grand Center's life as the theatre district, followed by the Rialto, a repurposed Knights of Columbus building with the same Gothic bent as many of the university's structures. The Fabulous Fox was decorated in the Siamese Byzantine style, a striking approach that still dazzles attendees today. The 1929 interior has been fully and authentically restored, from the unique carpet to the chandelier.

Vandeventer Place attracted the wealthy and prestigious with it emphasis on privacy, security, and gentility. The neighborhood, with its million-dollar mansions, was dotted with fountains and small parks. However, Vandeventer Place, like the rest of Grand Center, found new purpose in a new time, as it is now occupied by a veteran's hospital, built after the end of World War II.

FOOD AND DRINK

A surprisingly small concentration of restaurants and bar options occupy the district, given the sheer number of people that pass through for college classes or matinée culture. The upside? You often get to see worlds colliding in these establishments. (Think mink coats and pearls en route to the **Fabulous Fox**, queued up at the **Best Steak House**.)

A BITE TO EAT

CHUY ARZOLA'S
3701 Lindell Blvd.
314-644-4430
www.chuyarzolas.com
Tex-Mex and 'ritas

CITY DINER
541 N. Grand Blvd.
314-533-7500
saucemagazine.com/
citydiner
Retro-cool comfort food

THE GOOD PIE
3137 Olive St.
314-289-9391
thegoodpie.com
Neopolitan pizzas, tiny bar

GOVINDA'S
3926 Lindell Blvd.
314-535-8085
Hare Krishna-run
vegetarian lunch buffet

NADOZ
3701 Lindell Blvd.
314-446-6800
nadozcafe.com
Sandwich/crêpe/
dessert café

PAPPY'S SMOKEHOUSE
3106 Olive St.
314-535-4340
pappyssmokehouse.com
Moan-inducing BBQ,
Memphis-style

TRIUMPH GRILL
3419 Olive St.
314-446-1801
www.triumphgrill.com
Vintage motorcycle décor,
vast eclectic menu

VITO'S
3515 Lindell Blvd.
314-534-8486
vitosstl.com
Pizza and the best of Sicily

{ SPIKED SHAKES }

It's a wicked combination of ice cream and booze: at **Kota Wood Fire Grill** (522 N. Grand Blvd., 314-535-5577, kotawoodfiregrill.com), the "Kota 21" shakes carry a buzz, while at **The Fountain on Locust** (3037 Locust, 314-535-7800, fountainonlocust.com), ice cream martinis make a great nightcap.

{ RETURN OF THE BEER BARON }

This is, don't forget, a town that beer built; no surprise, then, that a craft-beer resurgence is upon us once again. Even handier, three newish brewers lie within a short cab ride of each other. **Six Row Brewing** (3690 Forest Park Ave., 314-531-5600, sixrowbrewco.com), **Buffalo Brewing** (3100 Olive St., 314-534-2337, buffalobrewingstl.com), and **Urban Chestnut Brewing** (3229 Washington Ave., 314-222-0143, urbanchestnut.com) all bring seriousness of purpose to the enterprise...and a sense of humor to their branding. Prefer the Whale Ale or the Buffalo Drool?

SOMETHING TO DRINK

EXO
3146 Locust St.
314-707-8709
exostl.com
Upscale & urban lounge

HUMPHREY'S
3700 Laclede Ave.
314-535-0700
humphreysstl.com
Penny pitcher nights and an endless supply of SLU kids

{ JOIN THE HERD }

Take your place in line at the **Best Steak House** (516 N. Grand Blvd., 314-535-6033, beststeakstl. com), squint to make out the lettering on the menu board, and above all, be ready! When you hear "Next!" from the line cooks, a moment's hesitation will get you A Look. And then another, more insistent, "NEXT!" Glamorous it's not, but high theatre in its own right, just down the way from some of our town's poshest performance venues. As for the food, it's cafeteria service and budget prices: 16-oz Porterhouse dinner (with all trimmings) will set you back under $20, and the Texas toast and fried okra are scrumptious.

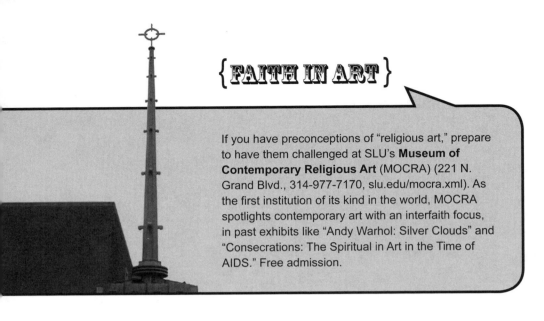

{ FAITH IN ART }

If you have preconceptions of "religious art," prepare to have them challenged at SLU's **Museum of Contemporary Religious Art** (MOCRA) (221 N. Grand Blvd., 314-977-7170, slu.edu/mocra.xml). As the first institution of its kind in the world, MOCRA spotlights contemporary art with an interfaith focus, in past exhibits like "Andy Warhol: Silver Clouds" and "Consecrations: The Spiritual in Art in the Time of AIDS." Free admission.

{ KIDZONE }

Outside (and even inside, despite a massive new a/c system), it's often hot as blazes, and you're there for a while with the crush of unwashed humanity spilling sno-cones on your feet...but when the lights go down and the band starts up, **Circus Flora** (on the parking lot behind Powell Hall, 718 N. Grand Blvd., 314-289-4040, circusflora.org) becomes a tent full of pure magic. Funny (and humane) animal acts, stunning acrobatics, and gut-busting clowning, all within a few feet of your seat. Few cities are blessed with such memory-making entertainment.

RECREATION

Culture vultures, art lovers, and urban revivalists converge on the institutions and upstart efforts in Midtown: many of our well-known venues, including the **Fabulous Fox Theatre** (527 N. Grand Blvd., 314-534-1678, fabulousfox.com), **Powell Hall** (718 N. Grand Blvd., 314-533-2500, stlsymphony.org/powell/index.htm), and **The Sheldon** (3648 Washington Blvd., 314-533-9900, sheldonconcerthall.org) are here, but take some time before sprinting to your car post-performance and discover that there's plenty going on beyond the brightest lights, too.

FESTIVITIES

DANCING IN THE STREETS
September
grandcenter.org
Hundreds of dancers from scores of troupes and styles take over stages throughout the Grand Center district

FIRST NIGHT
New Year's Eve
grandcenter.org/firstnight
Alcohol-free, family-friendly street party (with plenty of indoor fun, too!) of live entertainment, costumes, participatory art, and fireworks

MIDTOWN ALLEY STREET FEST
Late summer
midtownalley.com
Bands, beer, and food vendors; check the website for current info

EXERCISE

MOOLAH LANES
3821 Lindell Blvd.
314-446-6866
moolahlanes.com
Roll thunder til 3 a.m. nightly, and fuel your amazing athleticism with food and drink from the full menu and bar

{ HINT OF HISTORY }

On his way to becoming "the King of Ragtime," composer and pianist Scott Joplin made his way from Texas (by way of Sedalia, Mo.) to a second-floor flat in St. Louis in 1900, today the **Scott Joplin House State Historic Site** (2658A Delmar Blvd., 314-340-5790, mostateparks.com/scottjoplin.htm). For three years, Joplin and his wife lived here and he composed some of his most famous works, including "Elite Syncopations" and "The Entertainer."

Wondering how to transform your offspring from wild heathens to cultured citizens? You could start, about an hour at a time, with the **Family Concerts** offered by the St. Louis Symphony at Powell Hall (718 N. Grand Blvd., 314-533-2500, stlsymphony.org). The occasional Sunday matinées feature programs like Prokofiev's "Peter and the Wolf" to grab the attention of youngsters and their chaperones. A little squirming and stage-whispering is accepted, and parent-of-the-year types can use online program notes and activities to keep the discussion going at home or in the car.

ARTS, ENTERTAINMENT, & EDUCATION

THE BLACK REP
3610 Grandel Sq.
314-534-3810
theblackrep.org
The nation's largest professional African-American theatre company performs theatrical and dance works at the Grandel Theatre

BRUNO DAVID GALLERY
3721 Washington Blvd.
314-531-3030
brunodavidgallery.com
Nimble gallery showing emerging local and national/international contemporary artists, quite active in promoting STL arts scene

CINEMA ST. LOUIS
3547 Olive St.
314-289-4150
cinemastlouis.org
Portal to all things film in town, including screenwriting competitions, Oscar-night parties, free community movie screenings, and local film showcases

CONTEMPORARY ART MUSEUM
3750 Washington Blvd.
314-535-4660
camstl.org
Non-collecting institutional gallery housed in striking minimalist building, building bridges between international art world and local artists and collectors

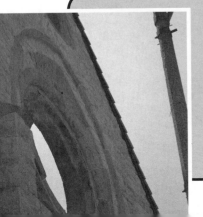

Now known as the **Spring Avenue Church**, the shell at 688 N. Spring Ave. was originally built by a Baptist splinter congregation in 1884 and underwent a succession of denominational and demographic changes (lastly as a Church of God in Christ Church) before being gutted by fire in 2001. Schemes for its revitalization as an urban sculpture garden have yet to materialize, but the remaining bones of the building were the backdrop for a recent installation of colorful lamps commissioned by the Pulitzer museum.

Sharing its era of provenance with other significant Art Deco skyscrapers like the Empire State Building and the Chrysler Building, the **Continental Life Building** (3615 Olive St., 314-652-3615, continental-building.com) provides one of the most striking points on the mid-city skyline. When built in the late 1920s, it was elaborately decorated inside and out and featured modern miracles like air-conditioning and a basement parking garage. The Depression, mismanagement, and other problems marred its early days, and although it remained a prestigious business address for decades, the building was emptied and boarded up in the late 1970s. Vandalized and element-weathered, it became an albatross too expensive to renovate and too expensive to raze. Developers rose to the considerable challenge, and after meticulous research and restoration, the building reopened in 2002 as an apartment high-rise.

CUPPLES HOUSE
3673 West Pine Mall
314-977-2666
slu.edu/x27031.xml
On campus of SLU, mash-up of Romanesque Revival mansion, with a straightforward Arts & Crafts interior sensibility, sets the scene for an ongoing display of Tiffany and Steuben glass, Western Jesuit Mission oil paintings, and more

DANTE'S
3221 Olive St.
314-652-2369
clubdantes.com
Weekend-only hotspot for Latin dance, reggaeton, salsa, and Spanish-tinged rock music and shows

FIREBIRD
2706 Olive St.
314-535-0353
firebirdstl.com
Smallish, largely ambience-free room still packs in crowds for local rock & indie touring acts

FUBAR
3108 Locust St.
314-289-9050
fubarstl.com
Rock/punk vibe at this frenetic, all-ages club featuring local and traveling acts

GYA COMMUNITY GALLERY & FINE CRAFT SHOP
2700 Locust St.
314-374-3282
Co-op exhibit and store space for the creations and events of a collective of woman artists and interested community members

JAZZ AT THE BISTRO
3536 Washington Ave.
314-534-3663
jazzstl.org/jazz-at-the-bistro
Reverent listening-room atmosphere for sophisticated sets from local, national, and international jazz luminaries

KRANZBERG ARTS CENTER
501 N. Grand Blvd.
314-289-1507
Black-box and studio spaces host cabaret and theatre groups

THE LOFT JAZZ CLUB
3112 Olive St.
314-225-2505
Not a loft, nor a jazz spot, but a
hip-hop/R&B dance club

MOOLAH THEATRE
3821 Lindell Blvd.
314-446-6868
stlouiscinemas.com
Gigantic single-screen theatre
shows first-run movies with sofa
seating and cocktails

NU-ART SERIES
2936 Locust St.
314-535-6500
thenu-artseries.org
Exhibition space focused on work (visual,
performance, musical, literary) of artists
of color: at the Metropolitan Gallery

PULITZER FOUNDATION
FOR THE ARTS
3716 Washington Blvd.
314-754-1850
pulitzerarts.org
Space by renowned architect Tadao
Ando is the backdrop for temporary
exhibits, pieces from the collection,
and fascinating interactions of
artistic disciplines

ST. LOUIS SHAKESPEARE
3610 Grandel Sq.
314-361-5664
stlshakespeare.org
Completionist professional company
is ¾ of the way to its goal to produce the
entire canon of Shakespeare,
with three of the Bard's works and one
non-Shakes show each season; at
the Grandel Theatre

SAINT LOUIS UNIVERSITY
BILLIKENS BASKETBALL
1 S. Compton Ave.
314-977-4758
slubillikens.com
Played at Chaifetz Arena; the Atlantic
10 Conference SLU team turns out
a respectable, engaged crowd for
home games

SAINT LOUIS UNIVERSITY
MUSEUM OF ART
3663 Lindell Blvd.
314-977-3399
slu.edu/sluma.xml
On-campus and exhibiting the
university's collections, including Asian
art and work from the Western Jesuit
Missions

SCHMIDT CONTEMPORARY ART
615 N. Grand Blvd.
314-575-2648
schmidtcontemporaryart.com
Showing top regional and national
contemporary artists

VAUGHN CULTURAL CENTER
3701 Grandel Sq.
314-615-3624
ulstl.org/vaughn_cultural_center.aspx
Art shows, concerts, and discussions
related to African-American history and
culture; at the Urban League

SHOPPORTUNITIES

Midtown is no shopaholics' paradise: head to the nearby Central West End for better boutiquing. Here, a smattering to explore.

GRAND WIG HOUSE
2911 Washington Ave.
314-533-6699
Yep, it's a wig store, for serious tress-seekers and costume-hunters alike

PRESTON ART GLASS
2651 Chouteau Ave.
314-772-2611
prestonartglass.com
Stained, leaded, beveled, and more: they can sell it, repair it, and even teach you how to make it

{ FLORIST ROW }

A concentration of flower, plant, and nursery product purveyors occupy a few blocks of LaSalle St. near Jefferson, in an otherwise light-industrial area off Chouteau. Though some are wholesale only, a handful of retail operations can net you bargains on cut flowers, plant baskets, floral arrangement supplies, glassware, and much more.

{ DIY }

Craft Alliance (6640 Delmar Blvd., 314-725-1177, craftalliance.org), long a staple in the Loop, has expanded to Grand Center. In addition to its gallery space, they offer a wide variety of adult and kids' classes and workshops, from handmade zines to metal cast jewelry.

{ GET YOUR MOTO RUNNING }

Need somewhere new to take dad for a field trip? Tool up to the **Moto Museum** (3441 Olive St., 314-446-1805, themotomuseum.com), a collection of rare and vintage mostly European motorcycles, dating from 1900 to 1975, give or take. Lovingly restored and displayed at eye-level, it'll give you a new appreciation for the machines, and the minds that built them. Limited hours, call to verify open times.

{ THE SHELDON'S OTHER SIDE }

Pretty sure we're contractually obligated to reference the concert hall's perfect acoustics, but here's something about **The Sheldon** (3648 Washington Blvd., 314-533-9900, thesheldon.org) you may not know: Just to the west of the auditorium, several art galleries exhibit photography, the history of jazz, children's art, architecture, and other compelling subjects. Well worth a visit on their own, or before your show.

FOREST PARK

CENTRAL WEST END ★ DE MUN ★ DOGTOWN ★ FOREST PARK
SOUTHEAST ★ THE GROVE ★ SKINKER-DEBALIVIERE

HISTORY

Forest Park occupies a special place in St. Louis's history. It was the site of the 1904 World's Fair, where many foods we take for granted were introduced or made popular. Hamburgers, hotdogs, lemonade, peanut butter, cotton candy, the debut of Dr. Pepper, the ice cream waffle cone, iced tea, as well as the first utterance of the axiom "an apple a day keeps the doctor away," all have a connection with the Fair. Forest Park and Washington University also played host to the first American-sponsored Olympic Games. The Fair brought in business from over sixty nations and forty-three of the forty-five states.

Many exhibits from the 1904 World's Fair remain an integral part of Forest Park. The Palace of Fine Arts evolved into the St. Louis Art Museum, built to resemble the Baths of Caracalla in Rome. The Smithsonian Institution commissioned the Flight Cage for the Fair, intending to move it to the National Zoo in Washington, D.C. St. Louisans rallied to keep the Flight Cage intact, and the city of St. Louis purchased it for $3,500 (the structure had originally cost $17,500 to construct). The cage served as the impetus for St. Louis to develop a full-fledged zoo—the first municipally supported zoo in the world and one of two U.S. zoos where admission is free.

The first memorial to honor Thomas Jefferson now serves as the headquarters of the Missouri History Museum, which has the largest collection of Lewis and Clark artifacts in the world. In 1936, one of the most iconic structures in St. Louis was built—a cantilevered, glass-and-wood Art Deco treasure known to St. Louisans as the Jewel Box. Originally designed to display native Missouri plants, it today is a destination for weddings and other events.

Forest Park Forever, a private, nonprofit organization, was founded in 1986 to restore, maintain, and sustain Forest Park as one of America's great

Few vestiges remain in Forest Park Southeast of the formerly hopping **Laclede Race Course**, built in 1865 from then-vacant common fields that lay far outside the city limits. The horse race track operated until 1869, when the area was parceled up for housing, in one of the first real subdivisions in town. Keep your eyes peeled for Race Course Avenue.

urban public parks. Over $94 million has been invested in the restoration of this community treasure in the past decade, restoring the park to its full-fledged glory.

The Central West End was developed during the time leading up to the 1904 World's Fair. St. Louis anticipated the influx of visitors and guests. Many of the wealthy were moving away from older city neighborhoods to the east, resettling here, so many of the avenues and boulevards in the area, designed as part of the Renaissance Revival and the Romanesque movements, possesses a grandeur and elegance only achieved through great expense. One of the most dominant features of this neighborhood is the Cathedral Basilica. This neighborhood, which has long prized heritage, tradition, and social responsibility, was home to the artistic set—including T. S. Eliot and Tennessee Williams (who set *The Glass Menagerie* here) and many early proponents of women's suffrage, including Kate Chopin, author of *The Awakening.*

Today, visitors and residents can stroll through the stately avenues and enjoy the culture and history—a communal habit of awareness of the present combined with preparation for the future.

FOOD AND DRINK

There's some serious eating, drinking, and clubbing to be had in this part of town, from nationally lauded chefs and envelope-pushing culinary trends to down-home goodness on a cafeteria tray. The concentration of restaurants in the Central West End make it an easy place to just park the car and wander until you find something to your liking. Manchester Avenue in The Grove is tailor-made for a bar crawl with your dedicated party people, with many bars open until 3 a.m. In De Mun, experience a pocket neighborhood of establishments so charming you may just want to rent an apartment and stay.

A BITE TO EAT

ATLAS
5513 Pershing Ave.
314-367-6800
atlasrestaurantstl.com
Solid, under-the-radar
neighborhood bistro

BAR ITALIA
13 Maryland Pl.
314-361-7010
baritaliastl.com
Italian, not overly
Americanized

BIXBY'S
Missouri History Museum,
2nd Floor
5700 Lindell Blvd.
314-361-7313
bixbys-mohistory.com
Great views of the park,
great plates of local food

BOBO NOODLE HOUSE
278 N. Skinker Blvd.
314-863-7373
bobonoodle.com
Sleek, chic pan-Asian dishes

BRASSERIE BY NICHE
4580 Laclede Ave.
314-454-0600
brasseriebyniche.com
Unfussy French, from
sweetbreads to coq au vin

CAFÉ OSAGE
4605 Olive St.
314-454-6868
bowoodfarms.com
Homey breakfast, lunch,
or afternoon tea, seasonal
and simple

CRÊPES ETC.
52 Maryland Pl.
314-367-2200
crepesstl.com
Savory or sweet,
always a treat

CULPEPPER'S
300 N. Euclid Ave.
314-361-2828
www.culpeppers.com
Wings are the thing,
plus pizza, beer, and
people-watching

DRESSEL'S
419 N. Euclid Ave.
314-361-1060
dresselspublichouse.com
Cozy, woody room for
Guinness and warming
pub grub

{ KIDZONE }

Give them a concrete example of what you mean with your archaic phrases like "a kid in a candy store" at **Oh Lolli Lolli** (802 De Mun Ave., 314-721-9600), a tiny retro candy shop with a bonanza of bins of licorice, gummies, sours, chocolates, and more. It's right next door to a pint-sized playground, where they can burn off that sugar high.

{ IT'S ALL AT THE CHASE }

Storied luxury hotel, exquisite dining, and entertainment (dancing or piano bar, anyone?), elegant lobby bars, in-house multi-screen cinema: it's hard to imagine why you'd ever need to leave the posh confines of the historic **Chase Park Plaza Hotel** (212-232 N. Kingshighway Blvd., 314-633-3000, chaseparkplaza.com). Impressive for date night, brunch with the out-of-towners, and just about any other occasion. Dining includes the swanky Tenderloin Room, buzzy Eau Café, & quietly elegant Eau Bistro.

THE DRUNKEN FISH
1 Maryland Pl.
314-367-4222
drunkenfish.com
Sushi, cocktails, and scene-making, not necessarily in that order

EVEREST CAFE
4145 Manchester Ave.
314-531-4800
everestcafeandbar.com
Nepalese and Korean, popular lunch buffet

HERBIE'S VINTAGE 72
405 N. Euclid Ave.
314-769-9595
herbies.com
Refreshed room for a revered, upscale bistro

JACKSON'S
6655 Manchester Ave.
314-645-4904
stl-jacksons.com
Casual eatery with a Big Easy nightclub vibe

JIMMY'S CAFÉ ON THE PARK
706 De Mun Ave.
314-725-8585
jimmyscafe.com
STL Sardi's, with local celeb caricatures on the walls

{ SHOWPLACE }

The **Cathedral Basilica** (4431 Lindell Blvd., 314-373-8242, cathedralstl.org), a.k.a. the "New Cathedral," completed in 1914, boasts among other treasures the largest indoor collection of mosaic art in the world...a fact mentioned with just a trace of envy by tour guides at St. Mark's Basilica in Venice, Italy (itself home to an impressive mosaic assemblage).

KAYAK'S
276 N. Skinker Blvd.
314-862-4447
Student-heavy coffeeshop,
tabletop s'mores

LA GRA
1227 Tamm Ave.
314-645-3972
ilovelagra.com
Italian tapas & wine bar

LATITUDE 26
6407 Clayton Ave.
314-932-5600
latitude26texmex.com
Tex-Mex cuisine

KALDI
700 De Mun Ave.
314-727-9955
kaldiscoffee.com
Veg-heaven menu from
local coffee-roasting empire

KOPPERMAN'S DELI
386 N. Euclid Ave.
314-361-0100
saucemagazine.com/
koppermans
Deli-market...and some
regrettable sandwich
names ("Ike and Tina Tuna,"
anyone?)

LA DOLCE VIA
4470 Arco Ave.
314-534-1699
ladolceviabakery.com
Homemade baked goods,
lauded weekend dinners

LILUMA
236 N. Euclid Ave.
314-361-7771
fialafood.com
Bistro treatment for
chicken, scallops, and
even burgers

LITTLE SAIGON
10 N. Euclid Ave.
314-361-8881
littlesaigoncafe.com
Fresh, light Vietnamese

LLYWELYN'S
4747 McPherson Ave.
314-361-3003
llywelynspub.com
Celtic pub, fam-
friendly food

NICK'S PUB
6001 Manchester Ave.
314-781-7806
nickspub.info
Wings, beer, darts, & pool

**NORTHWEST COFFEE
ROASTING**
4251 Laclede Ave.
314-371-4600
northwestcoffee.com
Beans-to-go, brewed
to drink

**OLYMPIA KEBOB
HOUSE & TAVERNA**
1543 McCausland Ave.
314-781-1299
Greek favorites

OR SMOOTHIE & CAFÉ
3 N. Euclid Ave.
314-367-8883
orsmoothieandcafe.com
Super-healthy choices for
carnivores to vegans

PI
400 N. Euclid Ave.
314-367-4300
restaurantpi.com
Cornmeal-crusted pizza-
of-the-moment

RACANELLI'S
12 S. Euclid Ave.
314-367-7866
racanellis.com
NY-style pizza

{ COMFORT, CAFETERIA-STYLE }

For old-school, down-home, gut-busting home cookin', get in line and don't ask
too many questions at **Sweetie Pie's** (4270 Manchester Ave., 314-371-0304)
or **Del Monico's Diner** (4909 Delmar Blvd., 314-361-0973): you'll get a tray
and a walk in front of some of the most mouth-watering veggies, meats, and
desserts this side of the South. The everyman appeal also makes these likely
rooms in which to spot politicians, business leaders, and other Big Deals.

{ SWEET SPOTS }

You almost don't want to know about Pie Fridays at **Sugaree Baking** (1242 Tamm Ave., 314-645-5496, sugareebaking.com): once you are aware of the wedding cake specialist's open hours, once you've tasted the whoopie pies and triple-berry pie and realized it's not just Friday but Saturday, too...well, it's the kind of place you'll fake other errands to "just happen to be in the neighborhood" for. At **The Cup** (28 Maryland Pl. Rear, 314-367-6111, cravethecup.com), the humble cupcake reigns supreme, in varieties like confetti and peanut butter cup, but a cakewich (born in an attempt to use up errant scrap ends from custom-ordered wedding cakes) deserves your attention as well. **Bissingers** (32 Maryland Pl., 314-367-7750, bissingers.com), a full-on chocolate lounge experience, stays open late on weekends for you to drown yourself in decadent desserts, paired with your wine of choice.

RASOI
25 N. Euclid Ave.
314-361-6911
rasoi.com
Indian flavors, eye-popping décor

SCAPE
48 Maryland Pl.
314-361-7227
scapestl.com
Date-night bistro

THE SCOTTISH ARMS
8 S. Sarah St.
314-535-0551
thescottisharms.com
Haggis, smoked salmon, and plenty of whiskey

SEAMUS MCDANIEL'S
1208 Tamm Ave.
314-645-6337
seamusmcdaniels.net
Irish bar, great burgers

SPAGHETTERIA MAMMA MIA
904 S. Vandeventer Ave.
314-531-9100
spaghetteriamammamia.com
Pastas, pizzas, handrolled meatballs

SUBZERO NEW AMERICAN BURGERS
308 N. Euclid Ave.
314-367-1200
20+ varieties, plus toppings like eel and fried egg

WILD FLOWER CAFÉ
4590 Laclede Ave.
314-367-9888
wildflowerdining.com
Whimsical, casual American food

{ ALL-IN-ONE-EVENING }

Like to park your car once and make an evening of it? Consider stopping by the **West End Grill & Pub/Gaslight Theatre** (354 N. Boyle Ave., 314-531-4607, westendgrillandpub.com) complex, where you can enjoy cocktails in the undeniably sensual bar, plus tasty appetizers or dinner, then scoot next door for a great theatrical production by resident company **St. Louis Actors' Studio** (stlas.org)...and head back to the restaurant side for post-show discussion and dessert! Win-win-win...win. That's four wins.

{ PLEASE KEEP ON THE GRASS }

Could be just another big-bucks donor that gets to have something named in his honor...but in the case of **Dwight F. Davis**, for whom the 18-court Forest Park tennis center is named, it's a well-deserved honorary nod. Davis was a native St. Louisan, champion tennis player, international politico, and funder of the Davis Cup; his passion was the free, public enjoyment of tennis and other park-based recreation. As the public parks commissioner in the early 1900s, he railed against the "Keep Off the Grass" crowd. Today, his namesake tennis courts are open to the public, and there's even still free play offered on a walk-up basis during much of the open season.

{ 24/7 PEOPLE-WATCHING PERCH }

Nothing attracts a crowd like a crowd...well, that and maybe coffee. From WiFi squatters to dog-walkers, **Coffee Cartel**'s (2 Maryland Pl., 314-454-0000, thecoffeecartel.com) prime location on the CWE's most prominent corner provides an amazing window on the neighborhood. Sit outside when it's clement, inside when it's not; either way, you'll never lack for street theatre.

{ ROASTED AND READY }

Drive down certain light industrial backstreets of The Grove/Central West End area, and if the breeze is right, you'll catch the distinctive aroma of coffee beans turning from green to glorious: at least four companies, from national brands to hometown beaneries, fire up the hoppers and set the good stuff en route to your cup. Within about four square blocks of Boyle and Papin, you'll find **Thomas**, **Kaldi's**, **Northwest**, and **Ronnoco** (plus their coffeehouse imprint, **Wildhorse Creek**).

SOMETHING TO DRINK

34 CLUB
34 N. Euclid Ave.
314-367-6674
Basic booze, divey digs

ATTITUDES
4100 Manchester Ave.
314-534-0044
GLBT-welcoming as
long as you dance,
dance, dance!

BIG MOE'S
1072 Tower Grove Ave.
314-324-8697
Drink specials and
freestyle rap nights

**BRENNAN'S/
MARYLAND HOUSE**
4659 Maryland Ave.
314-361-9444
Wine & cigar sales
downstairs, oddly
subdivided apartment
rooms for drinks upstairs

ERNEY'S 32
4200 Manchester Ave.
314-652-7195
erneys32.com
Vodka and video dancing
for GLBT crowd

FELIX'S
6335 Clayton Ave.
314-645-6565
felixsrestaurant.com
Martinis & live music

HANDLEBAR
4127 Manchester Ave.
314-652-2212
handlebarstl.com
Bike-themed watering
hole

JUST JOHN
4112 Manchester Ave.
314-371-1333
justjohnsclub.com
GLBT-friendly, bingo,
dance, & karaoke

THE LOADING ZONE
16 S. Euclid Ave.
314-361-4119
GLBT-friendly cocktail
and video bar

MAGNOLIA'S
5 S. Vandeventer Ave.
314-652-6500
magnoliasbar.net
GLBT-friendly dance bar

MANDARIN LOUNGE
44 Maryland Pl.
314-367-4447
mandarinlounge.net
Asian motifs, rooftop patio

NOVAK'S
4121 Manchester Ave.
314-531-3699
novaksbar.com
GLBT-friendly mainstay,
always celebrating
something

PREMIUM LOUNGE
4199 Manchester Ave.
314-367-3146
loungestl.com
Cocktails and light bites

REHAB
4054 Chouteau Ave.
314-652-3700
GLBT-welcoming
party corner

ROSIE'S PLACE
4573 Laclede Ave.
314-361-6423
Cheap drinks,
no pretensions

SANCTUARIA
4198 Manchester Ave.
314-535-9700
sanctuariastl.com
Inventive cocktails & tapas

SASHA'S WINE BAR
706 De Mun Ave.
314-863-7274
sashaswinebar.com
Wines, cheeses, & noshes

SUBZERO VODKA BAR
306 N. Euclid Ave.
314-367-1200
subzerovodkabar.com
300 vodkas, 25-ft ice bar

THE WINE PRESS
4436 Olive St.
314-289-9463
stlwinepress.com
Wine, beer, apps,
acoustic music

RECREATION

It's the 800-pound gorilla of recreational opportunities (to say nothing of culture and attractions; sorry, everywhere else!): Forest Park lies at the heart of these neighborhoods, and, really, is the heart of the entire region. At around 1,300 acres (500 more than New York's Central Park, not that we're bragging), this verdant oasis offers myriad outdoor amenities, including almost six miles of dual-surface trails given a nonstop workout by runners, walkers, cyclists, and bladers; hiking trails throughout the park's interior; fishing in the lakes and lagoons; two golf courses; 18,000 trees for arborists and avid birders; and an unbeatable smorgasbord of humankind.

FESTIVITIES

ANCIENT ORDER OF HIBERNIANS ST. PATRICK'S DAY PARADE
Dogtown
stlhibernians.com
March 17
It's as Irish as it gets, and you should bundle up and experience it at least once in your St. Louis tenure.

CWE ART FAIR & TASTE
Central West End
thecwe.org
June
Live entertainment, restaurant booths, and a village of both juried art and handmade crafts fill the neighborhood's streets.

GREAT FOREST PARK BALLOON RACE
Forest Park
greatforestparkballoonrace.com
September
Most hot air in town outside of political campaigning season, with many folks advocating the night-before-the-race "balloon glow" as the must-do

GREEK FESTIVAL
4967 Forest Park Blvd.
sngoc.org/GreekFest/default.htm
Labor Day weekend
St. Nicholas Greek Orthodox Church, where you can stuff your face with phyllo and catch some folk-dancing

GROVEFEST
September
Art, music, and general neighborhood mayhem draw big crowds to one of the city's latest hot districts.

HALLOWEEN IN THE CWE
Central West End
314-367-2220
thecwe.org
Halloween weekend
A nod to the kiddos with a morning parade and costume contest, but this is really all about grown-ups getting dressed-up and getting drinks.

TOUR DE GROVE
tourdegrove.com
May
Professional bicycling race draws big names and is a big payout for the winner; tons of auxiliary events (for kids, novice cyclists, art lovers, and curious spectators) round out an entire weekend of cycling.

CITY CYCLING TOURS

Forest Park Visitor's Center

314-616-5724

citycyclingtours.com

Bike, helmet, and water, along with expert narration, included on this three-hour tour of Forest Park (ignore fateful "Gilligan" theme in the back of your head...)

HANDBALL & RACQUETBALL IN FOREST PARK

fphcbigblue.com

Four wooden and four concrete courts are perfect for pick-up ball, just north of the Visitor's Center

THE HIGHLANDS GOLF & TENNIS CENTER

5163 Clayton Rd.

314-531-7773

highlandsgolfandtennis.com

Nine holes, state-of-the-art driving range, and clay tennis courts in Forest Park

IPOD WALKING TOURS OF FOREST PARK

Check out a free player pre-loaded with four narrated tours from the Visitor's Center, or visit forestparkforever.org to download the mp3s to your own player

NORMAN K. PROBSTEIN GOLF COURSE

6141 Lagoon Dr.

314-367-1337

forestparkgc.com

Three 9-hole courses, all a par 35, can be split up or played together, with equipment and pro shop on-site in Forest Park

STEINBERG SKATING RINK

400 Jefferson Dr.

314-367-7465

steinbergskatingrink.com

Practice your Rockefeller Center spins without big-city prices (or big-city credit card acceptance). Open Nov-March, weather permitting

{ FUNPLEX DUPLEX }

At **Atomic Cowboy** (4140 Manchester Rd., 314-775-0775, atomiccowboystl.com), you're as likely to see Mr. Leather 2010 tossing back shots at the bar as you are to find a suburban family with little kids munching chips and salsa at a booth on the patio...and that's just an average afternoon. Then come the burlesque shows, the cycling-themed poster art shows, raucous concerts, bonfire parties, and just about anything else you can think of. It's a cacophony that somehow works. And the burritos are tasty, too. Far more sedate, but equally multi-purpose, **Café Ventana** (3919 West Pine Blvd., 314-531-7500, cafeventana.com) steams from early morning til late at night on a crowd-pleasing mix of coffee, beignets, absinthe, bagels, and a Sunday jazz brunch, with a healthy dose of SLU students studying through it all.

{ KIDZONE }

Sure, **Forest Park** has many of the major attractions you know by heart. But if you're looking for fresh inspiration, here are some seasonal locations for you and your family. Climb to your heart's content at **Turtle Playground**, designed by artist Robert Cassilly. Or you can explore the **Variety Wonderland Playground**, with its fun-for-all-ages design. Pop into **Nora's** for picnic victuals, then spread a blanket out on the lawn of the **Missouri History Museum** for an outdoor concert. The **Boathouse** offers refreshments to fuel your afternoon boating, as well as paddle or rowboat rentals. In colder weather, visit **Art Hill**, one of the best sledding spots in St. Louis, then head to the **Visitor's Center** where a café can whip up some hot chocolate to warm those cold fingers. Too hot or too cold or too...whatever to be outdoors? It seems counterintuitive, but head to the **Saint Louis Zoo**. Start with indoor films and hands-on fun in the Living World building. From there, a short walk will get you to the fascinating **Insectarium**: you'll know it by the giant beetle sculpture outside. Finally, push on up the hill and duck into the **Bird House**, where you can get really close to hornbills, owls, roadrunners, and all manner of fowl.

TURTLE PLAYGROUND
Clayton Ave. at Art Hill Pl.

NORA'S
1136 Tamm Ave.
314-645-2705
norasindogtown.com

BOATHOUSE
6101 Government Dr.
314-367-2224

MISSOURI HISTORY MUSEUM
5700 Lindell Blvd.
314-746-4599
mohistory.org

VARIETY WONDERLAND PLAYGROUND
5595 Grand Dr.
314-877-1309

VISITOR'S CENTER
5595 Grand Dr.
314-367-7275

ST. LOUIS ART MUSEUM
1 Fine Arts Dr.
314-721-0072

SAINT LOUIS ZOO
1 Government Dr.
514-781-0900

ARTS, ENTERTAINMENT, & EDUCATION

CHESS CLUB & SCHOLASTIC CENTER OF SAINT LOUIS
4657 Maryland Ave.
314-361-2437
saintlouischessclub.org
Attractive storefront home for casual games, big-time tournaments, lessons, and more, all in the interest of promoting chess in the community

CLUB VIVA
408 N. Euclid Ave.
314-361-0322
clubvivastl.com
High-energy dance floor hosts reggae, world, and wildly popular salsa nights for 21+

THE CHAPEL
6238 Alexander Dr.
chapelvenue.com
Literal "sanctuary for the arts" in converted Gothic chapel offers free space for bands, musicians, poets and other artists to present work in lovely, intimate setting

{ ARCHITECTURAL ODDITY }

Where Kingshighway meets Washington, position yourself to admire **Holy Corners**, a designated National Register Historic District that encompasses six houses of worship, built between 1902 and 1908, concentrated at the intersection. It's also perhaps the only corner in the city from which you can test your knowledge on this point. Can you spot the three distinct architectural column styles? You're looking for Corinthian, Doric, and Ionic.

THE GRAMOPHONE
4243 Manchester Ave.
314-531-5700
thegramophonelive.com
Small live music venue with a bit of a loungey vibe, hosting everything from local blues to DJ spins to touring Americana bands, plus a comfy bar, 21+

HI-POINTE THEATRE
1005 McCausland Ave.
314-644-1100
hi-pointetheatre.com
Single-screen movie theatre, built in 1922 but upgraded charmingly over the years, is a spectacular place to catch a flick (with 500 of your closest friends)

KEMPER ART MUSEUM
One Brookings Dr.
314-935-4523
kemperartmuseum.wustl.edu/
On-campus at WashU and showcasing the university's 19th-21st century American and European treasures

MISSOURI HISTORY MUSEUM
LIBRARY AND RESEARCH CENTER
225 S. Skinker Blvd.
314-746-4500
mohistory.org
Archives (documents, photographs, objects) about St. Louis, the state, the Louisiana Purchase Territory, and regional river valleys, open to the public Tu-Sa (call for specific collection access requirements)

{ GALLERY WALK }

Immerse yourself in culture at some of the CWE's art galleries. **Atrium Gallery** (4728 McPherson Ave., 314-367-1076, atriumgallery.net; sculpture, mixed-media and large-scale work), **Duane Reed Gallery** (4729 McPherson Ave., 314-361-4100, duanereedgallery.com; glass, painting, photography, and fiber art), and **William Shearburn Gallery** (4735 McPherson Ave., 314-367-8020, shearburngallery.com) (sculpture, painting, and mixed-media) have established themselves as homes for the most promising and engaging regional and international artists.

{ DRINK IT IN }

Some people frequent art openings strictly to score a few plastic cups of Costco wine; why not upgrade to a more legit scene? At the **Vino Gallery** (4701 McPherson Ave., 314-932-5665, thevinogallery.com), the wine is front and center (and it's good stuff, too, with a concentration on small-production artisan wines), but local art hangs on the walls, giving you a chance to stretch those mental muscles a little.

THE MUNY
1 Theatre Dr.
314-361-1900
muny.org
Come sweat it out at the nation's oldest and largest outdoor theatre, which mounts crowd faves like *Annie*, *Roman Holiday*, and *West Side Story* each summer from June-Aug; 1,500 free seats for each show fill up fast, so line up early if you're averse to paying

THIRD DEGREE GLASS
5200 Delmar Blvd.
314-367-4527
thirddegreeglassfactory.com
Glass studio and gallery space most known for fun "Third Friday Open House," with free glassblowing demos, live entertainment, and food/drink for sale

UNION AVENUE OPERA
733 N. Union Blvd.
314-361-2881
unionavenueopera.org
Professional opera sung in their original languages, by composers from Bizet to Verdi

WHITE FLAG PROJECTS
4568 Manchester Ave.
314-531-3442
white-flag-projects.org
Nonprofit, cutting-edge gallery space exhibits local and national art, and recently garnered a grant from the Andy Warhol Foundation

SHOPPORTUNITIES

BOWOOD FARMS
4605 Olive St.
314-454-6868
bowoodfarms.com
Locally supplied plant nursery with
eclectic gift shop, too

CENTRO MODERN FURNISHINGS
4727 McPherson Ave.
314-454-0111
centro-inc.com
Sleek furniture & accessories from
Herman Miller, Alessi, & more

CHRISTIANE'S CUSTOM JEWELRY
449 N. Euclid Ave.
314-398-0636
cgdannajewelry.com
Organic forms in handmade silver jewelry

DOT DOT DASH
6334 N. Rosebury Ave.
314-862-1962
dotdotdashboutique.com
Comfy classic clothes for
moms and tots, many Euro lines

GOLDEN GROCER
335 N. Euclid Ave.
314-367-0405
goldengrocer.com
Natural health foods & supplements
in a crunchy ambiance

IVY HILL
304 N. Euclid Ave.
314-367-7004
ivyhillboutique.com
Stylish women's boutique for cute,
current clothes & gifts

{ MADE TO ORDER }

No mass merch will do for you: unique or nothing, right? Extend your sensibilities to your scent by mixing up your own custom fragrance at **Cassie's Fragrance Boutique & Scent Bar** (316 N. Euclid Ave., 314-454-1010, cassiesscents.com). More than 4,000 possibilities await your discerning sniff, and the result can be used to blend everything from spray perfumes to bath oils, aftershave to hair spray.

{ DECOR DIG }

If your idea of nesting is less "Restoration Hardware" and more "clambering around piles of—who knows what?—to find that perfect finial," **Fellenz Antiques** (439 N. Euclid Ave., 314-367-0214) might be your idea of hoarder heaven: vintage and salvage items from wood doors and wrought-iron gates to odd-sized doorknobs, escutcheon plates, and much more are piled willy-nilly (and seemingly priced that way, too) for your perusal. The hours and service might best be described as erratic, so don't expect a lot of hand-holding. Just across the street, **Art Glass Unlimited** (412 N. Euclid Ave., 314-361-0474, artglassunlimited.com) offers a more serene experience, with custom stained-glass work, and high-quality repair for the glass in your home (or church).

LIBBY'S
4742 McPherson Ave.
314-454-3003
Colorful cruisewear, separates &
eveningwear for gals of a certain age

THE LITTLE BLAQUE DRESS
1110 Tower Grove Ave.
314-531-9990
ilovethislook.com
Grown and sexy clothes, casual to
dressy, for regular & plus-sized women

MARY JANE'S
387 N. Euclid Ave.
314-367-8867
maryjanesshoes.com
Girly fashion & loads of accessories,
all from independent designers

MORIS FASHIONS
26 Maryland Pl.
314-361-6800
morisfashions.com
Men's & women's apparel, from
Ted Baker, Etro, Theory, William Rast

NEW MARKET HARDWARE
4064 Laclede Ave.
314-371-1720
Old-school dry goods for every nook
& cranny of your aging house

{ DELIBERATELY LITERATE }

The Central West End enjoys a reputation as a literati locus, with stalwarts of the scene set conveniently along Euclid Avenue. From **Left Bank Books** (399 N. Euclid Ave., 314-367-6731, left-bank.com; longstanding independent bookseller) to across-the-way **Duff's** (392 N. Euclid Ave., 314-361-0522, dineatduffs.com; restaurant hosting poetry readings and providing writers a hangout and hangovers for decades) to **Big Sleep Books** (239 N. Euclid Ave., 314-361-6100, bigsleepbooks.com; hole-in-the-wall devoted to mysteries) and the newish **Schlafly branch of St. Louis Public Library** (225 N. Euclid Ave., 314-367-4120, slpl.org), it's the kind of place you could bring your notebook (paper or digital), get a corner table, and get crackin' on the Great American Novel. Before long, your own sculpted author bust might be added to the installations at **"Writer's Corner"** (Euclid at McPherson), joining Tennessee Williams and T.S. Eliot.

ROTHSCHILD'S ANTIQUES & HOME FURNISHINGS
398 N. Euclid Ave.
314-361-4870
rothschildsstl.com
Need a giant Mayan head, vintage racetrack poster, or leather headboard? Head here.

ST. LOUIS STRINGS
6331 Clayton Ave.
314-644-6999
stlstrings.com
Violin, cello, and bass manufacture, repair, sales, & rental

THE SILVER LADY
4736 McPherson Ave.
314-367-7587
thesilver-lady.com
Stunning sterling silver jewelry for men and women, great customer service and advice

A TASTE OF LUXURIE
364 N. Boyle Ave.
314-534-3800
atasteofluxurie.com
Of-the-moment designer trends for ladies

UJAMAA MAKTABA
4267 Manchester Ave.
314-535-3238
Afro-centric book store/community center also carries African garments & artwork

WOLFGANG'S PET STOP
330 N. Euclid Ave.
314-367-8088
wolfgangspetstop.com
Treats, toys, grooming, and necessities for the furry set

TOWER GROVE

COMPTON HEIGHTS ★ OAK HILL ★ SHAW ★ SOUTHWEST
GARDEN ★ TOWER GROVE EAST ★ TOWER GROVE SOUTH

HISTORY

This collection of neighborhoods is home to the world-class Missouri Botanical Garden, a.k.a. "Shaw's Garden," after founder Henry Shaw. Tower Grove Park, with its Victorian-era pavilions, is another of Henry Shaw's legacies that continues to delight locals and visitors alike. Homes were built to attract a range of incomes, making the area accessible for working people as well as professionals. The developer also offered long-term financing to attract potential buyers—something new to St. Louis. Diversity of housing stock and residents is a case study of neighborhood stability through the years.

Truly a neighborhood of neighborhoods, Tower Grove—with its architecture, landscape of tree-lined streets, walkable shopping on South Grand, and beauty of the Missouri Botanical Garden and Tower Grove Park—is a wonderful place to be throughout the year.

COMPTON HEIGHTS

This magnificent neighborhood is also a national historic district of about 200 homes, planned in 1889 with the view that nature was a neighbor. Wide setbacks and curving streets were designed to create beautiful views. The Compton Reservoir Park with its historic water tower greets you at the neighborhood's Grand Blvd. entrance. This engineering marvel, completed in 1896, is one of just seven remaining in the United States, three of which are in St. Louis City. Also located at the park is a controversial statue called "The Naked Truth." Unveiled in 1914 it was considered quite daring for the times, so much so that a jury requested the image be in bronze versus white marble to hide some of the "nakedness."

SHAW

Named for Missouri Botanical Garden founder and philanthropist Henry Shaw, Shaw is one of the oldest and most intact neighborhoods of St. Louis City's 14 historic districts. There are beautiful grand homes on Flora and Shaw places as well as spacious multi-family dwellings. In a recent *New York Times* travel piece, the Shaw neighborhood was depicted as "the leafy neighborhood where stately architecture mixes with hip spots." Naturally, the locals knew all along this was right on the money.

SOUTHWEST GARDEN

Within the Southwest Garden neighborhood, you'll find a colorful historic collection of turn-of-the-century frame and brick homes, storybook bungalows, two- and four-family flats, and an area of newer single-family homes. Brick became the building material of choice after a fire destroyed 15 city blocks in 1849, and frame construction was officially banned. Clay deposits found west of Kingshighway helped to create a flourishing brick industry. German, Irish, and Italian immigrant factory workers and African-Americans working the railroad settled this area in the 1890s.

TOWER GROVE EAST

The location of four major streetcar lines made the neighborhood prime for institutional, cultural, and entertainment uses. The 7th District Police Station (check out the cool ironwork), Messiah Lutheran Church, and the Strassberger Music Conservatory (you can still see the composers' faces on the sides of the building), along with St. Elizabeth's Academy, are some of the places that created the neighborhood's character. Tower Grove East's eclectic fabric has contributed to its continuity through time. Be sure to drive down Halliday and Crittenden.

TOWER GROVE HEIGHTS

Tower Grove Heights is a mini-neighborhood—its boundaries are Utah (south), Gustine (west), Arsenal (north), and Grand (east)—built out as nearly a single piece between 1905 and 1908. It was required that all residential structures be constructed of brick or stone, two-and-a-half stories high, and set back from the street at a uniform distance. Hartford and Juniata were designated as single-family streets while Arsenal, Connecticut, Wyoming, and Humphrey were "two-family" streets. Tucked away in Tower Grove Heights you'll find coffeehouses and neighborhood pizza places, which are widely considered metro-area eating destinations. Check out the homes on Utah.

TOWER GROVE SOUTH

The city of St. Louis calls this area Tower Grove South. Another name used through the years is Oak Hill, the name given the area by the early landowner. Official boundaries are a bit flexible. Everyone agrees on the Gustine (east) and Arsenal (north) boundaries. City agencies have made Chippewa the southern boundary, and Kingshighway the western border. Most residents, however, see the neighborhood's southern boundary as Humphrey and the western boundary as Morgan Ford.

Is it Morganford or Morgan Ford? In typical St. Louis fashion, there seems to be more than one spelling. Residents seem to prefer Morganford; city officials use Morgan Ford. Either way, there is a spirited rebirth of the neighborhood's main street well underway. More local and intimate than Grand Blvd., this resurging shopping district has become both a hangout for the locals and a destination for metro-area residents.

FOOD AND DRINK

The neighborhoods surrounding the park are home to a wide range of ethnic eateries (at some of the region's most reasonable prices), from Bedouin/Afghani dishes like sambosas and grilled lamb kabobs at **Al Waha**, to the rare, chopped beef kitfo sopped up with sour injera bread at **Meskerem Ethiopian Cuisine**. Other global cuisines represented include Middle Eastern, Japanese, Chinese, Thai, Vietnamese, and Italian...and plenty of good ol' American food when you're craving familiarity. This variety makes the choices here especially friendly for vegetarian/vegan diners, and the health- and environment-conscious will feel right at home in the burgeoning locavore paradise along Morgan Ford Rd.

A BITE TO EAT

AL WAHA
3191 S. Grand Blvd.
314-644-3940
alwahastl.com
Bedouin/Afghani cuisine & hookah

BASIL SPICE
3183 S. Grand Blvd.
314-776-1530
basilspicethai.com
Thai cuisine

BLACK THORN PUB
3735 Wyoming St.
314-776-0534
Excellent pizza in grungy digs

CAFÉ MOCHI
3221 S. Grand Blvd.
314-773-5000
Sushi/Japanese cuisine

CAFE NATASHA
3200 S. Grand Blvd.
314-771-3411
cafenatasha.com
Middle Eastern; kabobs

DINER'S DELIGHT
1504 S. Compton Ave.
314-776-9570
dinersdelightstl.com
Cash only, cafeteria-style soul food

KING AND I
3157 S. Grand Blvd.
314-771-1777
thaispicy.com
Thai cuisine; a mainstay

LEMONGRASS
3161 S. Grand Blvd.
314-664-6702
lemongrass-rest.com
Vietnamese cuisine

MANGIA ITALIANO
3145 S. Grand Blvd.
314-664-8585
dineatmangia.com
Homemade pasta

{24-HOUR EATS}

Working late, done drinking for the night or just need a 3 a.m. stack of pancakes? Get your wee hours grub on at **Courtesy Diner** (3153 S. Kingshighway, 314-776-9059), **Uncle Bill's** (3427 S. Kingshighway, 314-832-1973), **The Buttery** (Tu-Sa only; 3659 S. Grand Blvd., 314-771-4443, cash only), and **City Diner** (F morning thru Su night only; 3139 S. Grand Blvd., 314-772-6100, citydiner.us).

MEKONG RESTAURANT
3131 S. Grand Blvd.
314-773-3100
Vietnamese cuisine

MESKEREM
3210 S. Grand Blvd.
314-772-4442
Ethiopian cuisine

MOKABE'S
3606 Arsenal St.
314-865-2009
mokabes.com
GLBT-friendly coffeehouse,
veg-friendly Su brunch

PHO GRAND
3195 S. Grand Blvd.
314-664-7435
phogrand.com
Vietnamese cuisine

SEKISUI SUSHI BISTRO
3024 S. Grand Blvd.
314-772-0002
sekisuiusa.com
Japanese cuisine; sushi

THE SHAVED DUCK
2900 Virginia Ave.
314-776-1407
theshavedduck.com
BBQ ribs/beef/pork/
chicken/duck

THREE MONKEYS
3153 Morgan Ford Rd.
314-772-9800
3monkeysstl.com
Cajun-influenced bar food
and pizza

THURMAN GRILL
4069 Shenandoah Ave.
314-772-8484
thurmangrill.com
Seafood gumbo, sandwiches

THE VINE
3171 S. Grand Blvd.
314-776-0991
the-vine-cafe.com
Middle Eastern cuisine

WEI HONG
3175 S. Grand Blvd.
314-773-8318
weihongrestaurant.com
Cantonese cuisine

YUMMIE'S SOUL FOOD
3149 Shenandoah Ave.
314-226-9800
yummiesrestaurant.com
Soul/Southern food

{ KIDZONE }

A popular neighborhood hangout in its own right, **Hartford Coffee Company** (3974 Hartford, 314-771-5282, hartfordcoffeecompany.net) has really earned its fame among the sleep-deprived, caffeine-seeking parents of Tower Grove South and beyond—with a large, somewhat sequestered children's play area featuring a train table, play kitchen, chalkboard, stocked bookshelves, and most importantly, other little kids, it's a welcoming spot for people whose party includes members of the shorter set. The staff whips up a mean chocolate milk, plus there's a kid's menu and plenty of grab-and-go cups of snacks like Goldfish crackers and Cheerios. At 5 p.m. on the first W of the month, there's a kid-centered concert; even the non-breeders here are reasonably tolerant. Bring your own Purell, if you're germ-averse, because there's no telling how many times a day those train pieces get chewed.

{ DRINKS AND DRAG }

At **The Grey Fox Pub** (3503 S. Spring Ave., 314-772-2150, greyfoxstl.com), you can get a drink, but the real attraction of this gay-friendly corner bar are the drag shows that take over the stage several nights a week. More seasoned performers strut their stuff for "La Cage Aux Foxes" on F and Sa nights, but it's hard to beat the sheer entertainment value of the aspiring dancers, singers, lip-synchers, jugglers, and more who get their turn under the lights at the Su night Variety Show.

{ SOMETHING SWEET }

Let's get straight to the good stuff: For a sweet tooth, a trio of worthy stops includes **World's Fair Donuts** (old-school, with your blueberry cake, plain glazed, or long johns dropped in white paper sacks, drip coffee in Styrofoam cups, and counter staff doing the math by hand, in pencil, on the back of a donut box; 1904 S. Vandeventer Ave., 314-776-9975, cash only), **SweetArt Bakeshop & Art Studio** (homemade sugary goodness centered on cute-as-pie cupcakes, including Come Hither Carrot, The Fauxstess, and Red Velvet, including vegan baked yummies; 2203 S. 39th St., 314-771-4278, sweetartstl.com), and rich, creamy gelato served in the handsome surroundings of **Gelateria del Leone** (3197 S. Grand Blvd., 314-776-3500, thegelateria.com).

{ CLASSIC SOUTH CITY }

How can you not have a soft spot for a bar that, in its early days, functioned as a de facto meeting hall for the local Catholic church? Fast forward eight decades, and **Friendly's Sports Bar & Grill** (3503 Roger Pl., 314-771-2040, friendlyssportsbar.com) is still going strong, thanks to its homemade fried chicken, cold beer, numerous TVs and, for the athletic set, pool, darts, skeeball, shuffleboard, and patio games out back in the beer garden.

SOMETHING TO DRINK

Plenty of corner taverns and neighborhood watering holes have crowds of regulars, but you'll find most welcoming to the first-timer, too; this being the ancestral home of the south St. Louis brewery worker, expect to find a lot of Anheuser-Busch products crossing the bar, and sometimes a game of washers or cornhole out back.

ABSOLUTLI GOOSED
3196 S. Grand Blvd.
314-771-9300
absolutligoosed.com
GLBT-friendly martini bar, appetizers

AMSTERDAM TAVERN
3175 Morgan Ford Rd.
314-772-8224
amsterdamtavern.com
Nonsmoking, soccer-mad

BLEEDING DEACON PUBLIC HOUSE
4123 Chippewa St.
314-772-1813
thebleedingdeaconpublic-house.com
Hipster bar, gourmet pub food

CBGB
3163 S. Grand Blvd.
314-773-9743
Smoky dive, big patio, live music

O'CONNELL'S PUB
4652 Shaw Ave.
314-773-6600
Award-winning burgers, house-made Mayfair dressing and historical ties to Gaslight Square make this dark-interiored pub appealing

PETRA CAFE HOOKAH LOUNGE
3177 S. Grand Blvd.
314-772-4888
petrasaintlouis.com
Lunch, dinner, hookah, coffee

RILEY'S PUB
3458 Arsenal St.
314-664-7474
Cozy booths, cheap pizza & pints

THE ROYALE
3132 S. Kingshighway Blvd.
314-772-3600
theroyale.com
Nonsmoking, top-notch hip cocktails & food

{ SERIOUSLY LOCAL }

We're in the heartland, so it only makes sense that the national obsession with locally and sustainably produced foodstuffs would take hold here. The twin epicenters in town are conveniently positioned across the street from each other, forming a small but well-fed empire on Morgan Ford Rd. **Local Harvest Grocery** (3108 Morgan Ford Rd., 314-865-5260, localharvestgrocery.com) and **Local Harvest Café & Catering** (3137 Morgan Ford Rd., 314-772-8815, localharvestcafe.com) seek a minimum of 50% of their store inventory (and café ingredients) from the best farmers/producers they can find within 150 miles of St. Louis. The list is long: vegetables, sure, but also bison, lamb, eggs, milk, peanut butter, honey, herbs, coffee, chocolate, wine, beer, soap, soup, goat cheese, pizza, baked goods, and on and on. Their business practices are green, too; all in all, it's garnered numerous awards for both operations.

SASHA'S ON SHAW
4069 Shaw Blvd.
314-771-7274
sashaswinebar.com
Wine bar + cheese/crepes/full menu

TIN CAN TAVERN & GRILLE
3157 Morgan Ford Rd.
314-865-3003
tincantavern.com
Plethora of canned beers, video games, comfort food

TOWER PUB
3234 Morgan Ford Rd.
314-771-7979
Pool table, loud music, plenty of beer

URBAN
3216 S. Grand Blvd.
314-772-3308
DJ spins, inventive cocktails

VAN GOGHZ
3200 Shenandoah Ave.
314-865-3345
vangoghz.com
Arty martini bar, full menu, breakfast

RECREATION

These neighborhoods and their community life are centered on the twin institutions of Tower Grove Park and the Missouri Botanical Garden, providing a green oasis amid the bricks and bustle of the city streets. It's a community of dog-walkers, softball players, stroller-pushers, and blanket-liers, from every age group, national heritage, and cultural demographic imaginable. And the park and surrounding streets (architecturally impressive) also provide backdrop for the numerous public **festivals** and **house tours** that happen every year.

FESTIVITIES

FESTIVAL OF NATIONS
August
314-773-9090
festivalofnationsstl.org
The world comes to Tower Grove Park at this massive international celebration of food, music, dance, arts, crafts, and culture

GRAND SOUTH GRAND HOUSE AND GARDEN TOUR
mid-April
Tour the majestic homes that surround Tower Grove Park

THE HISTORIC SHAW ART FAIR
October
314-773-3935
Juried show of art and fine craft from across the country, set along an elegant residential street

PAGAN PICNIC
June, Tower Grove Park
314-398-2992
paganpicnic.org
Rituals, workshops, and entertainment for Pagan families and interested others

PRIDEFEST
June, Tower Grove Park and S. Grand
314-772-8888
pridestl.org
Parade, information booths, food/drink/entertainment celebrating the gay/lesbian/bisexual/transgendered community

{ KIDZONE }

Located in a magical "cottage castle" (formerly living quarters for groundskeepers at Tower Grove Park), the **Saint Louis City Open Studio and Gallery (SCOSAG)** (4255 Arsenal St., 314-865-0060, scosag.org) has brought the wonder of the arts to kids (and now adults) through weekly open studio time, hands-on classes in disciplines from cartoon drawing to instrument making, and popular spring break and summer art camps for kids from kindergarten on up.

{ SHOWPLACE }

The **Missouri Botanical Garden** (4344 Shaw Blvd., 314-577-5100, mobot.org) enjoys a stellar international reputation for research and facilities and is locally beloved for its visitor amenities providing the backdrop for generations of family memories created at what old-timers still call "Shaw's Garden," after founder and benefactor Henry Shaw, a prominent merchant and amateur botanist who established this oasis in the 1850s. Worth a visit any time of year, favorite highlights include the geodesic dome Climatron (indoor tropical rain forest is a winter mood-booster), the annual Best of Missouri Market (great food, arts, toys and furniture, all from Missouri producers; first weekend in Oct.), and the Kemper Center for Home Gardening (spot-on advice and inspiration for your yard, from volunteer master gardeners).

{ A WALK IN THE PARK }

Visitors will discover their own delights among the 289 acres of the stunning Victorian **Tower Grove Park**, nestled in a thoroughly urban setting. A selection of the varied diversions includes: **Café Madeleine** (Sunday brunch spot inside the Piper Palm House, a brick conservatory with numerous windows on the park, 314-575-5658); **Tower Grove Farmers' Market** (Saturdays from May-October, near the center circle, with farmers and food producers from within 150 miles of town, tgmarket.org); the **Muckerman Children's Fountain** (pop jets and wading pool, open daily throughout the summer and free of charge); 12 hard tennis courts and 3 grass tennis courts, available for public use (small fee, 314-771-7776); and pony and horse-drawn carriage rides, available by reservation (314-771-2679).

At 170 feet, visible from miles around in many directions, the limestone/brick/terra cotta **Compton Hill Water Tower** (Grand Blvd. just south of I-44, 314-552-9000, watertowerfoundation.org) was built in 1898 as decorative camouflage for the water standpipe the city had designed to help regulate the flow of city water to what were then the booming edges of the metropolitan area. A lovely, landscaped park made the spot a popular gathering place for local families, visitors who wanted to climb the 198 inside steps for the view, and sightseers in town for the 1904 World's Fair. Asbestos and general deferred maintenance shut the tower in the mid-1980s, but a demolition threat in 1995 rallied local preservationists, who saw the value of keeping intact one of just a handful of towers remaining in the United States (two others are elsewhere in St. Louis). Today, $5 ($3 for kids 6-12) will get you in for a chance to make the climb yourself, from noon-4 p.m. on the first Saturday of each month, from April through November.

ARTS, ENTERTAINMENT, & EDUCATION

STRAY DOG THEATRE IN TOWER GROVE ABBEY
2336 Tennessee Ave.
314-865-1995
straydogtheatre.org
Regular season of stage performances (*Rocky Horror Show*, *Into the Woods*, and *Our Town* recently), plus serves as umbrella for other groups specializing in improv, youth workshops, and experimental theatre

SHOPPORTUNITIES

Neighborhood retail outlets tend toward the functional (post offices, groceries, and the like), but several spots offer great gift and gourmet shopping.

THE BUG STORE
4474 Shaw Blvd.
314-773-9251
Home and garden store

CHEAP TRX
3211 S. Grand Blvd.
314-776-7898
Tattoos, piercing, erotic gifts, gay pride merch

DUNAWAY BOOKS
3111 S. Grand Blvd.
314-771-7150
Stacks and stacks of used books

GARDEN GATE SHOP
4344 Shaw Blvd.
(at Missouri Botanical Garden)
314-577-0865
gardengateshop.org
Clothing, home décor, books, kids' toys, and plants

GRAND HABITAT ANTIQUES
3206 S. Grand Blvd.
314-771-9051
Antiques, collectibles

G & W BAVARIAN STYLE SAUSAGE COMPANY
4828 Parker Ave.
314-352-5066
Sausage, salsiccia, Polish, chorizo, and more, made on site, plus deer processing and free canned beer while you wait

{ RETRO-A-GO-GO }

Prefer your fashions, furnishings and home remedies from a decade other than our own? Clothe yourself in finery from the Age of Victoria on at **The Vintage Haberdashery** (3181 Morgan Ford Rd., 314-772-1927, vintagehab.com); and deep-clean the way your great-grandma did with time-tested products from the old-school **Watkins/Avon/Fuller Brush Distributors** (3179 Grand Blvd., 314-776-0009, fuller.com) storefront on South Grand.

In one of his first on-screen leading roles, actor Steve McQueen was among the cast of emotionally damaged bank robbers in *The Great St. Louis Bank Robbery*. This well-regarded 1958 bank heist film was based on true events in 1953 and directed by the acclaimed Charles Guggenheim (who also directed *Monument to the Dream* at the Gateway Arch, if you're playing STL movie trivia). The attempted robbery and the movie both went down at the real-life Southwest Bank branch, now renamed but still firmly anchored at the corner of Kingshighway and Southwest (you'll know it by the golden eagle rotating on top); other local spots making an appearance include the pagodas of nearby Tower Grove Park, to which the gang repairs to refine their dastardly plans. Many of the cops and other extras in the film are St. Louisans who were somehow involved in the events of that 1953 day.

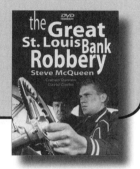

{ KIDZONE }

You can literally be a kid in a candy store: **General Candy Company** (4800 Oleatha Ave., 314-353-1133, general candy company.com) wholesales goodies from Jujyfruits and Mike & Ike to candy necklaces and wax mustaches (plus popcorn, nachos, mints, candy bars, bubble gum, and more), but the public can just walk right into the warehouse, too, and pretty much go crazy. If Willie Wonka had a working warehouse, this would be the scene.

GRINGO JONES IMPORTS
4470 Shaw Blvd.
314-664-1666
Multi-room jumble of jewelry, home accents, pottery, garden gear

GROVE FURNISHINGS
3169 Morgan Ford Rd.
314-776-7898
grovefurnishings.com
Frames, candles, gifts, Mission furniture, & lamps

JAY INTERNATIONAL FOODS
3172 S. Grand Blvd.
314-772-2552
Multi-ethnic grocery store

LITTLE SHOP AROUND THE CORNER
4474 Castleman Ave.
314-577-0891
littleshop.org
Antiques & collectibles, artwork, china

{ DON'T MISS }

Have you had a piece of Shakespeare's Pizza today? Mizzou alumni (and others) hankering for that familiar taste from 9th Street in Columbia make regular pilgrimages to the next best thing: the freezer case at **Gustine Market** (3150 Gustine Ave., 314-932-5141, gustinemarket.com). There, four varieties of Shakespeare's Pizza—cheese, veggie, sausage, and pepperoni—are yours for the buying and at-home baking.

CARONDELET

BEVO ★ BOULEVARD HEIGHTS ★ CARONDELET ★ CHEROKEE ★ DUTCHTOWN ★ GRAVOIS PARK ★ HOLLY HILLS ★ MARINE VILLA ★ MOUNT PLEASANT ★ PATCH

HISTORY

Carondelet and its neighborhoods are the essence of what St. Louisans affectionately call the South Side. Carondelet Park is where the community gathers to play. Its lakes, picnic grounds, playgrounds, baseball diamonds, and tennis courts are in constant use. The historic and beautiful boathouse dates to 1908. Sunday nights during the summer, lawn chairs line the grass and music fills the air with free concerts at Carondelet Park's Bandstand, built in 1898. Nearby is the Bevo Mill, a working windmill; Sugar Loaf Mound, one of the few surviving Indian mounds in St. Louis; and the always delicious Ted Drewes Frozen Custard stand on Grand Blvd.

CARONDELET

Until its annexation to St. Louis in 1870, Carondelet was an independent city. French explorer Clement Delore de Treget arrived in 1767, authorized by the Spanish to create a settlement. Carondelet's early days were a model of diversity, where Creoles (those of Spanish and French heritage) lived in peaceful coexistence with Native Americans and free African-Americans. A working-class community, Carondelet also earned the dubious nickname *Vide Poche*, or "empty pockets," apparently in reference to either the financial status or the gambling skills of the residents.

Des Peres School, the first public kindergarten west of the Mississippi, was founded in 1873. The Sisters of St. Joseph's Holy Family Chapel at the Carondelet Motherhouse is noted for its artifacts, hand-carved altar, and relics, said to date to the Roman Empire. The Steins Row Houses, built in the mid-nineteenth century and renovated in the twenty-first century, provide a glimpse of housing in the early Carondelet years. James Eads, of Eads Bridge fame, built Union ironclad gunboats on Carondelet's riverfront during the Civil War.

HOLLY HILLS

The name comes from combining the California city names of Hollywood and Beverly Hills. Holly Hills was marketed to buyers as "The California of St. Louis," a testament to the early twentieth century's infatuation with Hollywood. Federer Pl., Leona St., Bellerive Blvd., and Holly Hills Blvd. are part of a picturesque drive that is a must for natives and newcomers alike. The bluffs of Bellerive Park, built in 1908, offer visitors panoramic views of the Mississippi. Local legend says that 7-UP was invented in a basement lab in Holly Hills. Plus, Butch O'Hare, the World War II flying ace for whom Chicago's O'Hare Airport is named, is a neighborhood native son.

DUTCHTOWN

German immigrants who settled here earned the "Scrubby Dutch" nickname for their legendary insistence on cleaning everything right down to their front steps and brick façades. The massive Romanesque towers of St. Anthony of Padua Church are an impressive presence in Dutchtown. The Feasting Fox, or Busch's Inn, was built by August Busch Sr. in 1914 as a venue to show that beer could be served in a family establishment. The Feasting Fox is one of the few remaining places in St. Louis where German favorites such as schnitzel, sauerbraten, and strudel can regularly be found on the menu.

BEVO

No visit to the South Side is complete without a trip to Bevo Mill. This still-working replica Dutch windmill was built by August Busch in 1917. Honoring a German and Dutch tradition, the storks mounted on the chimney ensure good luck to visitors. The Mill Room, once the exclusive dining room of August Busch, features arches ending in stone-carved gnomes. Bevo Mill helped Anheuser-Busch market its popular Bevo Beverage, a 1% alcohol malt beverage, during Prohibition. In its time, Bevo Beverage was an integral part of popular culture. Irving Berlin referred to Bevo in song, as does the song "Trouble" from *The Music Man*, and Sinclair Lewis mentions Bevo Beverage in *Babbitt*.

The Bevo neighborhood grew up around the Bevo Mill. Today Bevo has added the nickname of "Little Bosnia," due to a recent influx of Eastern Europeans. Be sure to take the time to try a taste of the old country in one of the coffeehouses, bakeries, or restaurants of St. Louis's most recent immigrant community.

FOOD AND DRINK

A BITE TO EAT

BANH MI SO
4071 S. Grand Blvd.
314-353-0545
banhmiso1.com
Spring rolls and the
famous sandwich, that's
why you're here

BLACK BEAR BAKERY
2639 Cherokee St.
314-771-2236
blackbearbakery.org
Worker-owned collective;
lunch & brunch with a side
of anarchy

BOSNA GOLD
4601 Gravois Ave.
314-351-2058
Bosnian sausages,
cabbage rolls in
hunting-lodge ambiance

CAFE DEMENIL
3352 DeMenil Pl.
314-771-5829
cafedemenil.biz
Converted carriage
house lunchroom on
grounds of Chatillon-
DeMenil mansion

CHIMICHANGA'S
5425 S. Grand Blvd.
314-352-0202
Cheap and festive
Mexican, huge patio

FEASTING FOX
4200 S. Grand Blvd.
314-352-3500
feastingfox.com
German fare in charming
historic building

{ SPOOK PATROL }

Ghost tours—or, if you prefer, "paranormal
excursions"—will take the starch out of even
the most jaded participant at the historic **Lemp
Mansion** (3322 DeMenil Pl., 314-664-8024,
lempmansion.com). Local historians and
paranormal investigators set the scene, then
lead groups through the house, site of numerous
suicides and unexplained deaths during the
residence of the Lemp family. Feeling especially
brave? Book a tour with an overnight stay. And
keep your eyes on that door...

{ THE DEVIL INSIDE }

Perhaps not surprisingly, a lot of mystery and
misinformation surrounds the case of a possessed
young boy whose spiritual reckoning formed the basis
for the movie *The Exorcist*. Are the details sufficiently
murky to allow you not to shudder a bit when you pass
the old **Alexian Brothers Hospital** (3933 S. Broadway)
(now St. Alexius), supposed site of the casting-out?

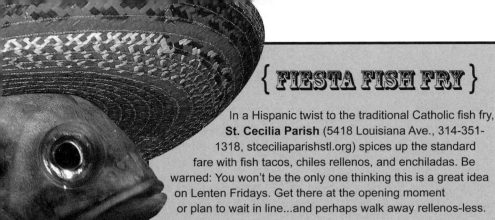

GARDUNO'S
2737 Cherokee St.
314-776-2315
Tacos, tamales, and tasty
salsas & guacamole

GRBIC
4071 Keokuk St.
314-772-3100
grbicrestaurant.com
Schnitzel, goulash, &
delights of Bosnia

THE HAVEN
6625 Morgan Ford Rd.
314-352-4283
thehavenpub.com
Fried pickles, awesome
meatballs, and desserts
from Federhofer's Bakery

IRON BARLEY
5510 Virginia Ave.
314-351-4500
ironbarley.com
Roasted pork & chicken,
smoked trout,
& the famous Ballistic
Elvis Sammiche

**LABEEBEE'S
MID-EAST CAFÉ**
2609 Cherokee St.
314-773-1200
labeebees.com
Lebanese fare: hummus,
baba ganoush, pizzas,
wraps

LEMMONS
5800 Gravois Ave.
314-481-4812
Black Thorn pub's pizza,
further south

THE MUD HOUSE
2101 Cherokee St.
314-776-6599
themudhousestl.com
Indie coffeeshop serves
full menu, breakfast
through early evening;
pretty back patio

ORIGINAL CRUSOE'S
3152 Osceola St.
314-351-0620
dineocr.com
Solid American bar-
comfort food, and
Mayfair dressing by the jar

TOWER TACOS
3147 Cherokee St.
314-256-1141
Tasty Mexican,
comfortable side patio

TAQUERIA EL BRONCO
2812 Cherokee St.
314-762-0691
Homey menu, tiny space,
and Mexican soap operas

URBAN EATS
3301 Meramec St.
314-558-7580
urbaneatscafe.com
You call it brunch,
they call it revolution:
the owners are dedi-
cated to neighborhood
revitalization...and boozy
smoothies

LA VALLESANA
2801 Cherokee St.
314-776-4223
Authentic Mex fare
from pork-cheek tortas
to fresh-made popsicles
(paletas, in the parlance)

{ SWEET STUFF }

Taste the sugary South Side at **Dad's Cookies** (3854 Louisiana Ave.,
314-772-3662, dadscookies.com; can't go wrong with the classic Scotch
oatmeal, plus STL-themed chocolates make great gifts); **Diana's Bakery**
(2843 Cherokee St., 314-771-6959; Mexican churros, enormous fruit-filled
pastries: just pick and point); **El Chico Bakery** (2634 Cherokee St., 314-
664-2212; addictive tres leches cake and fruit empanadas); **Carondelet
Bakery** (7726 Virginia Ave., 314-638-3519, carondeletbakery.com; old-
school spot for elephant ears, special occasion cakes, stollen, & donuts);
and **I Scream Cakes** (2641 Cherokee St., 314-932-5758, iscreamcakes.
com; from-scratch cakes and ice cream, in fanciful shapes from trophy deer
head to launch-ready rocket).

{ OH YEAH, THE RIVER }

It's just right over there: Spend an afternoon admiring it from the picnic-table
perch at **Bellerive Park** (S. Broadway and Bates St.). Let Old Man River roll by,
taking your cares along with him.

BROADWAY BEAN
7619 S. Broadway
314-659-8095
broadwaybeancoffee.com
Coffee, art, & music

FOAM
3359 S. Jefferson Ave.
314-772-2100
foamstl.com
Coffee, beer, music &
cultural events, and
funky decor

HALFWAY HAUS
7900 Michigan Ave.
314-256-0101
Beer & wine bar with
music on the patio

THE HEAVY ANCHOR
5226 Gravois Ave.
314-352-5226
theheavyanchor.com
Bar side & venue side,
hosting movie nights,
trivia, & bands

HUMMEL'S PUB
7101 S. Broadway
314-353-5080
Gay-friendly corner bar,
weekend drag shows

KICKER'S CORNER
6201 S. Broadway
314-832-7935
Head down for $5
Tuesday night pizza

LUNA LOUNGE
4561 Gravois Ave.
314-481-5862
letseat.at/Luna
Stealth restaurant-as-bar,
exposed brick walls, in
Bevo Mill's long shadow

POOH'S CORNER
6023 Virginia Ave.
314-351-5313
Beers with the police...
and fresh-laid eggs for
sale, as supply allows

RED'S EIGHTH INNING
6412 Michigan Ave.
314-353-1084
From cops at Pooh's
to firefighters (and bikers)
here, plus Ping-Pong
and a 6 a.m. open

SHOT HEAVEN
5233 Gravois Ave.
314-351-9606
shotheaven.com
Drinks & games
(pool, darts), karaoke

**THE SILVER
BALLROOM**
4701 Morgan Ford Rd.
314-832-9223
thesilverballroom.com
Pinball, punk rock juke-
box, and much-touted
Australian meat pies

SLO TOM'S
6728 S. Broadway
314-353-9618
Drink cheap, that's the
name of this game; maybe
shoot a little pool

THE STABLE
1821 Cherokee St.
314-771-8500
thestablestl.com
Soaring space
(guess what it used
to be?), craft brews
on tap, good food

SUPER'S BUNGALOW
5623 Leona St.
314-481-8448
Imagine crochety
Uncle Raymond turned
his house into a beer
bar, complete with a
tidy backyard patio

TIM'S CHROME BAR
4736 Gravois Ave.
314-353-8138
Live music and old-timer
dancing on weekends

{ SHAKE A TAIL FEATHER }

On the famous floating dance floor of the **Casa Loma Ballroom** (3354 Iowa Ave., 314-664-8000, casalomaballroom.com), good folks have been coming to Charleston, jive, swing, mosh, and noodle since 1935. The stage has hosted everyone from an unknown Frank Sinatra to Count Basie, and today still draws crowds for swing dancing, Latin music nights, and rock 'n' roll shows.

{ MISSISSIPPI MOUND }

Rising up prominently on Ohio St., and with a commanding view of the river, **Sugar Loaf Mound** (4420 Ohio St., sugarloafmoundstl.com) is the last surviving example of the Native American mound formations that once dotted the landscape this side of Big Muddy and lent St. Louis the "Mound City" moniker. The site's been dated to about 1050 AD, and ownership recently passed to the Osage Nation, which plans to restore a structure there and preserve its heritage.

RECREATION

This chapter's namesake, **Carondelet Park**, is the third largest park in the city at nearly 200 acres. It was built to provide a closer alternative to far South Siders than Forest Park. Today it houses two stocked fishing lakes, picnic and play areas, baseball/softball/tennis facilities, bike and walking paths, and a popular summer Sunday evening concert series.

EXERCISE

Carondelet Park Rec Plex (930 Holly Hills, 314-768-9622, carondeletparkrecplex. org). It's a joint venture of the city and the YMCA, but no membership is required to visit the most attractive feature, the fancy outdoor pool. Built to rival suburban water funplexes, the pool features an interactive kiddie splash/play structure, a walk-in rec pool, a lazy river, lap lanes, and waterslides. On weekends, you'll have to glom onto a member and also pay a day usage fee, but during the week, you just pay up and walk in.

St. Louis Skatium (120 Catalan St., 314-631-3922) Indoor roller rink with a limited and changing public schedule; well used, though, for private parties and rentals.

FESTIVITIES

CINCO DE MAYO
May
3407 S. Jefferson Ave.
314-632-6488
cincodemayostl.com
Fam-friendly free-for-all along Cherokee Street includes live entertainment (with a Main Stage and a Gringo Stage), the wildly random People's Joy Parade, tons of authentic foodstuffs & drink

CZECH FESTIVAL
April
4690 Lansdowne Ave.
314-752-8168
acec-stl.org
Gorge on roasted meats of all sorts, kolaches, Czech beer, and more while the fleet of foot take turns on the dance floor to the musical stylings of the St. Louis Czech Express

2720

2720 Cherokee St.
314-276-2700
2720Cherokee.com
Multilevel, multipurpose concert venue
and gallery space, special emphasis
on dubstep/reggae/funk/soul bands

IMPROV TRICK

2715 Cherokee St.
314-922-1998
theimprovtrick.com
Actor and impresario Bill Chott's
hometown studio, keeping the
city's improv acting and comedy
bona fides burnished with classes,
performances, and more

IVORY THEATRE

7620 Michigan Ave.
314-631-8330
theivorytheatre.com
Theatre space in a beautiful
renovated church, presenting
mostly musicals

OFF BROADWAY

3509 Lemp Ave.
314-773-3363
offbroadwaystl.com
Among the city's best concert venues:
pleasingly medium size, great series
of Sunday family matinee shows, and
crowds who (mostly) come to actually
listen to music

PHD GALLERY

2300 Cherokee St.
314-664-6644
phdstl.com
Sculptor Philip Hitchcock's clean, spare
gallery space presents challenging
work from local and international artists,
including frequent ruminations on
human sexuality

SNOWFLAKE

3156 Cherokee St.
snowflakecitystock.com
Gallery showing local and
international contemporary artists

{ KIDZONE }

Get messy and arty at the **South
Broadway Art Project** (3816
S. Broadway, 314-773-3633,
southbroadwayartproject.org),
a nonprofit studio dedicated to
giving kids (and the adults who
raise 'em) tools and means of
self-expression through the arts.
If all that sounds high-falutin',
dig on these birthday party
themes instead: Picassoesque
Portraits, Beatnik Batiks, Dada
Tea Party. Tell me you wouldn't
love that invite! Adult classes/
workshops/parties, too.

{ DIY OR DIE }

One of the most distinctive pockets of the region can be found along **Cherokee Street**, from its dusty antiquey east end clear through to the spunky, gritty arts corridor near Jefferson. A fascinating amalgam of an African-American residential core, a Hispanic-anchored business district, and a burgeoning art and activism haven, this street has it all. The newest energy centers on Cherokee's art community: upstarts like **The Firecracker Press** (2838 Cherokee St., 314-776-7271, firecrackerpress.com; letterpress print shop); **Cherokee Photobooth** (2637 Cherokee St., 314-757-8408, cherokeephotobooth.com; cheeky portrait studio dreaming up backdrops & photo fun); **Community, Arts, & Movement Project** (3022A Cherokee St., 314-827-4730, stlcamp.org; home to communal housing, bike repair shop, indy media center, and community engagement events); **All Along Press** (2712 Cherokee St., 314-827-6185, allalongpress.com; letterpress/ screenprinting coop); and **Fort Gondo Compound for the Arts** (3151 Cherokee St., 314-772-3628, fortgondo.com; exhibits, arts instigators, and granddaddy of 'em all.)

{ SERVING THE LORD AND SELLING FURNITURE }

Ever flipped by Channel 24 and seen an earnest old couple warbling old-time gospel music and swapping good-natured stories? Slim & Zella Mae Cox have been singing the Lord's praises throughout their more than six decades together and counted Roy Acuff & George Jones among their contemporaries and collaborators. The **Slim & Zella Mae Cox Furniture Company**'s (2831 Chippewa St., 314-865-2466) paid the bills during that time, and if you stop by today, you can see the recording studio in back where they prepare shows for broadcast, along with trophies and awards from their long careers.

SHOPPORTUNITIES

Among other pockets, Cherokee boasts a world-famous antiques district, worth exploring til you find your favorite.

HOME/GARDEN/BODY/GIFTS

APOP
2831 Cherokee St.
314-664-6575
apoprecords.com
Rare vinyl, zines, pop culture schtuff

THE ARCHIVE
3215 Cherokee St.
314-288-0712
archivescribe.com
Eclectic used bookstore

BOROUGH VINTAGE
447 N. Euclid Ave.
314-884-8436
boroughvintage.com
Best looks from the 1940s-80s

THE CRYSTAL WIZARD
7621 S. Broadway
314-638-7721
facebook.com/pages/The-Crystal-Wizard
Billed as Midwest's oldest occult shop, great when you're fresh out of fortune-telling supplies

FLOWERS TO THE PEOPLE
2317 Cherokee St.
314-762-0422
flowerstothepeople.biz
Sustainably sourced flowers, plus terrariums

GOOOLLL
3353 California Ave.
314-771-5966
facebook.com/pages/Gooolll
Whether you call it soccer or futbol, everything you need is here

{ CIVIC PRIDE, SOUTH SIDE }

Enter the vortex of STLphilia at two shops on Cherokee Street: the **STL Stylehouse** (3159 Cherokee St., 314-494-7763, stl-style.com; home of the awesome neighborhood-loving tees, bags, and maps from the brains and hearts of Jeff and Randy Vines, the proudest hometowners you ever did see) and the **St. Louis Curio Shoppe** (2301 Cherokee St., 314-771 6353, stlcurioshoppe.com; purveyors of everything local, from books and music to jewelry, foodstuffs, artwork, and backyard warshers sets.) Feel the love, people!

{ MUSIC ROW }

Gear up your garage band with sales, lessons, and service from **Midwest Guitar** (2610 Cherokee St., 314-962-8822, midwestguitar.com); **Saxquest** (2114 Cherokee St., 314-664-1234, saxquest.com; also housing a saxophone museum); and **Geoffrey Seitz Violins** (4171 Loughborough Ave., 314-353-1312, seitzviolins.com). If you want to build your own violin or guitar, your luthier dreams can come true.

PERIDOT
3159 Cherokee St.
314-771-3571
peridotstl.com
Gifts, bags, home decor, and more, handmade by local crafty types

REFABULOUS
3314 Meremac St.
314-353-1144
refabulous.com
Trend-savvy women's resale

ANTIQUES/COLLECTIBLES

CHINA FINDERS
2125 Cherokee St.
314-566-5694
chinafinders.com
Match just about any pattern and replenish that set of china you inherited

ELDER'S LTD.
2124 Cherokee St.
314-772-1436
Always good quality & selection, reliable hours

HAMMOND'S
1939 Cherokee St.
314-776-4737
hammondsbooks.net
Vintage and antiquarian books

PANORAMA ANTIQUES & WHIMSIES
1925 Cherokee St.
314-772-8007
panoramafolkart.com
Folk art & primitive crafts

RETRO 101
2303 Cherokee St.
314-762-9722
Kitsch and vintage fashion

RIVERSIDE ARCHITECTURAL ANTIQUES
1947 Cherokee St.
314-772-9177
cherokeeantiquerow.net/riverside
Wrought iron, doors, decorative hardware

COMESTIBLES

COMPANION EARLY BIRD OUTLET
4555 Gustine Ave.
314-352-4770
companionstl.com
All the Companion baked goods originate
here, and weekend mornings are the
time to stock up at by-the-pound pricing

EUROPA MARKET
5005 Gravois Ave.
314-481-9880
Specializes in Eastern European
staples and other groceries

MAUDE'S MARKET
4219 Virginia Ave.
314-353-4219
maudesmarket.com
Small all-local grocery, selling produce,
cleaning supplies, food items, and more,
plus shares in its own CSA

MERB'S
4000 S. Grand Ave.
314-832-7117
merbscandies.com
Bionic apples, molasses puffs, yes

{ HINT OF HISTORY }

We've barely scratched the surface of what there is to know about the
area, so stop by the **Carondelet Historical Society** (6303 Michigan Ave.,
314-481-6303, carondelethistoricalsociety.org) to get schooled on all the
rest; among the highlights is a reproduction of the classroom of educator
Susan Blow, founder of the first public kindergarten in the U.S., here in the
former Des Peres School.

NEAR SOUTH SIDE

BENTON PARK ★ BENTON PARK WEST ★ FOX PARK
★ LAFAYETTE SQUARE ★ LASALLE PARK ★ MCKINLEY
HEIGHTS ★ SOULARD

....

HISTORY

SOULARD, BENTON PARK, AND LASALLE PARK

Soulard is one St. Louis's earliest neighborhoods. Its heritage dates to early French landowners Antoine and Julia "Madame" Soulard. In the years leading up to the Civil War, Soulard experienced massive European immigration as well as an influx of Americans headed west. This spike in population created highly diverse architecture, with St. Louis putting its own spin on the Italianate, Federal, and Second Empire styles. The early twentieth century saw Soulard temporarily fall from grace into disrepair, but mid- to late-century urban pioneers brought revitalization with tremendous results.

Soulard celebrates its French lineage with one of the largest Mardi Gras celebrations in the United States and gives a post–July 4th nod to freedom in mid-July with its Bastille Day celebration. The French translation of *soulard* is to "make drunk," and Soulard lives up this meaning, with its pubs and bars that are notable for their support of local musicians. If it's live music you're looking for, Soulard offers some of the best anywhere in St. Louis. Art galleries and Soulard Market (since 1779) make Soulard a cool place to hang out any time of day or year.

LaSalle Park is a historic residential neighborhood with distinctive streetlights, brick sidewalks, and two homes dating to the Civil War era. Fortunately design standards require new construction be in the same style as the Federalist and Victorian architecture. Religious options reflect the diverse nature of LaSalle Park: You'll find the Religious Society of Friends (the Quakers), the LaSalle Baptist Church, St. John Nepomuk (the first Czech Catholic Parish in United States founded in 1854), and St. Raymond Maronite Cathedral (founded at the turn of the twentieth century by Lebanese and Middle Eastern immigrants).

Benton Park became a haven for the early brewers. The natural limestone cave system below the neighborhood, with its cooler temperatures, was perfect for storing beer. There is also a park in Benton Park, naturally named Benton Park—a perfect and frequent setting for neighborhood festivals and events with its picturesque bridge, fishing lake, and shady picnic spots. The restoration efforts of nearby Soulard eventually flowed into Benton Park.

LAFAYETTE SQUARE

Named for the famous Frenchman, the Marquis Jean de Lafayette, after his notable American tour brought him to St. Louis, Lafayette Square became St. Louis's first suburban neighborhood. Grand Victorian homes and beautiful vistas and landscaping became the hallmark of Lafayette Square. Lafayette Park, St. Louis's oldest city park, offers a beautiful green oasis amid one of St. Louis's premiere neighborhoods. As the population continued migrating west in the early to mid-twentieth century, the luster returned to this grand neighborhood. The Victorian homes have been restored to their rightful elegance. Boutiques, restaurants, coffeehouses, and even a chocolate bar can be found along Park Avenue. If your time is short in St. Louis, put Lafayette Square high on the must-see list.

LAFAYETTE PARK
ST LOUIS, MO.

AREA, 30 ACRES.

FOX PARK AND MCKINLEY HEIGHTS

Countering the French influence in Soulard, Fox Park shows a dominant German influence. In the 1880s, German immigrants began arriving, and they took on the task of carving a neighborhood for themselves, sometimes quite literally. Many early residents were craftsmen, a trait that can still be seen today with the meticulous attention to architectural detail. Unlike Lafayette and Soulard, the booming working class built this neighborhood. Each home was affordable but gorgeous. The molding on the homes and businesses is unique and artistic, and German influences can be spotted in the gables, towers, windows, and steep rooflines. St. Louis landmark St. Francis de Sales, a German Gothic cathedral, was built and paid for by neighborhood parishioners.

McKinley Heights is nestled east of Fox Park, south of Lafayette Square, and west of Soulard. Often overlooked in the presence of its more prominent neighbors, this unique, historic neighborhood's interior is filled with an eclectic array of small to large brick residences along tree-lined streets.

FOOD AND DRINK

A wide range of dining options, from blue-collar diners to some of the city's most cutting-edge cuisine, dot these neighborhoods, with plenty of 3 a.m. bars in the Soulard area to keep it rocking all year round.

A BITE TO EAT

1111 MISSISSIPPI
1111 Mississippi Ave.
314-241-9999
1111-m.com
Wine-country-inspired
bistro

BILLIE'S FINE FOODS
1802 S. Broadway
314-621-0848
Old-school diner serving
all-day breakfast, BBQ

BITTERSWEET BAKERY
2200 Gravois Ave.
314-771-3500
thebittersweetbakery.com
Schmancy baked goods &
homemade breakfast,
lunch specials

CHAVA'S
925 Geyer Ave.
314-241-5503
chavasmexican.com
Mexican fare (Guadala-
jara tacos recommended)
and chicken wings

**FERARO'S JERSEY-
STYLE PIZZA**
1862 S. 10th St.
314-588-8345
ferarospizza.com
Jersey-style is a real
thing, as evidenced by
sweet sauce, mozzarella
globs (and a Bon Jovi/
Springsteen audio loop)

FRANCO
1535 S. 8th St.
314-436-2500
eatatfranco.com
French-inspired fare,
great cocktails

FRAZER'S
1811 Pestalozzi St.
314-773-8646
frazergoodeats.com
One of the city's original
"chalkboard specials"
spots, serves fresh veg-
gies, seafood, steak

FRITANGA
2208 S. Jefferson Ave.
314-664-7777
fritangastl.net
Homestyle Nicaraguan
food, like empanadas &
carne asada

{ GET GOOEY }

Among our foodstuffs of local lore, gooey butter cake seems the most self-explanatory. It's gooey. It's buttery. It's cakey. But consider the possibilities: **Park Avenue Coffee** (1919 Park Ave., 314-621-4020, parkavenuecoffee.com) sure has. In their roster of 76 flavors (!), a few of the more unusual include banana split, chocolate key lime, espresso chip, and cranberry orange. They rotate through 'em all, 12-15 a day.

{ THE OTHER MARDI GRAS }

You don't need us to tell you about beads and such, but how about the ritual begging? **Twelfth Night** (314-771-5110), marking the official start of the Mardi Gras season, involves raucous "petitioning" from krewes, neighbors, and politicians demanding that Mardi Gras begin, followed by a procession unfurling the Mardi Gras flag, to firework accompaniment. Other don't-miss events include the deliriously frantic **wiener dog races**, a **Cajun/Creole cook-off** (watch chefs compete, sample culinary delights, drink hurricanes, and rock out to live music), and the **Family Winter Carnival** (with live music, crafts/art activities, children's parade), a good intro to the event for the younger set.

GAST HAUS
1740 Chouteau Ave.
314-621-4567
stlgasthaus.com
Schnitzel, strudel,
German beer

**HARDSHELL CAFÉ/
GEYER HOUSE**
1860 S. 9th St.
314-231-1860
soularddining.com
Gumbo, fresh oysters,
steaks & more, in two distinct rooms: Hardshell is
"indoor patio" and Geyer
is "historic wood-beamed"

HODAK'S
2100 Gravois Ave.
314-776-7292
hodaks.com
Famous fried chicken

LLYWELYN'S PUB
1732 9th St.
314-436-3255
llywelynspub.com
Upscale sports pub
atmosphere, fried pickles

LUVY DUVY'S CAFE
2321 Arsenal
314-776-5889
luvyduvys.com
Southern specialties &
hospitality

NICHE
1831 Sidney St.
314-773-7755
nichestlouis.com
Innovative cuisine from
a nationally lauded chef,
especially fond of the pig

RICARDO'S
1931 Park Ave.
314-421-4833
ricardositaliancafe.com
Cozy neighborhood Italian

RUE LAFAYETTE
2026 Lafayette Ave.
314-772-2233
ruelafayette.us
La vie en rose, with
croissants, quiche (&
antiques)

SAGE
1031 Lynch St.
314-256-1203
sageinsoulard.com
American food, upscale
atmosphere, dessert
shots

SIDNEY STREET CAFE
2000 Sidney St.
314-771-5777
sidneystreetcafe.com
Romantic spot for
seasonal food

**SOULARD COFFEE
GARDEN**
910 Geyer Ave.
314-241-1464
soulardcoffeegarden.com
Perennial weekend
breakfast/brunch fave

SOULARD'S
1731 S. 7th St.
314-241-7956
soulards.com
Fireside dining, good wine
list, Saturday breakfast

SQWIRES
1415 S. 18th St.
314-865-3522
sqwires.com
American cuisine in
"industrial/inviting"-style
décor

TUCKER'S PLACE
2117 S. 12th St.
314-772-5977
tuckersplacestl.com
Steaks, burgers,
potatoes in dark, woody
atmosphere

{ SANDWICH AND A SONG }

If primacy were determined solely on the basis of bumper sticker dominance, **Blues City Deli** (2438 McNair Ave., 314-773-8225, bluescitydeli.com) would be as ubiquitous as McDonald's: Just about every contractor-driven pickup truck in town sports one of the joint's stickers. You gotta figure these guys know where the eating's good, though. Memphis-style pulled pork, NOLA-inspired muffaletta, Chicago dogs, pastrami reuben, and a variety of po' boys comprise the menu. Throw in twice-a-week live music, and it's no secret why this joint is jumpin'.

{ KIDZONE }

Lafayette Fire Company No. 1 (1801 Park Ave., 314-621-5001, lafayettefirecompany.com) is chock-full of emergency rescuer gear (hoses, badges, ladders, lights, and the like, some from the fire/EMT personnel owners), so restless members of your dining party will have plenty to look at while waiting for genuine firehouse specials like pancakes, slingers, chili, burgers, dogs, meatloaf, ribs, and more. Sign on for the nightly "supper club" and get the chef's pick of the day. Goes without saying they've always been smoke-free.

{ PERFECT PATIOS }

Each with its distinctive charms, united by one theme: these are spots to covet in temperate weather. Join the crowds at **McGurk's** (1200 Russell Blvd., 314-776-8309, mcgurks.com; enormous, and with a lovely fountain; ask bartenders for fish food for kids to toss, pictured below); **Joanie's** (2101 Menard St., 314-865-1994, joaniespizzeria.com; sunny spot for pizza); **Vin de Set** (2017 Chouteau Ave., 314-241-8989vindeset.com; view of the Arch, downtown, bustling rooftop spot); **Venice Cafe** (1903 Pestalozzi St., 314-772-5994, thevenicecafe.com; psychedelic mosaic party paradise, but bring your cash); **Yemanja Brasil** (2900 Missouri Ave., 314-771-7457, yemanjabrasil.com; tropical oasis complete with hammocks); **Molly's** (816 Geyer Ave., 314-241-6200, mollysinsoulard. com; get shrimp & grits, or fried green tomatoes, alfresco); **Hammerstone's** (2028 S. 9th St., 314-773-5565, hammerstones.net; great spot for a breakfast pizza!); and **Square One Brewery** (1727 Park Ave., 314-231-2537, squareonebrewery.com; tranquil water feature & fantastic house brews/spirits).

SOMETHING TO DRINK

33 WINE SHOP & TASTING BAR
1913 Park Ave.
314-231-9463
33wine.com
Wine shop & tasting bar

1860 SALOON
1860 S. 9th St.
314-231-1860
soularddining.com
Live music & dancing
nightly, plus bar food

BASTILLE
1027 Russell Blvd.
314-664-4408
soulardbastille.com
1920s-era tiger-oak bar,
mostly gay clientele,
Monday drag shows

BENTON PARK CAFE
1900 Arsenal St.
314-771-7200
bentonparkcafe.com
Boozy brunch cocktails
& lip-smackin' spiked
coffees

BIG DADDY'S
1000 Sidney St.
314-771-3066
bigdaddystl.com
Party bar with free sports
shuttle

CARSON'S
1712 S. 9th St.
314-436-2707
Karaoke! Regulars make
this a don't-miss

CAT'S MEOW
2600 S. 11th St.
314-776-8617
catsmeowstl.com
Cheap & off the beaten
path, opens early and
takes washers seriously

CLEMENTINE'S
2001 Menard St.
314-664-7869
Favorite gay dive spot,
with Oh My Darlin' café
slinging steaks & more
in back

DB SPORTS BAR
1615 S. Broadway
314-588-2141
Wings, sports, and
women in their skivvies

ERNESTO'S WINE BAR
2730 McNair Ave.
314-664-4511
ernestoswinebar.com
Tucked-away spot for
wine & great apps

GLADSTONE'S
1800 S. 10th St.
314-231-6339
BBQ and barely-
concealed assets

GREAT GRIZZLY BEAR
1027 Geyer Ave.
314-231-0444
greatgrizzlybear.net
Bar apps, wraps, and a
pretty patio

ITAP
1711 S. 9th St.
314-621-4333
internationaltaphouse.com
Beer paradise (and nary
an A-B product in sight)

JOHNNY'S
1017 Russell Blvd.
314-865-0900
johnnysinsoulard.com
Raucous & scantily-clad;
with burgers

KEYPER'S
2280 S. Jefferson Ave.
314-664-6496
keypersstl.com
Piano bar, mostly gay
clientele, giant drinks

THE MAP ROOM
1901 Withnell Ave.
314-776-3515
themaproomstl.com
Cozy, quaint spot for a
nightcap or coffee

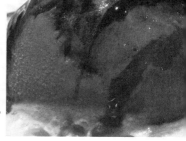

{ DEATH BY CHOCOLATE }

Bailey's Chocolate Bar (1915 Park Ave., 314-241-8100, baileyschocolatebar.com) is brown sugar meets red velvet, a chocoholic's paradise (with a nod to their friends, the cheeseheads): The stuff makes its way into cocktails, hot drinks, and decadent desserts, including the "Lover's Plate" of numerous dippable bites. Excellent beer selection and roses you can buy right from your table. Feel the love.

NADINE'S GIN JOINT
1931 S. 12th St.
314-436-3045
Darts, jukebox, and kickin' chili

THE SHANTI
825 Allen Ave.
314-241-4772
soulardshanti.com
Live music/open mics, easygoing hippie vibe

SOCIAL HOUSE
1551 S. 7th St.
314-241-3023
socialhousesoulard.com
DJs and dance

TRUEMAN'S PLACE
1818 Sidney St.
314-865-5900
truemanssoulard.com
Big menu, shots, sports shuttle, sand volleyball, darts, Wii

WAY OUT CLUB
2525 S. Jefferson Ave.
314-664-7638
Bric-a-brac packed and home to some mighty loud rock-punk shows

{ BUD PLUS }

The free tour is fine, but real brewing aficionados will be better served by **Anheuser-Busch's Beermaster Tour** (St. Louis Budweiser Tour Center, 12th & Lynch Sts., 314-577-2626, budweisertours.com/toursBeermaster.htm), an upgrade that for $25/person (or $10 for those 13-20) gets you behind the scenes to fermentation cellars, the historic Brew House, the Clydesdale Stable & Tack Room, a packaging/bottling line, and a private VIP tasting room. Some folks get super-excited, too, to sample Budweiser directly from a finishing tank. Reservations required, along with closed-toe shoes.

RECREATION

Plenty in the way of DIY-ethos diversions, plus a few heavy hitter annual events like **Mardi Gras** and **home tours** in Lafayette Square and Soulard. A smattering of galleries makes for an interesting arts scene, too.

FESTIVITIES

BENTON PARK
SUMMER CONCERT SERIES
Summer/fall
& CHALK ART FESTIVAL
Late fall
Monthly concerts bring a diverse musical range and crowd to the park, as does a pro & amateur chalk art exposition

LAFAYETTE PARK
SUMMER CONCERT SERIES
June-Sept, every other Sat., 6-9 p.m.
lafayettesqr.com

LAFAYETTE SQUARE
HOME & GARDEN TOUR
First weekend in June
& HOLIDAY PARLOR TOUR
December

314-772-5724 x9
lafayettesqr.com/Events/Tour/default.aspx
See how the Victorians and their latter-day real-estate inheritors live

MARDI GRAS
February-March
314-771-5110
From stuff-yourself-silly food events to parades to races, there's something for just about everyone over the weeks-long celebration

SOULARD HOLIDAY PARLOR TOUR
December
soulard.org/HistoricSoulardHoliday
ParlourTour.php
Inside scoop from homeowners & tour guides, with a variety of buildings included

EXERCISE

RAMP RIDERS
2324 Salena St.
314-776-4025
rampriders.net
Make all your BMX/skateboard/rollerblade dreams of glory come true; the indoor skatepark facility offers open sessions daily, private instruction, equipment rental, demonstrations, contests, and overnight events.

BUMBERSHOOT AERIAL ARTS
2200 Gravois Ave.
314-898-3259
sites.google.com/site/bumbershootaerialarts
Wants you to "find your inner monkey" by learning skills most of us have only seen at the circus. Trapeze, silks, hoop, juggling, and more are the specialties at this studio, with classes for kids, teens, and adults. Want to try before you buy? Stop by most any Saturday from 4-5 p.m. for a free hour on the trapeze (ages 13+), no experience necessary.

{ WHEEL FUN }

The **Gateway Cup** (gatewaycup.com) brings professional criterium cycling to both Lafayette Square and Benton Park (in addition to the Hill and St. Louis Hills) in multiple events over Labor Day weekend. Neighbors often turn their front sidewalks into party patios, kids on bikes and in wagons abound, and when the peleton whizzes by you at a corner turn, it'll blow your skirt up.

ARTS, ENTERTAINMENT, & EDUCATION

CONCRETE OCEAN GALLERY
2257 S. Jefferson Ave.
314-448-1796
concreteoceanart.com/1.html
Local contemporary artists, rotating monthly exhibits

GOOD CITIZEN GALLERY
2247 Gravois Ave.
314-348-4587
goodcitizenstl.com
Contemporary art in a wide range of styles and media...plus a bonus billboard atop the space that serves as one big piece of public art

KOKEN ART FACTORY
2500 Ohio Ave.
314-776-7600
kokenartfactory.com
Home of annual "Naughti Gras" erotica show, plus other themed happenings

**LEMP NEIGHBORHOOD
ARTS CENTER**
3301 Lemp Ave.
314-771-1096
lemp-arts.org
All-ages venue for underground shows from folk to math-rock, along with arts programs for community kids

MAD ART GALLERY
2727 S. 12th St.
314-771-8230
madart.com
Re-imagined former Art Deco police station, site of events and art happenings including traveling film fests, visual exhibitions, and live music

OLD ROCK HOUSE
1200 South 7th St.
314-588-0505
oldrockhouse.com
Three-level live music venue for local and touring shows

SOULARD ART MARKET
2028 S. 12th St.
314-258-4299
soulardartmarket.org
Artists' collective exhibits monthly, in range of media

SOUTH BROADWAY ATHLETIC CLUB
2301 South 7th St.
314-776-4833
southbroadwayac.org
Sheer oddball entertainment, in the form of monthly local wrestling matches, complete with grudges, girlfights, chair-breaking...and can't-look-away people-watching; family-friendly, if you don't mind your kid watching cartoonish violence and seeing drunk people

SHOPPORTUNITIES

COMESTIBLES

GRAND PETITE MARKET
2017 Chouteau Ave.
314-241-7799
grandpetitemarket.com
Specialty culinary goodies, from fancy
oils and salts to copper cookware,
picnic baskets, and table linens

KAKAO CHOCOLATE
2301 S. Jefferson Ave.
314-771-2310
kakaochocolate.com
Artisan chocolate including hand-dipped
truffles, indulgent hot chocolate mix, and
marshmallow pies

MILLER HAM
3345 Lemp Ave.
314-776-0190
Family-run and tucked-away, they sell to
some local meat markets and do private-
label product for Straub's, but you can
still walk in the door (a phone call before
Easter or other ham-loving holidays is
advised) and walk out with a ham

VINO VITAE
1637 S. 18th St.
314-771-8466
vinovitae.com
Cozy wine shop specializing in
"educational retail," which means
best experienced at one of the frequent
tasting events & classes, where you'll get
to sip (and nibble) your way to discover
new favorites from the wine, beer, and
spirits selection

{ TO MARKET, TO MARKET }

Another unbeatable people-watching spot,
Soulard Market (730 Carroll St., 314-622-
4180, soulardmarket.com) on a Saturday
morning provides both entertainment and
provisions (and if you're not careful, maybe a
pet). Market regulars have their own partisan
picks, but most agree that the mini-donut stand,
the Schmitz Spice Shop (averaging 600-800
pounds of spices sold per week!), and Scharf's
produce are tops. But if you need a kitten,
socks, or soap, you might just be in luck, too;
as one happy shopper put it, Soulard is one of
those rare locales that "continues to marinate in
its own freaky juices."

{ KIDZONE }

You can buy 'em on many city corners, but it's worth a pilgrimage to the mothership of **Gus' Pretzels** (1820 Arsenal St., 314-664-4010, guspretzels.com), where, in addition to the regular stick variety, you'll find numbers, letters, baby carriages, hearts, sports logos, the Arch, and many seasonal shapes. Visit before noon and you'll likely see some twisted behavior in the bakery. Sandwiches, pretzel dips, and other snacks available. Cash only.

HOME/GARDEN/BODY

LA BELLE HISTOIRE
2501 S. 12th St.
314-556-0156
soulardgypsyshop.com
French Quarter feel pervades this fanciful boutique full of jewelry, exquisite hand-made masquerade masks, candles, and incense

MISSOURI CANDLE & WAX
707 Park Ave.
314-241-3544
mocandle.net
Supplies for the home candlemaker, including paraffin wax, soy wax, beeswax, wicking, hundreds of fragrances, and more. In business for more than a century and willing to show you the ropes

PETS IN THE CITY
1919 S 12th St.
314-772-7387
thecitypet.com
Holistic pet supply store features food, treats, toys, bedding, and gear

GIFTS

LOOKING GLASS DESIGNS
1917 Park Ave.
314-621-3371
Handbags, scarves, baby gifts, and a emphasis on personalization and monogramming

THE PORCH
1700 S. 9th St.
314-436-0282
soulardporch.com
Combo wine shop and gift emporium is the perfect spot en route to a girlfriend birthday party; grab a fun present and a bottle of vino and you're good to go!

TROVA
1900 Park Ave.
314-776-2141
trovagifts.com
Refined gifty stuff, including handmade jewelery, journals almost too pretty to write in, luxury soaps, gourmet edibles

ANTIQUES/COLLECTIBLES

R. EGE ANTIQUES

1304 Sydney St.

314-773-8500

regeantiques.com

It's antiquing minus the fussy, with an eye here towards outsider and funky art, including industrial artifacts, former church furnishings, and whole gobs of curiosities and thingamajigs. Need a baby-doll head mold or antique bird cage? This is your spot

FABRICATION ARTS CENTER

1916 Park Ave.

314-776-4442

fabartscenter.com

A collection including art glass, wrought iron, lampwork beading, mosaic, and period lighting in one Lafayette Square storefront workspace. Shop or take a class!

SUTTONWOOD ANTIQUES

1301 Gravois St.

314-781-5444

suttonwoodinteriorsandantiques.com

Antique and new home furnishings, with a bent towards Oriental styles

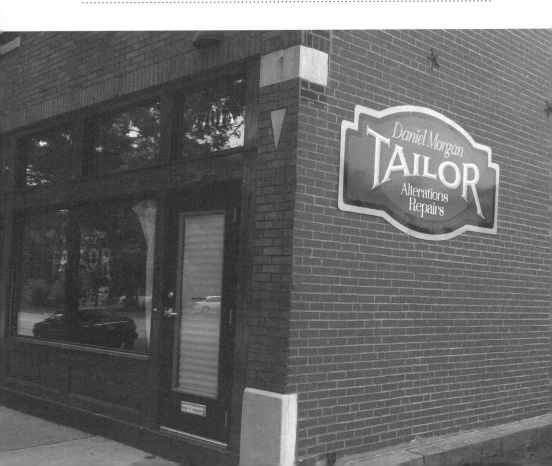

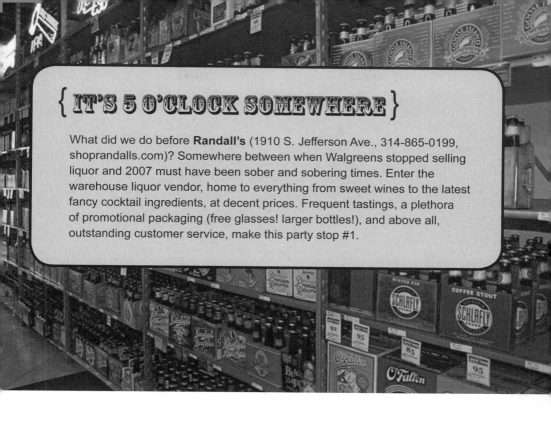

{ IT'S 5 O'CLOCK SOMEWHERE }

What did we do before **Randall's** (1910 S. Jefferson Ave., 314-865-0199, shoprandalls.com)? Somewhere between when Walgreens stopped selling liquor and 2007 must have been sober and sobering times. Enter the warehouse liquor vendor, home to everything from sweet wines to the latest fancy cocktail ingredients, at decent prices. Frequent tastings, a plethora of promotional packaging (free glasses! larger bottles!), and above all, outstanding customer service, make this party stop #1.

{ READY TO WEAR }

Easier than losing 15 pounds, more attainable than an Oprah makeover: get some clothes that actually fit! **Daniel Morgan, Tailor** (2701 S. Jefferson Ave., 314-664-6366), runs a ship-shape shop where you can take your current threads for fitting, nip/tucking, repair, and even pretty solid wardrobe advice. (He'll gently talk you out of the dated silhouettes that aren't doing you any favors.) And you won't feel a thing but fabulously fashionable.

As far as you can get from the Wii, take the family to St. Louis's **Perfectos old-time baseball game** (perfectos.vintagenine.com) in Lafayette Park and show them the meaning of "old school." In vintage uniforms, and playing by vintage rules, the team (taking on opponents like the St. Louis Brown Stockings, the University City Lions, and the St. Charles Capitals) is faithful to the game circa 1860. Among the differences? Ye olden men considered it "unmanly" to wear protective gear.

{ PILLARS OF FAITH }

Like so many city neighborhoods, this area has a wealth of religious institutions that have played pivotal historical roles. Two especially stand out: **St. John Nepomuk** (1625 S. 11th St., 314-231-0141, at right), dating from the mid-1800s and originally serving a Bohemian congregation (when the surrounding streets were known as "Bohemian Hill" and a Czech newspaper was published on site) and **St. Francis de Sales** (2653 Ohio Ave., 314-771-3100, institute-christ-king.org/stlouis), also called "the Cathedral of South St. Louis," an imposing Gothic edifice with a 300-foot-plus spire, and also home to a daily, traditional Latin mass.

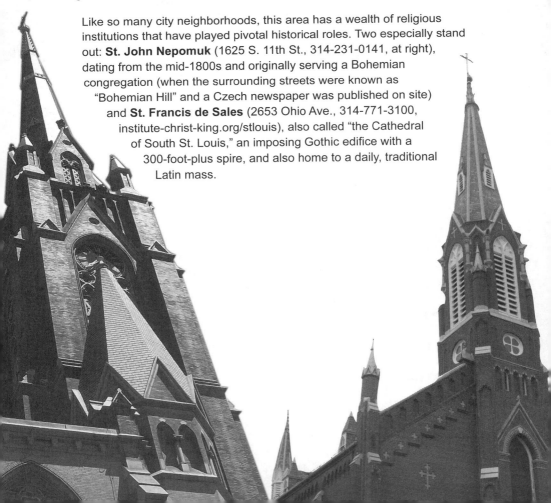

SOUTHWEST CITY

CLIFTON HEIGHTS ★ THE HILL ★ LINDENWOOD ★ NORTH HAMPTON ★ PRINCETON HEIGHTS ★ ST. LOUIS HILLS ★ SOUTHAMPTON

HISTORY

The southwest corner of St. Louis City teems with architectural charm, parks, and gourmet and family restaurants. Walkable, tree-lined neighborhoods, an abundant collection of city parks, annual block parties, and neighborhood festivals give these neighborhoods a small-town feel in a metropolitan city. It's no wonder this area is one of the top choices for the best of city living.

THE HILL

The Hill is a place where family businesses are owned for generations, where most folks know their neighbors, and where visitors will find some of the finest Italian food in the country. The Italian Immigrant monument in front of St. Ambrose Catholic Church pays homage to the immigrant heritage of the neighborhood. Fire hydrants on The Hill are red, green, and white in a nod to the colors of the flag of the mother country. There are lines on weekends and holidays at Volpi Salumeria and Viviano's Market for Italian delicacies. The Missouri Baking Co. is also a destination, known for its marvelous Italian-inspired baked goods. Hill restaurants are continually recognized for dining excellence.

Baseball fans know famed New York Yankee Yogi Berra and former St. Louis Cardinal and national baseball broadcaster Joe Garagiola are sons of The Hill. Both grew up on Elizabeth Avenue, now carrying the ceremonial name Hall of Fame Place. Beloved broadcaster Jack Buck bought his first home on Elizabeth. All three homes are marked with granite plaques.

ST. LOUIS HILLS

A ride or stroll through St. Louis Hills reveals Art Deco–influenced architecture and elegant stonework. Francis Park, the crown jewel and neighborhood centerpiece, has churches at all four corners and enjoys daily visits from walkers, joggers, and cyclists. Willmore Park is located in the neighborhood and has fishing lakes, bike trails, a playground, picnic areas, a dog park, tennis courts, a roller hockey rink, and ball fields.

SOUTHAMPTON

Southampton is architecturally similar to St. Louis Hills but with narrower lots, giving the neighborhood more of a gingerbread feel. Stunning art glass, faux fireplaces, Cuban mosaics, and hardwood floors, some with inlaid wood, are representative of a Southampton home. A walk through the neighborhood reveals few homes alike. Many of the homes built in the 1920s and 1930s took more than a year to build. Macklind Avenue is the heart of Southampton, with cafés, restaurants, and shops anchoring the neighborhood's renaissance.

CLIFTON HEIGHTS

Clifton Heights contains a magical little valley and lake, known as Clifton Park, in its neighborhood. Many homes surrounding the park have Victorian-inspired architecture. Other Clifton Heights homestyles include Arts and Crafts bungalows and frame homes. The neighborhood's natural topography with hills and prominent valleys is unique when compared to other city neighborhoods, rendering it both hidden and convenient.

LINDENWOOD

Parks are the anchors of many Southwest St. Louis neighborhoods, and Lindenwood is no exception. Lindenwood Park's soccer and baseball fields and roller hockey rink have hosted tournaments both formal and informal. Ivanhoe is the neighborhood's "downtown" with shops and cafés. Like neighboring Southampton and St. Louis Hills, Lindenwood has a significant number of homes that were built in the Art Deco style of the 1920s and 1930s with art glass and hardwood floors. A walk through the neighborhood or around Lindenwood Park is a treat any time of year.

FOOD AND DRINK

Southwest City has its share of award-winning eateries. **Aya Sofia** (6671 Chippewa St., 314-645-9919, ayasofiacuisine.com) is an upscale Turkish restaurant with an intimate atmosphere. Weekend entertainment offers belly dancing, an unexpected novelty in this part of St. Louis. **Onesto Pizza and Trattoria** (5401 Finkman St., 314-802-8883, onestopizza.com) is making the world better one meal at a time, using only local or organically grown produce as well as hormone- and antibiotic-free meats and fish. If you're looking for pizza of the non-provel persuasion, here you'll find some of the best in the city.

A BITE TO EAT

ADRIANA'S
5101 Shaw Ave.
314-773-3833
adrianasonthehill.com
Mouthwatering Italian sandwiches, pastas, salads for the lunch crowd

AMIGHETTI'S
5141 Wilson Ave.
314-776-2855
www.amighettis.com
Original location; Amighetti Special is a lunchtime favorite

ANTHONINO'S TAVERNA
2225 Macklind Ave.
314-773-4455
anthoninos.com
Pizza, Italian, and Greek for lunch or dinner; laid back and kid-friendly

ARI'S
3101 Hampton Ave.
314-644-4264
arisrestaurantstl.com
Greek-American, casual

BARTOLINO'S OSTERIA
2103 Sulphur Ave.
314-644-2266
bartolinosrestaurants.com
Italian fine dining

BIGGIE'S
3332 Watson Rd.
314-781-0060
biggiesrestaurant.com
Family friendly, made-from-scratch dressings and pasta sauces

BRAZIE'S
3073 Watson Rd.
314-481-5464
Classic Italian just south of The Hill

CHARLIE GITTO'S
5226 Shaw Ave.
314-772-8898
charliegittos.com
Italian; make a reservation, look spiffy

CUNETTO'S
5453 Magnolia Ave.
314-781-1135
www.cunetto.com
Traditional Italian, family owned, and worth the wait

DA BALDO'S
3518 Hampton Ave.
314-832-6660
italystl.com/baldo
Italian, old-school style

DOMINIC'S
5101 Wilson Ave.
314-771-1632
dominicsrestaurant.com
Italian dining with romantic ambience; reservations recommended

EOVALDI'S DELI
2201 Edwards St.
314-771-5707
delionthehill.com
The Godfather or the Meatball sandwiches are favorites

EL PAISANO
3315 Watson Rd.
314-645-7455
Mexican cuisine and
entertainment (often
mariachi)

FASSI SAUSAGE AND SANDWICH FACTORY
2323 Sublette Ave.
314-647-5158
joefassisandwiches.com
Italian deli decorated with
local baseball memorabilia

FARMHAUS
3257 Ivanhoe Ave.
314-647-3800
farmhausrestaurant.com
Contemporary American,
can be a tough seat to get

FAVAZZA'S
5201 Southwest Ave.
314-772-4454
favazzas.com
Laid back Italian, outdoor
seating in season

FIVE BISTRO
5100 Daggett Ave.
314-773-5553
fivebistro.com
Fresh, locally sourced,
New American menu

GIAN-TONY'S
5356 Daggett Ave.
314-772-4893
gian-tonys.com
Southern Italian fare; fresh
herbs and vegetables
from garden

GIOIA'S DELI
1934 Macklind Ave.
314-776-9410
gioiasdeli.com
Italian deli; Hot Salami
sandwich is their
signature item

GIOVANNI'S ON THE HILL
5201 Shaw Ave.
314-772-5958
giovannisonthehill.com
Four-star Italian
establishment; jacket is
required

GUIDO'S PIZZERIA & TAPAS
5046 Shaw Ave.
314-771-4900
guidosstl.com
Casual Italian, tapas, and
Basque fare

HARRY'S BAR AND GRILL
4940 Southwest Ave.
314-771-5077
Mouthwatering half-pound
burgers

JOEY B'S ON THE HILL
2524 Hampton Ave.
314-645-7300
joeybshill.com
Sports bar and Italian
restaurant

LA TROPICANA MARKET AND CAFE
5001 Lindenwood St.
314-353-7328
latropicana.com
Pan Latin fare,
seasonal outdoor dining

LILY'S
4601 S. Kingshighway
Blvd.
314-352-1894
lilysstl.com
Mexican food; casual

LORENZO'S TRATTORIA
1933 Edwards St.
314-773-2223
www.lorenzostrattoria.com
Contemporary Northern
Italian; house-made
risotto and gnocchi and
patio dining

LORUSSO'S CUCINA
3121 Watson Rd.
314-647-6222
lorussos.com
Italian dining, business
casual

LOU BOCCARDI'S
5464 Magnolia Ave.
314-647-1151
louboccardis.com
Great version of St. Louis-
style pizza

MAMA CAMPISI'S
2132 Edwards St.
314-776-3100
mamasonthehill.com
Allegedly, the birthplace
of the world-famous St.
Louis toasted ravioli

MAMA TOSCANO'S
RAVIOLI
2201 Macklind Ave.
314-776-2926
www.mamatoscano.com
Handmade ravioli regular
or toasted to take home

MANZO'S SAUSAGE
KITCHEN & MARKET
5346 Devonshire Ave.
314-481-5200
manzosausage.com
Handcrafted since
1955; deli and market
features Greek, Italian,
and Eastern European
specialties

MODESTO TAPAS
5257 Shaw Ave.
314-772-8272
www.modestotapas.com
Bona fide taste of Spain

MURDOCH PERK
5400 Murdoch Ave.
314-752-9126
murdochperk.net
Coffee house, breakfast,
lunch, & dinner; crepes
are a customer favorite

PLATO'S CAFÉ
5912 Hampton Ave.
314-678-5912
Coffee house, outdoor
seating, cash only

PIETRO'S
3801 Watson Rd.
314-645-9263
pietrosdining.com
Italian, pizza, homestyle
comfort food

PIZZA-A-GO-GO
6703 Scanlan Ave.
314-781-1234
pizzaagogo.blogspot.com
Serving St. Louis–style
pizza since 1967; no
alcohol; cash only

PIZZA TIVOLI
5861 S. Kingshighway
Blvd.
314-832-3222
Brick-oven pizza

{(ALMOST) 24-HOUR EATS}

After a night of continuous happy hour excitement or when you're
craving breakfast after dinner, head on over to the 24/7 **Courtesy
Diner** (1121 Hampton Ave., 314-644-2600) or **Chris' Pancake and
Dining** (5980 Southwest Ave., 645-2088), which serves weekends
until 1:30 a.m.

{ CLASSIC SOUTHWEST CITY }

For tweens and teens, the deli-markets of Southwest City are what the hamburger stand was to the *Happy Days* set. **Mom's Deli** (4421 Jamieson Ave., 314-644-1198), **LeGrand's Market** (4414 Donovan Ave., 314-353-4059, legrandsmarketcatering.com), and **Macklind Avenue Deli** (4721 Macklind Ave., 314-481-2435, macklindavenuedeli.biz), are where the after school set in the know heads to cure hunger pangs on weekday afternoons, weekends, and school vacations.

PUEBLO SOLIS
5127 Hampton Ave.
314-351-9000
pueblosolisstl.com
Award-winning Mexican fare

RIGAZZI'S
4945 Daggett Ave.
314-772-4900
rigazzis.com
32-ounce frozen fishbowl beer

SOUTHWEST MARKET
5224 Columbia Ave.
314-776-5220
Lunch sandwiches

STELLINA PASTA CAFÉ
3342 Watson Rd.
314-256-1600
stellinapasta.com
Italian, housemade pastas and great salad

SPIRO'S RESTAURANT
3122 Watson Rd.
314-645-8383
spirossouth.com
Greek family-owned family restaurant

TRATTORIA MARCELLA
3600 Watson Rd.
314-352-7706
trattoriamarcella.com
Spiffy, "be seen," highly rated

ZIA'S
5256 Wilson Ave.
314-776-0020
www.zias.com
Classic Italian and St. Louis–style cuisine, with a wait most nights

SOMETHING SWEET

You can still get your kicks on Route 66, but one can also satisfy even the most serious sweet tooth. **Gooey Louie** (6483 Chippewa St., 314-352-2253, gooeylouiecake.com) offers up favorite treat, gooey butter cake. And if that's not enough sugar to make you comatose, **Donut Drive In** (6525 Chippewa St., 314-645-7714) can seal the deal with their hand-cut donuts. Loyal customers come from miles around. **Gelato Di Riso** (5204 Wilson Ave., 314-664-8488) offers the authentic Italian confection in flavors such as lemon, pear, and pistachio, as well as espressos, lattes, teas, and smoothies.

{ LANDMARK }

On any given summer evening, traffic barriers slow the cars as the crowds make their way to **Ted Drewes Frozen Custard** (6726 Chippewa St., 314-481-2652, teddrewes.com), the frozen custard mecca on Route 66. Winters thin the crowds a bit but locals and tourists alike crowd around the sidewalk heaters while enjoying concrete treats like All Shook Up, (Elvis-inspired banana and peanut butter cookie), Terramizzou (a pistachio treat inspired by the University of Missouri), and Dutchman Delight (in honor of the Scrubby Dutch of the South Side).

{ DRINKS FOR MARTINI MAVENS }

The Famous Bar (5213 Chippewa St., 314-832-2211, thefamousbar.com) pours some of the best around. Their seasonal selections alone are reason enough to stop in and toss back a martini. Lovers of the local music scene will not be disappointed. With plenty of parking in back for those with designated drivers, it's a destination for lovers of martinis and music alike.

SOMETHING TO DRINK

Classic South Side bars with games, pub food, and locals are in plentiful supply. However, aspiring sommeliers now too have a place to call their own at **3500 Winehaus** (3500 Watson Rd., 314-353-9463, 3500winehaus.com).

BABE'S TAVERN
3215 Ivanhoe Ave.
314-647-3436
babestavern.com
Classic South Side bar; spring, summer, and fall beer garden

DOUBLE-D'S DEN
5204 Hampton Ave.
314-481-4794
Not for serious non-smokers; fun place to sing karaoke on weekends

JOHNNY GITTO'S
6997 Chippewa St.
314-781-8111
3 a.m. karaoke bar

THE MACK
4615 Macklind Ave.
314-832-8199
Great burgers and pub food

MILO'S BOCCE GARDEN
5201 Wilson Ave.
314-776-0468
www.milosboccegarden.com
As the natives say, "If you want to play bocce you gotta come to The Hill"

POP'S BLUE MOON
5249 Pattison Ave.
314-776-4200
popsbluemoon.com
Tucked-away dive with friendly patrons and frequent live music, cash only

SHAW'S COFFEE, LTD.
5147 Shaw Ave.
314-771-6920
shawscoffee.com
Dark-roasted, European-style espresso and non-coffee drinks, pastries, and confections

SOUTHTOWN PUB & SMOKE SHACK
3707 S. Kingshighway Blvd.
314-832-9009
A great place to watch the game or play games while you have a beverage

{ SERIOUSLY LOCAL }

Go back in time and experience Old World–style grocery shopping—no need for a trip across the pond. A sensory experience awaits: imported and domestic cheeses, olives and oils, meats, spices, pastas, and so much more. Everything a cook needs to prepare gourmet Italian dinners can be found at Di Gregorio's, Vivianos, or Urzi's markets. Volpi is nationally recognized as a premier salumeria; be sure to visit for scrumptious samples. A lemon ice from Urzi's hits the spot on hot St. Louis summer days. There are not many U.S. cities with as many family-owned (for decades) shopping treasures all in one neighborhood.

DI GREGORIO'S MARKET
5200 Daggett Ave.
314-776-1062
digregoriofoods.com
Italian corner market; authentic and tasty homemade specialties available for lunch; a wide variety of pastas, sauces, specialty oils, and herbs

MISSOURI BAKING COMPANY
2027 Edwards St.
314-773-6556
Vast assortment of traditional, fabulous, Italian baked breads, biscotti, cannoli, and more; cash only

SALUME BEDDU
3467 Hampton Ave.
314-353-3100
salumebeddu.com
Artisan-cured meats garnered national attention when *Forbes* called it "the best salami in the country"; try the soppressata Siciliano, with fennel and red wine; great spot for lunch, too

URZI'S MARKET
5430 Southwest Ave.
314-645-3914
Family-owned, authentic Italian market with many specialty items; cash only

VITALE'S BAKERY
2130 Marconi Ave.
314-664-4108
vitalesbakerystl.com
Breads, cannolis, pizza shells, and Italian cookies (sesame and anise)

VIVIANO AND SONS
5139 Shaw Ave.
314-771-5476
shopviviano.com
Step into this Old-World Italian grocery filled with enticing authentic specialties: pastas, spices, domestic and imported cheeses, wines; everything imaginable for an Italian kitchen

VOLPI
5258 Daggett Ave.
314-772-8550
volpifoods.com
Lovingly handcrafted Italian salami and cured meats; nationally known gourmet salumeria treasure

RECREATION

Residents of the city of St. Louis treasure their parks, and Southwest City is no exception. **Francis, Willmore, Lindenwood, Clifton, Tilles,** and **Christy Parks** provide a gathering place for joggers, dog-walkers, picnics, concerts, and festivals. A variety of athletic practice fields provide exercise within walking distance for neighborhood kids or big kids still living in their glory days. Willmore Park is home to the **Southwest City Dog Park**, a fenced-in oasis where dog owners allow their canine companions to run and play off-leash.

FESTIVITIES

CHRISTMAS

Yearly lighting contests create a magical look during the Holiday Season. Candy Cane Lane and Snowflake Street, along with neighboring blocks, always do a bang-up job. Candy Cane Lane collects donations on weekends during the season to help the less fortunate. A home on the corner of the 6300 block of Devonshire and Childress, called by some "The Mary House," features a house-sized painting of the Nativity, a gift to the original owners years ago.

CHRISTMAS ON THE HILL & CHILL ON THE HILL RUN

thehillstl.com
First weekend in December
Visitors enjoy carolers, carriage rides, Nativity scenes around the neighborhood, and a concert at St. Ambrose Church.

COLUMBUS DAY

thehillstl.com
October
This annual celebration honors the gentleman from Genoa, Italy. Festivities include a parade, food (it is The Hill after all), music, and fun at Berra Park.

GATEWAY CUP 2011

gatewaycup.com
Fall
Francis Park brings cyclists from across the country to St. Louis for the second leg of the Gateway Cup. The Hill hosts the longest-standing bike race in St. Louis—the Giro Della Montagna, the third stop of the 2011 HF Realty Gateway Cup.

HALLOWEEN

October 31
Halloween brings out hundreds of ghosts, ghouls and goblins in the annual quest for treats. Be sure to have a joke ready if you're out and about in Southwest City.

SHOPPORTUNITIES

Johnnie Brock's Dungeon (40 Hampton Village, 314-481-8900) has everything for just about any festivity. Locally owned and operated, this 18,000-square-foot costume and party place is both a city and Missouri landmark. From Santa suits to ghouls, Mardi Gras to leprechauns, and Uncle Sam on July 4—if it's costume fun you'll most likely find it here. Note: The Dungeon in the basement is not for the faint of heart.

ARCHANGELS BOOKS
3461 Hampton Ave.
314-645-2256
archangelsbooks.com
An Orthodox store (Greek, Russian, Romanian, Bulgarian, etc.) with a unique and interesting gift selection

BERTARELLI CUTLERY
1927 Marconi Ave.
314-664-4005
bertarellicutlery.com
Top-notch cutlery and cooking accessories store; in-house sharpening

BIG RIVER RUNNING COMPANY
5352 Devonshire Ave.
314-832-2400
bigriverrunning.com
Shoes and gear for runners

CATHOLIC SUPPLY OF ST. LOUIS
6759 Chippewa St.
314-644-0643
catholicsupply.com
Gifts, books, and supplies for the faithful

THE FUTURE ANTIQUES (TFA)
6514 Chippewa St.
314-865-1552
tfa50s.com
1950s vintage furniture and furnishings store

GIRASOLE GIFTS & IMPORTS
2103 Marconi Ave.
314-773-7300
store.girasolegiftsandimports.com
Italian imported and themed merchandise

HANNEKE HARDWARE
5390 Southwest Ave.
314-772-5120
hanneke.com
Expert home restoration advice

HERBARIA
2106 Marconi Ave.
866-OAT-SOAP
herbariasoap.com
Natural soaps and gifts made on site; take a tour and learn how their soaps are made

KNITORIOUS
3268 Watson
314-646-8276
knitorious.com
Well-stocked with yarns from basic to fancy, notions, designer patterns, lots of helpful advice, and comfy chairs

SKIF INTERNATIONAL
2008 Marconi Ave.
314-773-4401
skifo.com
Fashion designer Nina Ganci creates and sells one-of-a-kind, natural fiber, USA-made garments from her Hill studio

{ VINYL LIBRARY AND MORE }

Housed in a former library, **The Record Exchange**'s (5320 Hampton Ave., 314-832-2249, 247actionauction.com) collection also includes cassettes and CDs. Perhaps overwhelming to the rookie, it's nirvana to the serious collector. Not for those looking for the latest hits. Be sure to give yourself plenty of time to take it all in.

{ GREEN GENERAL STORE }

For those looking to lower their carbon footprint, **Home Eco** (4611 Macklind Ave., 314-351-2000, home-eco.com) is a neighborhood general store showing shoppers and visitors how easy it really is to live a greener, healthier, sustainable lifestyle. Good products; good advice.

{ LOCAL FLAVOR }

Move over Frito-Lay. **The Billy Goat Chip Company** (4993 Loughborough Ave., 314-353-4628, billygoatstl. com) has become a homegrown success with hand-selected, sliced, seasoned, packaged potato chips.

{ DON'T MISS }

Most of Southwest City's architecture—gingerbread bungalows, Arts and Crafts styled abodes, stately homes with turrets (affectionately called Pencil Houses)—were built in the 1930s, and often took almost a year to build. Hardwood floors, leaded glass, rounded doorways and walls (some over one foot thick) are prevalent in this part of St. Louis City. Fireplaces are often decorative; homeowners didn't want the bugs from firewood and smoke but still desired the ambience of a fireplace. These homes with their distinctive and unique architectural features make this area a sought-after place to live in St. Louis.

{ A WALK IN THE PARK }

Join the locals in a stroll around or through **Francis Park** (bounded by Tamm, Eichelberger, Donovan, and Nottingham), the crown jewel of the St. Louis Hills neighborhood. The park features Francine the Mermaid and other eclectic mosaic sculptures, a state-of-the-art playground, soccer and baseball fields, tennis courts, and a roller hockey court. On summer Sunday evenings, bring a lawn chair (and some bug spray) and enjoy the sounds of music courtesy of the Compton Heights Concert Band's summer series. Best of all, it's free.

NORTH CITY

BADEN ★ BELLEFONTAINE AND CALVARY CEMETERIES ★
FOUNTAIN PARK ★ O'FALLON PARK ★ PENROSE PARK ★
RIVERVIEW ★ THE VILLE

HISTORY

THE VILLE

Elleardsville, named for its location near the farm of horticulturist Charles Elleard, is today known by its nickname, the Ville. The Ville is renowned as the cradle of African-American culture in St. Louis. Early twentieth-century restrictive covenants on property ownership banned African-Americans from living in many areas of St. Louis. The Ville, an unrestricted area, became the self-contained neighborhood of choice for the upper and middle African-American classes.

Annie Malone, the Ville's most prominent resident and a beloved philanthropist and civic leader, was one of the first African-American woman millionaires in the United States. Solid cultural institutions, like Homer G. Phillips Hospital and Annie Malone's Poro College, provided neighborhood employment.

In 1948, restrictive covenants were finally ruled unconstitutional. As in many other neighborhoods, residents of the Ville began moving to the suburbs, and the Ville lost a significant chunk of its population between 1950 and 1970.

Sumner High School was the first high school in St. Louis and also west of the Mississippi open to African-Americans. It was named after U.S. Senator Charles Sumner, the first U.S. politician to call for full emancipation of African-Americans. Noted Sumner High alumni include Chuck Berry, Tina Turner, and tennis great Arthur Ashe.

BADEN

Extensive German migration in the 1840s and 1850s helped Baden earn the nickname "Germantown." With the establishment of a post office in 1853, Germantown was formally named Baden to honor the German city Baden-Baden. True to St. Louis's eccentric habit of mispronouncing its ancestral namesakes, Baden is pronounced "BAY-den" versus its German namesake's pronunciation "BAH-den." Evidence of German heritage can be found in the neighborhood's architecture. Baden was another location of several Indian mounds, lost to development.

....

PENROSE PARK

Neat as a pin, the architecture of Penrose mirrors the Scrubby Dutch brick bungalow and hobbit-esque houses of its sister neighborhoods on St. Louis's South Side. Penrose Park was once the headquarters of Rexall Drugs until its 1985 closing. It still is home to the Mathews-Dickey Boys Club, which was founded in 1959 by two neighborhood baseball coaches and has served more than 40,000 metro-area youth. Ashland School's ornamental details are the signature of famed architect William Ittner. St. Elizabeth's Church contains stained glass created by world-famous St. Louisan Emil Frie.

....

O'FALLON PARK

The country estate of John O'Fallon is today known as O'Fallon Park. O'Fallon, a nephew of William Clark (of Lewis and Clark), was one of St. Louis's most highly regarded benefactors, donating the land for St. Louis University.

O'Fallon Park anchors the neighborhood. Visitors may note the park's boathouse architecture is similar to that of Carondelet Park in St. Louis's South Side. Both parks were part of a compromise that established parks in both North and South St. Louis City as conditions for the approval of building Forest Park, and similar architectural plans were used.

The O'Fallon Park Jazz Concert Series, a new jogging path, renovated basketball courts, and a renovation of the boathouse are drawing residents back to the area. The new multimillion-dollar O'Fallon Park Recreation Complex will open in 2011. More information can be found at ofallonpark.org.

....

RIVERVIEW

This lightly populated neighborhood alongside the Mighty Mississippi feels like you are in the country while within the St. Louis City limits. Riverview's northern boundary is Chain of Rocks Road, leading to the historic Chain of Rocks Bridge.

FOOD AND DRINK

A BITE TO EAT

BIGG DADDY'S FRIED RIBS
2812 N. Grand Blvd.
314-531-7427
biggdaddysfriedribs.com
Known for catfish and cobbler

BISSELL MANSION RESTAURANT
4426 Randall Pl.
314-533-9830
bissellmansiontheatre.com
Historic home of Captain Lewis Bissell, built in the mid-1820s—St. Louis's oldest home—serves as a comedy/mystery dinner theatre

COUNTRY GIRL'S PIE SHOP
3330 Union Blvd.
314-383-8509
Southern and soul food

CRISTO'S
8901 Riverview Dr.
314-388-0700
Generational family-owned eatery known for its steaks and good value

C-W FRIED & GRILL
9009 Riverview Dr.
314-867-6899
St. Paul sandwich is a specialty

GOODY GOODY DINER
5900 Natural Bridge Ave.
314-383-3333
goodygoodydiner.com
Since 1948; try the chicken and waffles

MAMMER JAMMER
5124 Natural Bridge Ave.
314-381-1617
Foodies know this is where to find the best "soul" steak sandwich around, "The Mammer Jammer"—hoagie bun, sizzling steak, and melted cheese sandwich with a bite to remember

SOMETHING TO DRINK

Bars on the north side tend to have a heavy pour when it comes to mixed drinks, so be aware and plan your intake accordingly. And don't be surprised to find establishments that proclaim themselves "30 and up" or even "35 and up"...these spots are only for the grown and sexy people. For the fun fact file: there is an active, and hotly contested, North Side tavern dart scene. Here are a few suggestions to get you started.

BEULAH'S RED VELVET LOUNGE
4769 Martin Luther King Dr.
314-652-6154
Pool and darts, music, pull tabs, & drinks

HARLEM TAP ROOM
4161 Martin Luther King Dr.
314-531-2965
Friendly corner bar in business for decades

J'S HIDEOUT
4257 Martin Luther King Dr.
314-531-4050
Cozy spot for a nightcap or a birthday celebration

PREMIER LOUNGE
5969 Martin Luther King Dr.
314-288-0500
Upscale night out, with plenty of room for private parties

VALERIE'S SIT & SIP
3701 Sullivan Ave.
314-531-5085
Mature crowd and cozy booth seating mean you really can sit and sip

{ VANTAGE POINTS }

OUR LADY OF THE HOLY CROSS CHURCH
(8115 Church Rd., 314-381-0323, ourladyoftheholycross.com/index.htm). Built in 1909, spires from this Baden house of worship are visible for miles.

CHAIN OF ROCKS BRIDGE
(10950 Riverview Dr., 314-436-1324 x 107). An engineering marvel when it opened in 1929. The bridge's 22-degree bend let shipping pass through without hitting the castle-like water intake towers located nearby in the center of the river. Spanning the Mississippi River, the Chain of Rocks Bridge shortened travel time between St. Louis and Edwardsville and was part of the nostalgic Route 66 between 1936 and 1968.

The 5,353-foot-long bridge is on the National Register of Historic Places and is one of the world's longest bicycle and pedestrian bridges. It is a vital link in the bi-state trail system, connecting the St. Louis Riverfront Trail to the MCT Confluence Trail on the Illinois side of the river. Visitors will wax nostalgic at historic Route 66 displays.

LANDMARKS

ANNIE MALONE CHILDREN AND FAMILY SERVICE CENTER

2612 Annie Malone Dr.
314-531-0120
anniemalone.com
In 1922, at age 50, Annie Malone donated $10,000 to help fund a permanent location for St. Louis Colored Orphans Home. On the National Register of Historic Places, it continues its service to and is an anchor of the Ville Neighborhood.

BELLEFONTAINE CEMETERY

4947 W. Florissant Ave.
314-381-0750
bellefontainecemetery.org
Take a journey into St. Louis's past with a trip through Bellefontaine Cemetery where some of the finest memorial art in the United States can be found. Adolphus Busch (amazing mausoleum); Thomas Hart Benton, Missouri's first U.S. senator and experienced dueler; William Clark of Lewis and Clark; "Beat Generation" writer William Burroughs; and poet

Sarah Teasdale are laid to rest here. Visitors will also see many family names recognizable today as local place names like Eads, Cupples, Hawken, Lemp, McDonnell, and Campbell.

BISSELL WATER TOWER

a.k.a. "New Red"
Built in 1885-1886, it was the second of three standpipe water towers in St. Louis. The 196-foot Bissell tower was designed to regulate water pressure rather than to store water. The water tower was used through 1912 and remains a favorite local landmark. Located at Bissell St. and Blair Ave.

CALVARY CEMETERY

5239 W. Florissant Ave.
314-381-1313
Following the 1849 Cholera Epidemic, city ordinance mandated all future cemeteries be built outside the city limits. In 1853, Catholic Archbishop Peter Kenrick purchased the estate of James Clay, son of legendary Kentucky politician Henry Clay. The archbishop used half of the property as his summer residence. The remaining half became Calvary Cemetery. Calvary was once an ancient Native American burial

ground and also the final resting place of soldiers from nearby Fort Bellefontaine. The Native American and military remains were collected and buried in a mass grave under a large crucifix, located at one of the highest points of the cemetery. Wandering through Calvary, you will see familiar names from your history books like Dred Scott, General William "War is Hell" Sherman, and playwright Tennessee Williams.

HALLS FERRY CIRCLE ROUNDABOUT
One of the few roundabouts in Missouri and one of just a handful in the U.S. when it opened in 1933, this area was still "in the country"; the intersections of Lewis and Clark Blvd., Riverview Blvd. (east), Halls Ferry Rd. (south), Riverview Blvd. (south), Goodfellow Blvd., and Halls Ferry Rd. (northwest) meet here.

HOMER G. PHILLIPS HOSPITAL
In segregated times, this hospital served the Ville Neighborhood. A civic achievement for African-Americans who long lobbied for a hospital of their own. Attorney Homer Phillips, who was killed before it opened, was instrumental in getting the project financed. When desegregation finally came about, the area suffered large population losses. The hospital closed in 1979. Lovingly restored, this North Side landmark on the National Register of Historic Places now provides 220 units of housing for the elderly.

KULAGE HOUSE
This home, at 1904 E. College Ave., was reconfigured in the early twentieth century, adding a pipe organ with 1,700 pipes housed in a stone tower. Still a private residence.

MARTIN LUTHER KING JR. STATUE
The Fountain Park neighborhood is home to a bronze statue honoring the late Dr. King. Inscribed with the message "His Dream, Our Dream," this is the only statue of Martin Luther King Jr. in St. Louis.

NORTH GRAND WATER TOWER
This landmark 154-foot Corinthian column served as a standpipe water tower between 1871 and 1912. Local legend wants to believe it was built by Jeff Whitman (brother of famed poet, Walt); however, Walter Barnett was the actual builder. No slouch himself, Barnett also built Shaw House in the Botanical Garden, and his sons designed the New Cathedral on Lindell. This landmark, with lights added in the 1930s, served as a navigational beacon so pilots (including Charles Lindbergh) could find Lambert Field on foggy nights. Located at N. Grand Blvd. at 20th St.

ROBISON FIELD
Today the site of Beaumont High School. From the Browns came the Perfectos, which were to become St. Louis's beloved Cardinals. From 1893 until 1920, this was home to the Redbirds. From 1911 to 1917 the St. Louis Cardinals had the first female owner in major league baseball, Helen Hathaway Robison Britton. A commemorative marker can be found at Beaumont.

UNION AVENUE CHRISTIAN CHURCH
Built during the 1904 Romanesque Revival; the architect, Albert Groves, also designed City Hall and numerous CWE manses. Located at 733 Union Blvd.

RECREATION

PARKS AND RECREATION

FAIRGROUND PARK

3715 Natural Bridge Ave.

314-289-5330

stlouis.missouri.org

Built in 1855 with land purchased from John O'Fallon, annual fairs were held in the park until 1902. Fairground Park housed St. Louis's first zoological garden, monkey house, bear pits (these gates still stand at Grand and Natural Bridge), carnivore house, and an aviary that once housed a 12,000-seat amphitheater, the largest in the U.S. in its time, with standing room for 10,000 more. In 1902, St. Louis's first auto race was held here. The winner's average speed was 33 mph. The 1904 World's Fair at Forest Park as well as the abolition of horse racing in 1905 led to the demise of the fairs. The fairgrounds were abandoned and sold to the city as a park, which opened in 1909. Today, visitors enjoy a nine-acre stocked fishing lake, a swimming and spray pool, as well as tennis, softball, baseball, soccer, and basketball fields.

O'FALLON PARK

1900 E. Adelaide Ave.

314-584-5020

stlouis.missouri.org

In the compromise that added the establishment of parks in North and South St. Louis as conditions for the approval of the Forest Park plan, O'Fallon Park was the North Side entrant. Amenities include the boathouse, picnic shelters, tennis and basketball courts, softball field, and a spray pool.

THE PENROSE PARK VELODROME

brings cyclists from all over to St. Louis for the rare track cycling experience. One of only 14 cycling tracks left in the nation, the Penrose Park Velodrome is located at Bircher Blvd. Built in 1962 for the national championships, this track replaced one located near Forest Park, which had been removed for the building of Highway 40 (I-64). The 1/5-mile track has seen a rebirth in recent years as volunteers have secured corporate donations and have worked to restore the track and ensure its continuity. Local cycling shop Big Shark sponsors weekday track races during the summer months.

SPORTSMAN'S PARK

Stan the Man had his glory years playing at Sportsman's Park. Located at Grand and Dodier, today it's the site of the Herbert Hoover Boys and Girls Club. From 1881 until the opening of "old Busch Stadium" in 1966, this is where Cardinal Nation gathered to take in the National Pastime. The 1940, 1948, and 1957 All-Star games were played here as well as ten World Series: 1926, 1928, 1930, 1931, 1934, 1942, 1943, 1944, 1946, 1964.

{ HOLY GROUND }

Mount Grace Convent and the Pink Sisters (1438 E. Warne Ave., 314-381-5686, mountgraceconvent.org). "The Pink Sisters" get their name from the rose-colored habits they wear. Although this is a cloistered convent, the chapel and some of the gardens are open to the public. Pope John Paul visited St. Louis in January 1999. The Pink Sisters prayed for good weather for months before the visit. Some of the best winter weather in St. Louis history occurred during Pope John Paul's visit. The local media had a field day with this legend when the day of the parade turned out to be nearly 70 degrees. Winter returned within hours of the Pope's departure.

NEAR COUNTY

BRENTWOOD ★ CLAYTON ★ GLENDALE ★ KIRKWOOD ★ LADUE ★
MAPLEWOOD ★ OAKLAND ★ OLIVETTE ★ RICHMOND HEIGHTS ★ ROCK
HILL ★ UNIVERSITY CITY ★ WARSON WOODS ★ WEBSTER GROVES

HISTORY

St. Louis County is a separate entity from St. Louis City, which is also a county. Outside of the state of Virginia—whose state constitution makes them a special case—Baltimore, Maryland, and Carson City, Nevada, are the only other major U.S. cities with this unusual governmental arrangement.

In 1876, the city of St. Louis chose to separate itself from its countrified cousins and split from St. Louis County. After much consideration, county officials chose **Clayton** as the county seat. The site was donated by two native Virginian farmers, Ralph Clayton and Martin Hanley. Hanley's 129-year-old farmhouse still stands on the edge of downtown Clayton, a testament to the city's unique combination of urban flair and quiet community.

Most municipalities in this area began as satellite communities based around transportation hubs. **Brentwood**, incorporated in 1910 to avoid annexation by the nearby city of Maplewood, was a stop on the Manchester trail. **Olivette** grew around the intersection of Olive and Price roads. Other towns, like **Glendale** and **Oakland**, were developed from country estates for the wealthy.

Named for Peter Ladue, a French pioneer, and established in the mid-1930s, **Ladue**'s median income is more than triple the national average. Ladue is notorious for its strict enforcement of codes some might find strange or antiquated. A couple was forced to marry or move in 1985, political yard signs until recently were verboten, and city government sparred with the police chief about escorting drunk drivers home versus arresting them.

Maplewood was laid out by James C. Sutton on a tract of land purchased in 1835. It was permanently settled in 1848, when Sutton built a log cabin in this area. The city adopted its present name in the 1890s and was incorporated in May 1908.

Richmond Heights was incorporated in 1907. Local legend has Robert E. Lee surveying in the area during his pre-Civil War stay in St. Louis. He named it Richmond Heights because the area reminded him of his native Richmond, Virginia.

KIRKWOOD

Kirkwood was platted in 1852 and named for James P. Kirkwood, the first chief engineer of the Missouri Pacific Railroad. After the Cholera Epidemic and the Great Fire of 1849, Kirkwood's higher elevation and spacious lots offered an appealing alternative for the middle and upper class.

Kirkwood's historic train station is a step into the past. Travelers daily leave by train for Chicago or Kansas City from the station. Kirkwood maintained strong ties to the city of St. Louis in part because of rail travel. Whether going to work or to a cultural event, St. Louis City was just a 40-minute train ride away. A drive through downtown or nearby neighborhoods is proof positive that Kirkwood's diligent efforts to preserve its past are a big success.

UNIVERSITY CITY

U. City was developed by E. G. Lewis, who published the popular *Woman's Magazine*. The octagonal City Hall was originally the magazine's headquarters. The Delmar Loop was the turnaround in U. City for the Delmar Street Car Line. The Loop is a great example of a cultural alliance between business and the arts and a top choice for locals to get out to eat, drink, listen to music, dance, or shop.

WEBSTER GROVES

Webster's location along the Pacific Railroad line led to its development as a suburb. Families could escape the noise of the city and live in a more bucolic environment. Businessmen could commute by train to work in the city.

The area took its name from Webster College, established by Artemas Bullard, a New Englander, in honor of fellow New Englander Daniel Webster. When establishing a post office, it turned out there was already a Webster, Missouri. In light of this and because of the area's many trees, "Groves" was added to the name. Today, the natives have reverted to the original name, referring to their town as simply "Webster."

FOOD AND DRINK

A BITE TO EAT

BRENTWOOD

CARL'S DRIVE IN
9033 Manchester Rd.
314-961-9652
Known for delicious homemade root beer and outstanding burgers

THE GUMBO SHOP
9501 Manchester Rd.
314-918-8747
gumboshopstl.com
Hole in the wall gumbo joint that's been around for many years

TRAINWRECK SALOON
9243 Manchester Rd.
314-962-8148
trainwrecksaloon.com
Burgers are mouthwatering at one of the oldest continuously operating taverns in the area

CLAYTON

ALMOND'S RESTAURANT
8127 Maryland Ave.
314-725-1019
almondsrestaurant.com
Southern, soul, and Cajun-influenced menu

ARAKA
131 Carondelet Pl.
314-725-6777
araka.com
Trendy, elegant, look-spiffy kind of place; Mediterranean cuisine

BARCELONA TAPAS RESTAURANT
34 N. Central Ave.
314-863-9909
barcelonatapas.com
Small plates and homemade sangria

BLACKBERRY CAFE
7351 Forsyth Blvd.
314-721-9300
theblackberrycafe.com
Mom and pop coffee shop, specializing in Greek food and soups

CAFE MANHATTAN
511 South Hanley Rd.
314-863-5695
Known for their burgers and soda fountain

CAFE NAPOLI
7754 Forsyth Blvd.
314-863-5731
cafenapoli.com
Romantic, highly regarded Italian

{ AN INNOVATOR }

In 1980, Mai Lee left her native Vietnam with her husband and young son in search of a better life. She worked as a waitress at St. Louis–area Chinese restaurants in order to make ends meet for her family. In 1985, Mai Lee opened a small, six-table Chinese restaurant on Delmar. Vietnamese dishes were added over time to honor of her homeland, to enthusiastic response from her customers. **Mai Lee Restaurant** (8396 Musick Memorial Dr.; 314-645-2835; maileerestaurant.com) has thrived for more than 20 years, known for its enormous menu, delicious Pho soup, spring rolls, and coffee. She moved to a more spacious Brentwood location, but the tradition of offering some of the finest Vietnamese and Chinese food to be found in St. Louis continues.

CARDWELL'S IN CLAYTON
8100 Maryland Ave.
314-726-5055
cardwellsinclayton.com
Classic restaurant, reservations recommended; dress nice and be sure to try the ribs

CARL'S DELICATESSEN RESTAURANT
6401 Clayton Rd.
314-721-2393
Home of the famous overstuffed sandwich; reubens are a customer favorite

CHEZ LEON
7927 Forsyth Blvd.
314-361-1589
chezleon.com
Local favorite Chef Marcel Keraval provides the classic French fine dining experience; look spiffy and expect prices to match the dress code

CLAYTON DINER
6 S. Central Ave.
314-727-2828
Old-school diner serving up Buck burgers and slingers

COMPANION
8143 Maryland Ave.
314-352-4770
companionstl.com
Left Coasters need look no further for sourdough that's as good or better than San Francisco's

THE CROSSING
7823 Forsyth Blvd.
314-721-7375
fialafood.com
Serving American, Italian, and French food; seasonal menu ensures locavores will be happy

THE FATTED CALF
12 South Bemiston Ave.
314-726-1141
fattedcalfburgers.com
This long-running Clayton standout is the self-proclaimed "Hamburger Lover's Heaven" but also serves delicious swordfish sandwiches

I FRATELLINI
7624 Wydown Blvd.
314-727-7901
saucemagazine.com/ifratellini
Moderately priced Italian, serving lunch and dinner

ICHIGO
7443 Forsyth Blvd.
314-726-0033
ichigomodern.com
Skip the buffet and head straight for the sushi

JENNIFER'S PHARMACY & SODA SHOPPE
30 N. Central Ave.
314-862-7400
jenniferspharmacy.com
Jennifer's is the real deal; try an egg salad sitting at the counter, old school on a stool

JOHN P. FIELDS PUB & RESTAURANT
26 North Central Ave.
314-862-1886
jpfields.com
A hockey fan favorite serving pub fare

MISO
16 N. Meramec Ave.
314-863-7888
misolounge.com
Sushi and pan-Asian

NORTHWEST COFFEE ROASTING CO.
8401 Maryland Ave.
314-725-8055
northwestcoffee.com
Bring the kiddos; fun, dynamic atmosphere

OCEANO BISTRO
44 N. Brentwood Blvd.
314-721-9400
oceanobistro.com
Delicious seafood, booth ambience

POMME RESTAURANT
40 N. Central Ave.
314-727-4141
pommerestaurants.com
Lovely high-end café

POSH NOSH
8115 Maryland Ave.
314-862-1890
poshnoshdeli.com
A don't-miss; ask for the free pickles (not on the menu) kept behind the counter

PROTZEL'S DELICATESSEN
7608 Wydown Blvd.
314-721-4445
protzelsdeli.com
Kosher Jewish deli
in the spirit of NYC's
Carnegie Deli

REMY'S KITCHEN & WINE BAR
222 S. Bemiston Ave.
314-726-5757
allgreatrestaurants.com
Greek and Mediterranean
fare; browse-worthy wine
list

ROXANE ON MERAMEC
12 N. Meramec Ave.
3314-721-7700
roxaneonmeramec.com
This eclectic bistro is a hot
spot for happy hour

TANI SUSHI BISTRO
16 S. Bemiston Ave.
314-727-8264
tanisushi.com
The OMG roll is a favorite,
but check out the Hot
Rock Beef cooked in front
of you on a 400-degree
hot rock

KIRKWOOD

AMIGOS CANTINA
120 W. Jefferson Ave.
314-821-0877
amigoskirkwood.com
Traditional Mexican fare
in the heart of Kirkwood

CITIZEN KANE'S STEAKHOUSE
133 West Clinton Pl.
314-965-9005
citizenkanes.com
A top choice if you're
looking for beef

DEWEY'S PIZZA
124 N. Kirkwood Rd.
deweyspizza.com
Real pizza, good salads;
kitchen windows allow the
kiddos to watch the pizza
skins fly

FILOMENA'S ITALIAN KITCHEN
9900 Manchester Rd.
314-961-9909
filomenasitalian
kitchen.com
Authentic red sauce and
Italian wedding soup at a
reasonable price; BYOB,
no corkage fee

HIGHLANDS RESTAURANT & BREWERY
105 E. Jefferson Ave.
314-966-2739
highlandsbrewing.com
If beer is your bailiwick,
then give this hometown
brewer a try; plenty of
food options

KING DOH CHINESE RESTAURANT
10045 Manchester Rd.
314-821-6988
kingdoh.com
Local favorite of
residents and food
critics for many years

MIKE DUFFY'S PUB & GRILL
124 W. Jefferson Ave.
314-821-2025
mikeduffys.com
Old-school burgers
with all the fixings,
served until 1 a.m.

ONE 19 NORTH TAPAS & WINEBAR
119 N. Kirkwood Rd.
314-821-4119
one19north.com
Unique selections,
sangria, live but not
too loud music

PEPPE'S APT. 2
800 S. Geyer Rd.
314-909-1375
peppesapt2.com
Authentic Italian food,
generous portions

RICHARD'S RIBS
10727 Big Bend Rd.
314-966-1015
The place for ribs in
Kirkwood; kid-friendly

SPENCER'S GRILL
(a.k.a. Kirkwood Grill)
223 S. Kirkwood Rd.
314-821-2601
Hometown old-school
grill filled with the locals

STEAK & RICE
951 S. Kirkwood Rd.
314-965-2082
Basic but consistent
Chinese

LADUE
FLACO'S COCINA
8400 Delmar Blvd.
314-395-4343
flacoscocina.com
Try the fish tacos or
freshly made guacamole

HOUSE OF INDIA
RESTAURANT
8501 Delmar Blvd.
314-567-6850
hoistl.com
Authentic Indian,
vegetarians have a lot
to choose from; great
lunch buffet

LESTER'S SPORTS
BAR AND GRILL
9906 Clayton Rd.
314-994-0055
lestersrestaurant.com
Deli sandwiches have
meat stacks measured
in inches; peruse all the
local sports memorabilia
after lunch or dinner

SPORTSMAN'S PARK
RESTAURANT
9901 Clayton Rd.
314-991-3381
Get the wings, baby; a
Ladue institution

MAPLEWOOD
ACERO
7266 Manchester Rd.
314-644-1790
fialafood.com
An intimate Northern
Italian dining spot; try the
daily ragu special

BOOGALOO
7344 Manchester Rd.
314-645-4803
boogalooswings.com
Enjoy Cuban food or
happy hour from a swing;
seriously, the bar seats
are swings instead of
stools

HOME WINE KITCHEN
7322 Manchester Rd.
homewinekitchen.com
Risk no-menu Monday for
a chef's-choice meal

MAYA CAFE
2726 Sutton Ave.
314-781-4774
mayacafestl.com
Distinctive pan-Latin food
and margaritas

MICHAEL'S
BAR & GRILL
7101 Manchester Ave.
314-644-2240
Longtime favorite/institu-
tion for Mediterranean
fare; the lamb shanks,
gyro salad, lemon soup,
and chicken wings are
favorites

MONARCH
RESTAURANT &
WINE BAR
7401 Manchester Rd.
314-644-3995
Delicious Southern-
influenced food in a lovely
space; if you want to
impress a date take them
here

PICCADILLY
AT MANHATTAN
7201 Piccadilly Ave.
314-646-0016
thepiccadilly.com
Family owned and
operated for three
generations; comfort food
menu and casual decor

SCHLAFLY
BOTTLEWORKS
7260 Southwest Ave.
314-241-2337
schlafly.com
Burgers, real brews, and
a menu featuring locally
grown produce; brewery
tour; farmer's market on
summer Wednesdays

OLIVETTE

DURANGO TAQUERIA AND GROCERY
10238 Page Ave.
314-429-1113
Fried pig esophagus for the adventurous, tacos for the conservative

HAVELI INDIAN RESTAURANT
9720 Page Ave.
314-423-7300
havelistl.com
Authentic, vegetarian (and non-vegetarian) Indian cuisine with varying degrees of spice

I LOVE MR. SUSHI
9443 Olive Blvd.
314-432-8898
mrsushistl.com
Good sushi in a small space; sushi chef has nice singing voice

LAND OF SMILE
9641 Olive Blvd.
314-989-9878
landofsmilethaifood.com
Thai and crab Rangoon, spring rolls, gui-cha; kid-friendly

LU LU SEAFOOD RESTAURANT
8224 Olive Blvd.
314-997-3108
luluseafood.com
Dim Sum available weekends; fresh, fast

MEI HUA CHINESE RESTAURANT
9626 Olive Blvd.
314-569-0925
meihuastl.webs.com
Skip the buffet and instead order hot braised pork or scallops in hot chili sauce

MS. PIGGIES SMOKEHOUSE
10612 Page Ave.
314-428-7776
mspiggiessmokehouse.com
Ribs, pork steaks, catfish, and chicken; pass the homemade BBQ sauce!

NOBU'S JAPANESE RESTAURANT
8643 Olive Blvd.
314-997-2303
Sushi is the menu mainstay; sake and other beverages of the Asian persuasion available; one of the first sushi places in the region

OLIVETTE DINER
9638 Olive Blvd.
314-995-9945
Traditional diner fare, bring cash and coin

PHO LONG
8629 Olive Blvd.
314-997-1218
Vietnamese; good for pho and spring rolls

RAY'S DONUTS (FORMERLY LAMAR'S)
9614 Olive Blvd.
314-989-1101
raysdonutsandcoffee.com
Donuts and holes that will more than satisfy any sugar addiction

ROYAL CHINESE BBQ
8406 Olive Blvd.
314-991-1888
Chinese BBQ, congee (rice porridge), and shark fin soup are menu mainstays

SHU FENG
8435 Olive Blvd.
314-983-0099
shufengstl.com
Chinese and Korean menu for lunch and dinner; one of the few Asian restaurants serving sizzling rice soup

RICHMOND HEIGHTS

FRANK PAPA'S RISTORANTE
2241 S. Brentwood Blvd.
314-961-3344
frankpapas.com
Local favorite on the Richmond Heights–Clayton corridor; a taste of Italy served in a cozy, intimate atmosphere

HARVEST SEASONAL MARKET CUISINE
1059 S. Big Bend Blvd.
63117, 314-645-3522
harveststlouis.com
Seasonal menu using locally sourced and organic produce whenever possible; always looking for sustainable methods and delicious practices

KATIE'S PIZZERIA CAFE
6611 Clayton Rd.
314-727-8585
katiespizzeria.com
Be it provel or mozzarella on your pizza, both are done well here

OLYMPIA KEBOB HOUSE & TAVERNA
1543 McCausland Ave.
314-781-1299
Greek; be sure to try the saganaki (flaming cheese); *Opa!*

POINTERS PIZZA
1023 S. Big Bend Blvd.
314-644-2000
pointersdelivery.com
A long-time local favorite

STARRS
1135 S. Big Bend Blvd.
314-781-2345
starrs1.com
Restaurant and wine shop with wines available from just about anywhere in the world

YEN CHING
1012 S. Brentwood Blvd.
314-721-7507
Exactly what everyone expects Chinese food to be

ROCK HILL

A'MIS
9824 Manchester Rd.
314-963-1822
amispizza.com
Italian food and pizza à la New York, Chicago, or St. Louis style

CHARCOAL HOUSE
9855 Manchester Rd.
314-968-4842
charcoalhouse.us
Think of this as "your parents" steakhouse; a special occasion, old-school, dressy kind of place

FAROTTO'S ITALIAN RESTAURANT & PIZZERIA
9525 Manchester Rd.
314-962-0048
farottos.com
St. Louis–style pizza institution if you're into provel on your pies, and popular happy hour spot

HACIENDA MEXICAN RESTAURANT
9748 Manchester Rd.
314-962-7100
hacienda-stl.com
Enjoy 'ritas and the party on the patio at this happy hour spot

{ FULLY CAFFEINATED }

City Coffee House and Creperie (36 N. Brentwood Blvd.; 314-862-2489; citycoffeeandcreperie.com); **Foundation Grounds** (7298 Manchester Rd.; 314-601-3588; foundationgrounds. com); **Meshuggah Cafe** (6269 Delmar Blvd.; 314-726-5662; meshuggahcafe.com) offer your morning fix in an independent environment.

{ (ALMOST) ANYTIME EATS }

Tiffany's Original Diner (7402 Manchester Rd., 314-644-0929) is a real diner with counter seating, good food, and fun. Open 24 hours except Sunday from 2 until 5 on Monday.

NACHOMAMA'S
9643 Manchester Rd.
314-961-9110
nachomamas-stl.com
Fresh & fast Tex-Mex, from burritos to tamales, plus frequent daily specials

U. CITY

AL-TARBOUSH DELI
602 Westgate Ave.
314-725-1944
Falafel is freshly made; you can purchase hummus, tabbouleh, dolmahs, and tahinis to go along with a hookah

BLUEBERRY HILL
6504 Delmar Blvd.
314-727-4444
blueberryhill.com
Restaurant/music club filled with pop-culture memorabilia; burgers, soups, and Chuck Berry in the Duck Room

CHEESE-OLOGY MACARONI & CHEESE
6602 Delmar Blvd.
314-863-6365
cheese-ology.com
Comfort food mavens and vegetarians will be happy and leave full

CICERO'S
6691 Delmar Blvd.
314-862-0009
ciceros-stl.com
Huge beer selection, Italian eats; people watch from your sidewalk café table spot on a St. Louis summer evening

ECLIPSE
6177 Delmar Blvd.
314-726-2222
eclipsestlouis.com
Interplanetary culinary adventure in the Moonrise Hotel; also check out the rooftop bar

FITZ'S AMERICAN GRILL & BOTTLING WORKS
6605 Delmar Blvd.
314-726-9555
fitzsrootbeer.com
See how root beer, orange soda, and cream soda are made, right from your table; plenty of healthy food options so you won't feel guilty about the root beer float

FRANK & HELEN'S PIZZERIA
8111 Olive Blvd.
314-997-0666
frankandhelens.com
Pizza with mozzarella cheese! The fried chicken is very good; the only other place in St. Louis where you can get Crown Candy ice cream besides Crown Candy

LA PIZZA
8137 Delmar Blvd.
314-725-1230
lapizzamenu.com
Hand-tossed New York–
style pizza

MI RANCHITO
887 Kingsland Ave.
314-863-1880
mi-ranchitostl.com
Mi Ranchito offers good,
inexpensive, authentic
Tex-Mex

MOMOS
630 North & South Rd.
314-863-3511
saucemagazine.com/
momos
Authentic Greek with a
tapas-style menu and
belly dancers

QUEEN OF SHEBA
6665 Olive Blvd.
314-727-7057
Ethiopian food; try the
goat curry

RANOUSH
6501 Delmar Blvd.
314-726-6874
ranoush.com
Syrian food with a
multitude of options for
vegetarians; baklava is
made fresh daily

SEKI'S JAPANESE RESTAURANT
6335 Delmar Blvd.
314-726-6477
Authentic Japanese food
with full sushi bar

U-CITY GRILL
6696 Enright Ave.
314-721-3073
Korean specialties just off
Delmar in The Loop; the
bulgogi beef is a favorite,
cash only

WEI HONG SEAFOOD RESTAURANT & BAKERY
7740 Olive Blvd.
314-726-0363
weihongseafood.com
Local favorite for Dim Sum

WINSLOW'S HOME
7213 Delmar Blvd.
314-725-7559
winslowshome.com
A cool place for breakfast
or lunch; try the scrump-
tious blueberry pancakes

WEBSTER

BIG SKY CAFE
47 S. Old Orchard Ave.
314-962-5757
allgreatrestaurants.com
Great place to begin or
finish an evening at the
Rep

CHINA INN
9737 Manchester Rd.
314-968-8823
Serves a mean "Happy
Family"

C.J. MUGG'S
101 West Lockwood Ave.
314-963-1976
cjmuggs.com
Come for martinis before
the Rep or sip while
people watching from the
sidewalk in the summer;
local music venue for
the over-30 crowd

CYRANO'S
603 E. Lockwood Ave.
314-963-3232
cyranos.com
Scrumptious desserts
before or after the Rep
or a play at Nerinx Hall
High School

HWY 61 ROADHOUSE & KITCHEN

34 S. Old Orchard Ave.
314-968-0061
hwy61roadhouse.com
Cajun, Creole, and BBQ;
local brews and music

MILAGRO MODERN MEXICAN

20 Allen Ave., Ste. 130
314-962-4300
milagromodernmexican.
com
An upscale taste of
Mexico; enjoy freshly
made margaritas at happy
hour; house-made chorizo
and grilled fish tacos

RACANELLI'S

8161 Big Bend Blvd.
314-963-1111
racanellis.com
Local-based NY-style
pizza chain

ST. LOUIS SPORTS ZONE

113 Kenrick Plz.
314-961-3366
stl-sportszone.com
Good place to get your
game on; ask for the
"Trashed Wings"

STRATTON'S CAFE

8103 Big Bend Blvd.
314-961-2900
strattonscafe.com
A good bet for breakfast;
also try the housemade
gelato

{ REMINDERS OF OUR PAST }

Hanley House (7600 Westmoreland
Ave.; 314-467-0712; hanleyhouse.
blogspot.com) is reminder of how Clayton
was in the early days. **Hawken House**
(1155 South Rock Hill Rd.; 314-968-
1857 historicwebster.org/HawkenHouse/
tabid/55/Default.aspx) is the 1857 home
to the rifle manufacturing Hawken family.
Quinette Cemetery (12120 Old Big Bend
Blvd.) is a historic African-American burial
ground was established in 1866 and is
one of the oldest west of the Mississippi.

CHILL
7610 Wydown Blvd.
314-932-5010
chillwydown.com
Frozen yogurt creations
by you, in stylish
surroundings

**CHOCOLATE
CHOCOLATE
CHOCOLATE**
112 N. Kirkwood Rd.
314-965-6615
chocolatechocolate.com
Enjoy handcrafted
chocolate on the day it
was made

**DR. JAZZ
SODA FOUNTAIN**
29 N. Gore Ave.
314-961-5299
drjazzwebstergroves.com
Cedar Crest Ice Cream
from Wisconsin is one
of the world's best

HANK'S CHEESECAKES
1063 S. Big Bend Blvd.
314-781-0300
hankscheesecakes.com
Scrumptious, a favorite
is the white chocolate
raspberry cheesecake

JILLY'S CUPCAKE BAR
8509 Delmar Blvd.
314-993-5455
jillyscupcakebar.com
Enjoy the 6-cheese mac
and cheese; stay for the
delectable cupcakes,
oversized and filled

**LAKE FOREST
CONFECTIONS**
7801 Clayton Rd.
314-721-9997
www.lakeforest
confections.com
If it's Hanukkah gold
coins you need, don't go
anywhere else; staff has
more than 100 years of
combined confectionary
experience

**LUBELEY'S
BAKERY & DELI**
7815 Watson Rd.
314-961-7160
lubeleysbakery.com
Stollens, (the German
pastry treat), hot cross
buns, and a cool retro
highway sign

**SERENDIPITY HOME-
MADE ICE CREAM**
8130 Big Bend Blvd.
314-962-2700
serendipity-icecream.com
Sold by the ounce, Seren-
dipity is currently served
in 100 local restaurants

SUGAR SHACK
151 W. Argonne Dr.
314-966-0065
kirkwoodsugarshack.com
Old-time sweets, sodas,
phosphates, floats, and
cake balls; parties with
theme names like Candy
Carnival, Candy Land,
and Pirate Party

**SWITZER
CANDY COMPANY**
27 N. Gore Ave.
314-961-1101
switzercandy.com
This is authentic,
traditional candy; known
nationally for licorice but
also try the many fruit
twist flavors as well as
Buttermels, a favorite of
Switzer Candy's founder,
Grandfather Frederick
Switzer

YO MY GOODNESS
237 W. Lockwood Ave.
314-963-3590
yomystl.com
Sold by the ounce; non-fat
and low-calorie frozen
delights in a variety of
flavors

DELMAR RESTAURANT AND LOUNGE

6235 Delmar Blvd.
314-725-6565
delmar-lounge.com
This is the granddaddy of The Loop's cocktail lounges; enjoy jazz on Friday nights

FALLON'S PUB

9200 Olive Blvd.
314-991-9800
Irish-themed sports bar with 16 TV screens; happy hour features live music, weekly trivia contests, patio dining, live music on the weekends

POST SPORTS BAR & GRILL

7372 Manchester Rd.
314-645-1109
thepostsportsbar.com
Learn the art of "Posting"; gameday specials

ST. LOUIS BUBBLE TEA

6677 Delmar Blvd.
314-862-2890
stlouisbubbletea.com
Refreshing on a hot, humid St. Louis summer evening, plus warming winter selections

SPORTS ATTIC

8212 Manchester Rd.
314-963-7829
Traditional local watering hole and popular spot for the after-work crowd

WINE A LITTLE

BRANICA'S WINE BAR

449 S. Kirkwood Rd.
314-984-9595
trattoriabranica.com
Kirkwood hot spot for happy hour; limited late-night dining menu

GRAPEVINE WINES AND CHEESE

309 S. Kirkwood Rd.
314-909-7044
grapevinewinesand-cheese.com
Over 1,000 wines to choose from plus 60 malt scotches, gourmet cheeses, foods, and accessories

ROBUST WINE BAR, SHOPPE & CAFE

227 W. Lockwood Ave.
314-963-0033
robustwinebar.com
An elegant spot for wine flights and thoughtful food pairings

ST. LOUIS CELLARS

2640 S. Big Bend Blvd.
saintlouiscellars.com
Tops local "best of" and "A-lists" for its selection, classes, tastings, and events

SASHA'S WINE BAR & MARKET

706 Delmar Blvd.
314-863-7274
Very nice wine bar; seasonal outdoor atmosphere is delightful

WINE AND CHEESE PLACE

7435 Forsyth Blvd.
314-727-8788
wineandcheeseplace.com
Wine, as the name says, gourmet foods, classes, and events

THE WINE MERCHANT

20 S. Hanley Rd.
314-863-6282
winemerchantltd.com
Considered a top stop for wine, this also was one of the first wine stores in St. Louis

CLAYTON

Public art abounds; a trip through town reveals works by Renoir as well as Milles

Folke Filbyter, *by Carl Milles*
Located in front of City Hall, 10 N. Bemiston. Milles studied with Renoir and also created the Meeting of the Waters at St. Louis's Union Station. On loan from the St. Louis Art Museum

Venus Victorious, *by Pierre-Auguste* Renoir located in Shaw Park's Centennial Garden On loan from the St. Louis Art Museum.

The Uncertainty of Ground State Fluctuations, *by Alice Aycock*
Located in front of the Center of Clayton at 50 Gay Avenue

FM6 Walking Jackman, *by Earnest Trova* at the intersection of Maryland Ave. and Brentwood Blvd.

Clayton Caryatid, *by Howard Ben Tre*
Located at 150 Carondelet Pl.

Still Point, *by Ruth Keller Schweiss*
Located in front of the Ritz Carleton at 100 Carondelet Pl.

KIRKWOOD

The Kirkwood Chairs
The work of Marianist Brother Mel Meyer
A whimsical stack of colorful chairs located at the entry to the Kirkwood Farmers' Market on Argonne Ave.

UNIVERSITY CITY

Gates of Opportunity are the Gateway to The Loop and are a beloved landmark of all St. Louisans

Rain Man, *by Gregory Cullen*
Rain Man, at Delmar and Kingsland, Epstein Plaza, was intended to be a temporary seven-month display. Its removal created an uproar. A group formed to raise funds for a more permanent bronze statue and the rest, as they say, is history.

Lion in the Grass, *by Robin Murez*
Sits playfully in the center of a rotary surrounded by native Missouri tall grass at Skinker and Olive. Murez also has art on display at St. Louis's Francis Park.

Musical Lion Benches, *by Robert Cassilly*
In front of University City's City Hall at Delmar and Trinity a saxophone-playing lion and a lute-playing lion invite you to sit and enjoy the view.

St. Louis Walk of Fame
This walking lesson in local history was the brainchild of Joe Edwards in 1988. Honorees must have been born in St. Louis or spent their formative or creative years here. Their accomplishment must have had a national impact on our cultural heritage. Currently there are more than 130 honorees, each represented by a brass starred sidewalk plaque.

Chuck Berry Statue, *by Harry Weber*
Unveiled in 2011 in honor of one of St. Louis's favorite sons, the legendary rock 'n' roller Chuck Berry. The eight-foot-tall bronze stands near beloved music venue and eatery Blueberry Hill, site of many Chuck Berry performances in that venue's Duck Room.

CHUCK BERRY

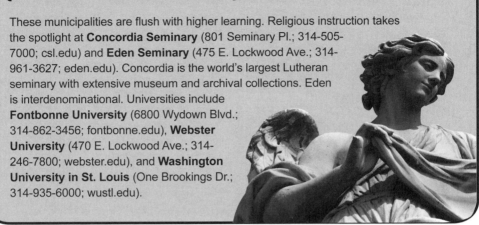

RECREATION

FESTIVITIES

ART AND AIR

June

Webster Groves

Art and Air features more than 100 artists in 12 categories on the grounds of beautiful Eden Seminary. Purchase the best of fine food and enjoy the sights and sounds of great music. Now that you're feeling artsy, head to the Art and Air Studios and create your own masterpiece. Free parking.

ART OUTSIDE

7260 Southwest Ave.

314-241-BEER

Art Outside is a three-day, juried alternative art fair featuring affordable works from St. Louis–based artists. With Bottleworks as the host, the opportunity to multi-task supporting both local art and beer is just too good to pass up.

GREEN TREE FESTIVAL

September

Geyer and Adams, Kirkwood

September drought and Dutch Elm disease were taking a serious toll on Kirkwood's trees. In 1961, Kirkwood offered several varieties of trees for sale for just a dollar. This gradually grew into a festival that draws crowds from across the metro area. There is also a Folk Life festival. Artisans dress in period costumes from the 1700s and 1800s and bring history to life with crafts, foods, and fiddle music. There is a Kids Dog Show and a canine Frisbee competition, crafters, and entertainment. Admission and parking are free.

LET THEM EAT ART

July

Maplewood

An inner-ring burb Bastille bash, featuring whimsical costume contest, public art, unique performances (music in all styles, belly dance, hooping), face painting, film screenings, and more, throughout downtown Maplewood.

LOOP ICE CARNIVAL

January

University City

Ice, Ice Baby. Dozen of ice sculptors and their creations; there is a Snow Ball (as in dance) and for the brave, a Frozen Buns Run. Free for all.

POTPOURRI SALE

April

Ladue

755 S. Price Rd.

314-993-4040

Sponsored by John Burroughs School, this is an annual 500-family yard sale. Bring cash, a backpack, and get there early for best parking. There's no yard sale quite like this one. Food available for purchase.

ST. LOUIS ART FAIR

September

Clayton

Clayton Business District

314-863-0278

Billed as the top art fair in the nation, it takes over the heart of downtown Clayton

ST. LOUIS INTERNATIONAL FILM FESTIVAL

November

University City

Hosted at the beautiful Tivoli Theatre in University City, which dates to 1924, this is local film lovers' best bet to catch new international films, documentaries, features, and short features.

TURKEY BOWL

Thanksgiving

For the past 100 years or so, Kirkwood and Webster Groves High Schools have met up for a classic football rivalry, one of a handful still in existence. To the winner goes the coveted Frisco Bell Trophy and to the loser, the little brown jug—kept at school until the following year's Turkey Bowl. There are many other events leading up to the big game, including bonfires, chili cook offs, alumni gatherings, and a Friendship Dance held at the school not hosting that year's Turkey Bowl.

WEBSTER COMMUNITY DAYS

4th of July

This is an all-American, family-friendly, 4th of July celebration that includes a parade, carnival, BBQ, and fireworks after dark.

{ TOE-TAPPING }

Now in its eleventh year, **Old Webster Jazz and Blues Festival** (*September*, Webster Groves; 314-961-4656; oldwebsterjazzfestival.com) offers non-stop jazz and blues from two stages. Street entertainers, jugglers, face painters, and balloon artists make the festival a family-friendly affair. Local restaurants sell food and drink to go with the music. Strollers and lawn chairs are welcome at this award-winning festival, which showcases some of the best musical talent St. Louis has to offer. Best of all, admission is free. A portion of the festival food and drink sales proceeds are donated to music programs in the Webster Groves School District.

PARKS AND REC

St. Louis's immigrant population left behind a European world where parks were primarily for the wealthy and noble classes. Their legacy to future generations is a long list of green spaces accessible to the masses. Although these communities have a number of excellent parks, take special note of Oak Knoll and Shaw parks, both in Clayton.

Oak Knoll Park is home to one of the last large native stands of 150-year-old Post Oak trees along with walking paths, native plant area, rain, sunken and flowering island gardens, and popular Musical Nites, a summer concert series on the fourth Sunday, June-September. The St. Louis Artists Guild, a fabulous art space and gallery, also calls Oak Knoll Park home.

The 47-acre Shaw Park is an urban oasis and Clayton's oldest and largest park, named in honor of former Clayton Mayor Charles Shaw. Centennial Gardens hosts sculpture by Renoir (on loan from the St. Louis Art Museum) in its bicentennial garden. There is also an aquatic center with a 50-meter competition pool, and an outdoor ice rink.

{ FULL-STEAM AHEAD }

Transport the family back in time with train and trolley rides at the **Museum of Transportation** (3015 Barrett Station Rd., 314-615-8688, museumstlouis.org). Steam locomotives from the late 1800s, classic cars, aircraft, and more. This kid-friendly interactive museum will entertain the entire family. Allow the better part of a day to take in all the fun and make sure to book a session in the air-conditioned Creation Station.

{ PINHEADS }

Step back in time at the retro (and historic) **Saratoga Lanes** (2725 Sutton Blvd., #A, 314-645-5308, saratogalanes.com). They've been rolling here since 1916, but improvements, like a second-story patio, keep the crowds coming back. **Pin-Up Bowl** (6191 Delmar Blvd., 314-727-5555, pinupbowl.com) takes a different approach with posh surroundings and fancy cocktails.

ARTS, ENTERTAINMENT, & EDUCATION

BLACK CAT-PIWACKET THEATRE
2810 Sutton Blvd.
314-781-8300
blackcattheatre.org
This 180-seat New York–style cabaret theatre has joined forces with Piwacket Children's Theatre. In addition to shows there are classes, camps, and special events.

THE FOCAL POINT
2720 Sutton Blvd.
314-781-4200
thefocalpoint.org
An eclectic mix of local art and culture. Hear a concert, listen to a poetry reading, watch dancing, or sit in on a jam session. While no beverages are served you can bring a margarita or two in from the Maya Café, located in the same building.

THE FOLK SCHOOL
3155 Sutton Blvd.
314-781-2244
folk-school.org
Grassroots group dedicated to preservation & propagation of traditional music & folk arts, with concerts, workshops, and classes for all ages on fiddle, ukulele, banjo, guitar, and more.

FRANK LLOYD WRIGHT HOUSE IN EBSWORTH PARK
120 N. Ballas Rd.
314-822-8359
ebsworthpark.org
Dubbed FLWHEP, this pristine example of Wright's architectural and design aesthetic (including original Wright-designed furniture and fabrics) is one of just five in the state. Tours by appointment only, W-Su.

THE GREEN CENTER
8025 Blackberry Ave.
314-725-8314
thegreencenter.org
Acres of prairie, wetlands, and woods, along with demonstration gardens, make this nonprofit environmental education center worth a visit; grounds open daily, visitor headquarters open W only.

{ INTERESTING, BUT DON'T TRY IT }

If you stood in the middle of Price Road where Delmar ends, you'd be in three cities at one time! (Olivette, University City, and Ladue)

THE REPERTORY THEATRE (THE REP)
130 Edgar Rd.
314-968-4925
repstl.org
St. Louis's premier live theatre at the Loretto-Hilton Center for the Performing Arts located on the grounds of Webster University. This architectural gem was the first of its kind in the U.S., designed to house both a professional acting company and an undergraduate arts department. Conrad Hilton, in appreciation for the education given to him by the Sisters of Loretto, donated the building funds. Backstage tours are offered free to school or community groups, around production schedules, September through March.

STAGES ST. LOUIS
THE ROBERT G. REIM THEATRE
Kirkwood Civic Center
111 S. Geyer Rd.
314-821-2407
stagesstlouis.org
One of the fastest-growing musical theatres around, in the heart of Kirkwood, in its 24th season of classic American musicals

{ LANDMARK }

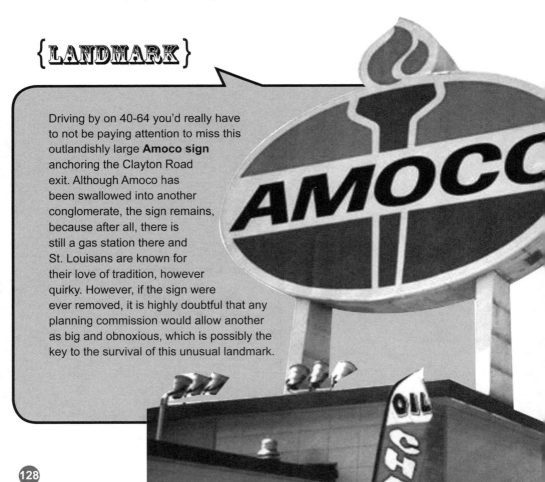

Driving by on 40-64 you'd really have to not be paying attention to miss this outlandishly large **Amoco sign** anchoring the Clayton Road exit. Although Amoco has been swallowed into another conglomerate, the sign remains, because after all, there is still a gas station there and St. Louisans are known for their love of tradition, however quirky. However, if the sign were ever removed, it is highly doubtful that any planning commission would allow another as big and obnoxious, which is possibly the key to the survival of this unusual landmark.

SHOPPORTUNITIES

Fans of local, independent business will jump for joy. Many towns are unique shopping destinations unto themselves. This list is only the tip of the retail iceberg.

SEASONAL PROVISIONS

CLAYTON FARMERS' MARKET
8282 Forsyth Blvd.
314-913-6632
claytonfarmersmarket.com
Saturdays, May through October

KIRKWOOD FARMERS' MARKET
150 East Argonne Dr.
314-822-0084
downtownkirkwood.com/kirkwood-farmers-market.asp
April through September,
Monday-Saturday

MAPLEWOOD FARMERS' MARKET
7260 Southwest Ave.
314-241-2337
Wednesdays, May through October
at Schlafly Bottleworks

WEBSTER GROVES FARMERS' MARKET
4 East Lockwood Ave.
314-963-5696 x888
webstergrovesfarmersmarket.com
May through October

{ ERIN GO BRAUGH }

St. Louis has a large Irish population, and two excellent shops offer wares straight from the Emerald Isle. **Kerry Cottage** (2119 S. Big Bend Blvd.; 314-647-0166; kerrycottage.com) offers clothing, jewelry, Waterford, and other fine crystal and china. **O'Malley's Irish Gift Shop** (2718 Sutton Blvd.; 314-645-8779) sells authentic, hard-to-find Irish gifts, music, and gear.

{ ALL ABOARD! }

Kirkwood Train Station (at S. Kirkwood Rd. and Argonne Dr.) was an endangered species saved from closure by a unique Amtrak and Kirkwood partnership. In 2003, the city of Kirkwood purchased the historic train station from Amtrak. Since then, the station has been staffed by a legion of volunteers who give out schedule information, help passengers embark, issue parking passes (which must be obtained in advance of your trip), and keep the station open from approximately an hour prior to the first passenger train of the day until about an hour after the last one. Tickets can be purchased at the station via an automated machine or direct from Amtrak. Next time you're pining for a ride on the rails, do it old-school style and leave from Kirkwood.

{ THE LANDMARK LIONS }

Gates of Opportunity:

The feline gatekeepers of University City sit 49 feet above the entry. Commissioned by E.G. Lewis (U. City founder), artist George Zolnay was a prominent designer and sculptor for the 1904 World's Fair. This art treasure symbolizes all things University City.

BRENTWOOD

Manchester Road's shopping opportunities weave through multiple municipalities, including Brentwood.

THE GIFTED GARDENER
8935 Manchester Rd.
314-961-1985
thegiftedgardener.com
Great home touches and gifts for those who love their little backyard slices of heaven: fancy hand tools, gloves and clogs, plus urns, welcome mats, birdbaths, fountains, pots, and gardening books

K. HALL DESIGNS
8416 Manchester Rd.
314-961-1990
khalldesigns.com
Serene apothecary ambience is retail home for STL-made (and nationally sold) fragrances, candles, diffuser oils in natural scents like sugared magnolia and Siberian fir; small selection of ceramics and fine linen gifts, too

T. HARGROVE FLY FISHING
9024 Manchester Rd.
314-968-4223
thargrove.com
Learn what you need to from passionate practitioners, buy what you need to tie flies, and then go out and practice your cast in the front lot! Drive by any temperate weekend morning and see for yourself

CLAYTON

As the signs say, "This is Clayton, Missouri." Trendy, upscale, must-have, and luxe describe the shopping options here.

BARUCCI GALLERY
8101 Maryland Ave.
314-727-2020
baruccigallery.com
Original paintings and contemporary art, glass, framing, and jewelry. Nationally recognized as a Top 100 Gallery in the U.S.

BYRON CADE, INC.
7901 Clayton Rd.
314-721-4701
byroncadegifts.com
China, crystal, silver, and much more!

DOTDOTDASH
6334 N. Rosebury Ave.
314-862-1962
dotdotdashboutique.com
Boutique that features casual urban children's and women's clothing and accessories

LAURIE SOLET
8228 N. Forsyth Blvd.
314-727-7467
lauriesolet.com
A boutique featuring ladies' clothing and accessories from NY and LA

LOLA & PENELOPE'S
7742 Forsyth Blvd.
314-863-5652
lolaandpenelopes.com
Fashions, food, and grooming services for the pampered pet

LUSSO
165 Carondelet Pl.
314-725-7205
lussohome.com
Find all the best names in home decor, candles, clothing, and accessories

SCHOLARSHOP
8211 Clayton Rd.
314-725-3456
scholarshopstl.org
St. Louis shoppers in the know come here first for quality men's, women's, and children's clothing and accessories. For more than 40 years, Scholarshop has raised money for the Scholarship Foundation of St. Louis, assisting thousands of now-successful St. Louisans with their education by providing interest-free loans. Check out the Webster Groves shop too, for a full day of scholar-shopping.

131

SU-ELLEN
8115A Maryland Ave.
314-862-5050
wsw.su-ellen.com
Classic women's clothing for day and
evening; sportswear to ball gowns,
dresses, coats, and accessories

WORLD NEWS, LTD.
4 S. Central Ave.
314-726-6010
Extraordinary newsstand with over 2,000
periodicals, newspapers, and local books
and a general store

DOWNTOWN KIRKWOOD

Grab the girls and shop til you drop. Start at Down by the Station, go buggy
at the Bug Store, re-decorate the home at Christopher's, or get your gourmet
kitchen on at Cornucopia. Theses are just a few of more than 100 unique
shopportunites that await in Downtown Kirkwood.

BLUSH BOUTIQUE
110 N. Clay Ave.
314-965-4411
shopblushboutique.com
Fashion forward designer
boutique, appears on local
"best of" lists

THE BUG STORE
113 W. Argonne Dr.
314-966-2287
Unique gifts and decor

CHECKERED COTTAGE
135 W. Jefferson Ave.
314-909-7233
checkeredcottage.com
Arts and craft supplies,
home products, plus sea-
sonal gift items

CHRISTOPHER'S
127 E. Argonne Dr.
314-909-0202
christophersgifts.com
Cool stuff for your casa;
gifts and kid stuff you
won't find elsewhere

CLAY & COTTON
157 W. Argonne Dr.
314-394-1400
clayandcotton.com
Home goods in cheerful
colors, unique fashion,
hostess gifts

CORNUCOPIA
107 N. Kirkwood Rd.
314-822-2440
cornucopiakitchen.com
15,000 gourmet items in
stock; coffees, teas, candy,
food, cookware, and cutlery

DOWN BY THE STATION
150 W. Argonne Dr.
314-965-7833
downbythestation.com
Unique gifts, scented wax
bowls, and collectibles

**LASS AND LADDIE, A
CHILDREN'S BOUTIQUE**
161 W. Jefferson Ave.
314-822-1886
lassandladdiehandmade.com
Modern, vintage, and
handmade items for kids

**O.K. HATCHERY
FEED AND GARDEN
STORE, INC.**
115 E. Argonne Dr.
314-822-0083
Since 1927, has supplied
feed, pet supplies, outdoor
decor, and garden accessories; shoppers appreciate the
old-school style; it's worth a
visit to check out even if you
don't need anything

PAPERDOLLS
110 E. Jefferson Ave.
314-965-3655
shoppaperdollsboutique.com
Women's clothing and
accessories

VELLUM
120 W. Monroe Ave.
314-909-1640
velluminc.com
Hip and haute from the
world of stationery and
invitations

LADUE

Creativity and fashion abound on Clayton Road.

GIDDYUP JANE
9670 Clayton Rd.
314-993-9944
giddyupjane.com
Handmade belt buckles, gorgeous boots, and Western wear for Midwestern ladies

IMAGINATION TOYS
9737 Clayton Rd.
314-993-6288
imagination-toys.com
Awesome toys, games, and diversions for kids of all ages & interests, with great advice (and free gift wrap) if you're en route to a birthday party and don't know much more than the kid's age

SALLIE HOME
9821 Clayton Rd.
314-567-7883
salliehome.com
Enter a dream world of bed/bath/home, with vignettes of linens, frames, china, candles, serving ware, and much more

THE SERVICE BUREAU
9773 Clayton Rd.
314-991-1104
stlservicebureau.com
Charitable shopping, you can call it: fine stationery and paper goods, mono-grammed gifts, and home decor, with all profits donated to local charities

MAPLEWOOD

Maplewood turned their downtown upside down with stellar results. Boutiques like Femme and Maven are regular stops on professionally guided shopping tours. Its eclectic, walkable shopping has topped off a textbook revitalization effort by Maplewood.

FEMME
7270 Manchester Rd.
314-781-6868
Step inside and you'll see unique high-end fashion and accessories; there's a yoga class one evening a week

MAVEN
7290 Manchester Rd.
314-645-1155
Bath and beauty boutique featuring Maven's own line of soaps, candles, and skin care; they also offer apparel, jewelry, and lighting

MEZZANINE
2741 Sutton Blvd.
314-645-2777
shopmezzanine.com
Boutique women's cloth-ing store, well-curated for the modern gal

ST. LOUIS SALT ROOM

2739 Sutton Blvd.

314-647-2410

mysaltspa.com

Take the cure of halotherapy, a European import involving spending time in a full-salt-surround environment, from walls to floor; it's a practice its beneficiaries swear by to alleviate symptoms of everything from asthma to pneumonia

TIGERLILY

7328 Manchester Rd.

314-646-0061

tigerlilystl.com

Mom and her two girls have a cute boutique and their tagline says it all: "For Baby, For You, For Home, For Fun"; women's accessories, tabletop, baby apparel, and monogramming

WEBSTER GROVES

Webster has two local shopping areas, Old Webster and Old Orchard. Each is home to independent bookstores, restaurants, boutiques, and more.

APPLE OF YOUR EYE

20 N. Gore Ave.

314-968-9698

appleofyoureyegifts.com

Fun to funky personalized gifts for over 30 years

DAISY CLOVER BOUTIQUE

8146 Big Bend Blvd.

314-962-4477

daisy-clover.com

Contemporary fashion size 0-16; makes top "best of" lists for boutiques

INITIAL DESIGN

25 N. Gore Ave.

314-968-8300

Monogramming of just about anything you can imagine

KRUEGER POTTERY SUPPLY

8153 Big Bend Blvd.

63119, 314-963-0180

kruegerpottery.com

Come out and play; classes for all skill levels, supplies for all things clay

LUCKY DOG

38 N. Gore Ave.

63119, 314-961-7877

luckydogstl.com

Cool stuff for pooches and their owners

PUDD'NHEAD BOOKS

8157 Big Bend

314-918-1069

puddnheadbooks.com

Classic independent bookstore with intriguing themed displays that hosts many events and is home to numerous book clubs

RED LEAD

27 N. Gore Ave.

314-962-0433

redleadpaperworks.com

Paper, art, and stamp store for the creative type

ROLLING RIDGE NURSERY
60 N. Gore Ave.
314-962-3311
rollingridgenursery.com
Keeping Webster's landscape well planted with plants of merit; holiday decoration and Christmas tree destination for more than 50 years

SALT OF THE EARTH
8150 Big Bend Blvd.
314-963-1919
salt-earth.com
Handcrafted treasures from Mexican and Italian artisans

WEBSTER GROVES BOOKSHOP
100 W. Lockwood Ave.
314-968-1185
Independent store with a cozy, comfortable literary ambience; wide selection of local books

WEBSTER RECORDS
117 W. Lockwood Ave.
314-961-4656
websterrecords.com
Hard-to-find vinyl, extensive CD collection; buys and sells

VIVA!
132 W. Lockwood Ave.
314-968-8482
shopvivaonline.com
Handbags, jewelry, gifts, and names like Firefly, Anna Marie Chagonon, and Vera Bradley

YUCANDU ART STUDIO
20 Allen Ave., Ste. 110
314-963-4400
yucandu.com
No appointment needed; drop in to paint, collage or do mosaics; classes for all ages and skill level and parties, too

....

ROCK HILL
Quaint shopping along Manchester Road.

THE BOOK HOUSE
9719 Manchester Rd.
314-968-4491
bookhousestl.com
It's a real house—circa 1863 and haunted, btw—stock floor-to-ceiling with new and used books in every genre, knowledgeable staff, and the bargain basement, which alone is worth the browse

RUNG
9739 Manchester Rd.
314-918-0575
shoprung.org
Dot.org? Yep, it's a retail store, with on-trend women's looks for both business and fun, which donates 100 percent of its profits to the Women's Foundation of Greater St. Louis, bringing the female focus full circle

THE LOOP IN UNIVERSITY CITY

It's hip, it's fun, and there are many options. Vintage clothing and Vintage Vinyl, fair trade shopping, artist guilds and galleries, even cool duds for the small fry. Shop, dance, or drink until you drop. It's so cool, in fact, it's one of America's "10 Great Streets," according to the American Planning Association. The Loop shopping district is loaded with public art and friendly to those on foot, bikes, or blades.

CITY SPROUTS
6303 Delmar Blvd.
314-726-9611
citysprouts.com
A fun place to grab gear for the kids; wide and unique selection; gift registry for expectant parents

CRAFT ALLIANCE
6640 Delmar Blvd.
314-725-1177
craftalliance.org
Nonprofits arts education, gallery and shop; great place for a one-of-a-kind gift shopping and jewelry

GOOD WORKS
6323 Delmar Blvd.
314-726-2233
goodworksfurniture4u.com
A different kind of furniture store; contemporary or traditional designs; you'll want one of everything

KNITTY COUTURE
6148 Delmar Blvd.
314-727-6500
knittycouture.com
A boutique knitting store in the heart of The Loop

LORI COULTER
6138 Delmar Blvd.
314-727-9870
loricoulter.com
Made-to-order swimwear

MACROSUN INTERNATIONAL
6273 Delmar Blvd.
314-726-0222
macrosun.com
Fair trade items from places like Thailand, Nepal, India, Tibet, and Sri Lanka; global jewelry and international fashions, exotic decor

MISS M'S CANDY
6193 Delmar Blvd.
314-721-7000
missmscandy.com
Classic candy store—every kid's, and many adults', dream

PLOWSHARING CRAFTS
6271 Delmar Blvd.
314-863-3723
plowsharing.org
Staffed primarily by volunteers, this store offers fair trade handicrafts from 40 countries and 3 continents

SILVER LADY
6364 Delmar Blvd.
314-727-0704
thesilver-lady.com
A jewelry store that specializes in silver and artist-made pieces

SOUL AND BLUES
6317 Delmar Blvd.
314-863-3600
soulandblues.com
Cutting-edge shoes for men and women; jewelry and accessories; shoe mavens should definitely have a look

{ HOT WAX }

Vintage Vinyl (6610 Delmar Blvd., 314-721-4096, vintagevinyl.com) is a destination with a national reputation. It has an extensive collection of rare CDs and vinyl, both new and used, plus concert DVDs, T-shirts, and merch from your favorite bands. You can often catch free in-store performances from national acts coming through town. Allow plenty of time, and enjoy the soundtrack from the live DJ while you shop.

SUBTERRANEAN BOOKS
6275 Delmar Blvd.
314-862-6100
store.subbooks.com
Independent urban bookstore

SUNSHINE DAYDREAM
6608 Delmar Blvd.
314-727-9043
sunshinedaydream.com
A 1970s flashback that fits well in the new millennium

ZIEZO
6394 Delmar Blvd.
314-725-9602
myspace.com/ziezo
Trendy women's boutique features emerging designers, as well as hot names from LA and NYC; for the fashionista with her own individual style

WARSON WOODS

The Manchester Road shopping continues through Warson Woods.

AMERICAN VISIONS
9999 Manchester Rd.
314-965-0060
american-visions.com
Exquisite and functional craft pieces from the U.S. and Canada, from measuring spoons to handbags

KANGAROO KIDS
10030 Manchester Rd.
314-835-9200
kangarookidsonline.com
Mecca for new parents, especially those into breastfeeding and attachment parenting: free support and educational groups are popular; buy a sling, learn to use it, and buy/sell quality consignment kids' clothes and gear

SHOPPING FOR A CAUSE

"For over 125 years this **Women's Exchange** (9214 Clayton Rd., 314-997-4411, woexstl.org) helps those in need lead productive lives through their own industry," it is known as one of *the* top places in the metro area for unique, handmade children's clothing and locally known for the Cherry Dress. The Tea Room at the Women's Exchange is where the girls gather for the Women's Exchange Salad Bowl with Mayfair Dressing or a piece of lemon meringue pie. Dinner is served and there is a takeout menu as well. It's a St. Louis tradition, which helps those in need. Win-win.

FOODSTUFF

BAUMANN'S FINE MEATS
8829 Manchester Rd.
314-968-3080
baumannsfinemeats.com
Experienced full-service
meat shop

EXTRA VIRGIN, AN OLIVE OVATION
143 Carondelet Pl.
314-727-6464
extravirginoo.com
A celebration of cooking
and all things olive

FREDDIE'S MARKET
9052 Big Bend Blvd.
314-968-1914
freddiesmarket.com
Third-generation family-
owned neighborhood
market with organic items,
hand-cut meats, farm-
fresh produce

GLOBAL FOOD MARKET
421 N. Kirkwood Ave.
314-835-1112
globalfoodsmarket.com
Globetrot while you
shop; local produce and
household products from
England to Pakistan

KAKAO CHOCOLATE
7272 Manchester Rd.
314-771-2310
kakaochocolate.com
For the serious chocolate
lover, mind-blowing treats

MCDONNELL'S MARKET PLACE
12309 Big Bend Blvd.
314-821-3544
A Kirkwood favorite
known for its fine
selection of meats and
handcrafted sausage

PENZEY'S SPICES
7338 Manchester Rd.
314-781-7177
penzeys.com
More than 250 herbs and
spices, plus advice on
what to do with them

SAPPINGTON INTERNATIONAL FARMER'S MARKET
8400 Watson Rd.
314-843-7848
sappingtonfarmersmkt.com
Local produce and
international foods

SEAFOOD CITY GROCERY STORE
8020 Olive Blvd.
314-993-2800
Top retail location for
seafood

STRAUB'S IN CLAYTON
(Original location)
8282 Forsyth Blvd.
314-725-2121
straubs.com
Local gourmet supermarket

VOM FASS
7314 Manchester Rd.
314-932-5262
vomfassusa.com
Vinegars, oils, wines, liqueurs
straight from the cask

SOUTH COUNTY

AFFTON ★ CONCORD ★ CRESTWOOD ★ JEFFERSON BARRACKS ★ LEMAY ★ MEHLVILLE ★ OAKVILLE ★ SHREWSBURY ★ SAPPINGTON ★ SUNSET HILLS

HISTORY

While the affluent built Victorian homes and European-style avenues, hardy pioneers moved to the fertile land of the Meramec floodplain to farm and raise families. The winding river reminded the many German immigrants of their homeland's Rhine, and their love of the land is shown in city planning for these communities, as many towns were planned around the natural sweeping curves and dips instead of typical city grids. In most cases, they made special efforts to preserve trees or other nature-made beauties.

These farmlands stretched from the Mississippi River to the Meramec. After World War I and World War II, the surrounding areas—including Crestwood, Shrewsbury, Sunset Hills, Mehlville, and Oakville—began to see an influx of residents seeking an escape from the city, and the population expanded in just a few short years. Today, these communities still have that mid-century suburban feeling.

AFFTON

Affton was originally a plantation owned by a Scotsman, but it became known as "Aff's Town" for the man who opened a general store and became the postmaster. Back in the days of buggies and carriages, the only road markers were buildings; Aff's general store became known as the "Ten Mile House," as it was ten miles away from the courthouse. This neighborhood was briefly a stand-alone village and enjoyed its own police force. However, the Affton residents voted to disincorporate in 1935 due to lack of revenue. It is now a part of St. Louis County but still has much of its charm, as many of its homes were built before World War II.

JEFFERSON BARRACKS

As the oldest operating military base in the country, Jefferson Barracks has seen much of America's history. Founded on the day of President Thomas Jefferson's death in 1826, it played host to Civil War generals Robert E. Lee and Ulysses S. Grant, as both men were stationed here. Strategically important in multiple wars and Westward Expansion, it was home to the nation's first permanent cavalry unit, the Dragoons. Its military hospital treated more than 18,000 soldiers during the Civil War, and the base served as the main training grounds for the Spanish-American War. During World War I, it became the first base to train soldiers in aviation parachuting and then during World War II it was one of the first Army Air Corps bases. Today, much of its land has been sold to the county for parks and residential developments, and the nearby National Cemetery is one of the nation's oldest military cemeteries. More than 20,000 soldiers are buried here, including 1,000 Civil War casualties interred according to their home state.

LEMAY

Crossing the Mississippi has always featured prominently in St. Louis's economic and cultural history. Fragments of the mom-and-pop contributions of ferry river crossing remain. Such is the case with Lemay. Francis LeMais and his son operated a ferry across the Meramec River, and a road was laid out in 1834 from their ferry to Carondelet. As Lemay became a bustling epicenter of river traffic, it was briefly considered as a candidate for our nation's capital, due to its strategic importance and central location in the rapidly expanding country.

FOOD AND DRINK

A BITE TO EAT

BARTOLINO'S SOUTH
5914 S. Lindbergh Blvd.
Affton
314-487-4545
bartolinosrestaurants.com
Fine Italian, seafood, and
steaks since 1982

BERIX
2201 Lemay Ferry Rd.
Mehlville
314-845-3711
berixcoffee.com
Eastern European specialties and Turkish coffee
produced in-house

CAFE AFFTON
8713 Gravois Rd.
Affton
314-457-8000
cafeaffton.com
Classic SoCo sports bar
with better food than you'd
expect

CRUSOE'S
RESTAURANT & BAR
5591 Oakville Shopping Ctr.
Oakville
314-892-0620
American; "Feed the Crew"
family special for takeout
orders

DRUNKEN NOODLES
TASTE OF THAI
5496 Baumgartner Rd.,
Ste. 109
Oakville
314-845-8808
A taste of Pad Thai deep in
South County

FORTEL'S PIZZA DEN
7932 Mackenzie Rd.
Affton
314-353-2360
fortelspizzaden.com
Where little leaguers and
big leaguers go after a
game to chow down

FRAILEY'S
SOUTHTOWN GRILL
4329 Butler Hill Rd.
Concord
314-892-1866
fraileysrestaurant.com
Traditional American;
try the wings

GARVEY'S GRILL
5647 Telegraph Rd.
Oakville
314-846-8881
garveysgrillonline.com
Traditional pub fare, with a
solid following among the
Oakville crowd

HELEN FITZGERALD'S
3650 S. Lindbergh Blvd.
Sunset Hills
314-984-0026
helenfitzgeralds.us
Pub, Italian, and American
fare; a happening party
spot on weekends and
especially on St. Paddy's

KING EDWARD'S
CHICKEN AND FISH
8958 Watson Rd.
Crestwood
314-843-3474
kingedwardschicken.com
Family-owned Southern-
style (Louisiana, to be
exact) chicken

LEMAY WOK
4530 Lemay Ferry Rd.
Mehlville
314-487-8834
A hole-in-the-wall-esque
Chinese eatery that's
worth the wait

PENNIE'S BBQ
4265 Reavis Barracks Rd.
Lemay
314-544-1661
Home of the 18-ounce
pork steak and the
24-ounce top sirloin

PHIL'S BBQ
9205 Gravois Rd.
Affton
314-638-1313
Home of the St. Louis
pork steak; an old-
school original

P'SGHETTI'S PASTA &
SANDWICHES
5540 S. Lindbergh Blvd.
Concord
314-849-5332
psghettis.com
Feed the masses for a
song

RICH & CHARLIE'S SOUTH COUNTY
4487 Lemay Ferry Rd.
Mehlville
314-894-1600
richandcharlies.com
Longtime eatery that changed the way St. Louis ate salad and pasta (Its next generation of restaurants became the Pasta House Company)

ROBERTO'S TRATTORIA
145 Concord Plaza Shopping Ctr.
Concord
314-842-9998
robertosstl.com
A favorite off-the-Hill Italian spot in the heart of SoCo

RUMA'S DELI
1395 Covington Manor Ln.
Mehlville
314-892-9990
rumasdeli.com
Hometown Italian deli, hot sandwiches, and mostaccioli

SAM'S STEAKHOUSE
10205 Gravois Rd.
Affton
314-849-3033
samssteakhouse.com
Romantic neighborhood gem, aged steaks

SMUGALA'S PIZZA PUB
10150 Watson Rd.
Crestwood
314-842-5900

6346 Telegraph Rd.
Oakville
314-846-9500
smugalas.com
Mozzarella-provel pizza with game room

SOCO'S GYROS
5530 S. Lindbergh Blvd.
Concord
314-843-7600
Gem of a Greek deli

SYBERG'S
7802 Gravois Rd.
Affton
314-832-3560
sybergs.com
A local favorite known for their wings, the building's resident shark appears about to dive onto Gravois

SOMETHING SWEET

THE DONUT STOP
1101 Lemay Ferry Rd.
Lemay
314-631-3333
thedonutstopinc.net
Listed in Bon Appetit's 2010 "Top 10 Best Places for Donuts" in the U.S.; closes 12:30 p.m. daily

MCARTHUR'S BAKERY
3055 Lemay Ferry Rd.
Mehlville
314-894-0900
mcarthurs.com
Main location; also in Kirkwood and Chesterfield; paczki available for a limited time right before Lent

SPANKY'S FROZEN CUSTARD
11616 Concord Village Ave.
Concord
314-843-9529
Traditional custard stand in heart of South County

You can't miss the cool 1950s neon sign at **Federhofer's Bakery** (9005 Gravois Rd., 314-832-5116, federhofersbakery.com), which in itself tells you to check out this old-school bakery—from birthday cakes to king cakes, stollens, and hot cross buns.

SOMETHING TO DRINK

FRANKIE G'S BAR AND GRILL
4565 Chestnut Park Pl.
Oakville
314-894-9292
frankiegs.com
Enjoy a burger or trashed wings with your adult beverage

GROWLERS PUB
3811 S. Lindbergh Blvd.
Sunset Hills
314-984-9009
More than 100 beers on tap, frequent drinker program, huge beer garden

HESSLER'S PUB
11804 Tesson Ferry Rd.
Concord
314-842-4050
Traditional pub fare, karaoke, and keno

O'LEARY'S
3828 S. Lindbergh Blvd.
Sunset Hills
314-842-7678
Affton's John Goodman is an owner of this bar and grill

THE PINK GALLEON
4010 Butler Hill Rd.
Mehlville
314-845-2386
pinkgalleon.com
Neon pool tables, darts, arcade games, and shot specials in enormous club

TEN MILE HOUSE
9420 Gravois Rd.
Affton
314-638-9082
thetenmilehouse.com
Live music, games, trivia, cold beer

SHOPPORTUNITIES

**BAKED GOODS
POTTERY**
11557 Gravois Rd.
Sappington
314-842-0110
www.bakedgoodspottery.
com
Ceramic and art glass
studio; parties for kids of
all ages

HANNEKE HARDWARE
10042 Gravois Rd.
Affton
314-631-6250
www.hanneke.com
Old-school advice for old-
house homeowners free
with every purchase

JOHNNY'S MARKET
11555 Gravois Rd.
Sappington
314-843-5760
www.johnnysmkt.com
From groceries to gourmet
with many hard-to-find
foods, friendly service at
no extra charge

{ LANDMARK }

Jefferson Barracks County Park (345 North Rd., stlouisco.com/parks/j-b.
html) was a military post which was opened in 1805, following the Lewis
and Clark expedition, and became a fort in 1826 with the closing of Fort
Bellefontaine. Names from history like Robert E. Lee, William Sherman,
Zachary Taylor, and Dwight Eisenhower were stationed here. It served as a
gathering point for troops and supplies for wars beginning with the Mexican
American War through World War II. Now a county park with biking/hiking
trails, corkball, soccer, softball, and baseball fields and picnic shelters.
World War II Weekend is held the last weekend in April and draws 15,000
spectators for the three reenacted battles and numerous encampments. Kids
get to pick up the spent shell casings after each battle for souvenirs.

KENRICK'S MEAT MARKET

4324 Weber Rd.

Affton

314-631-2440

kenricks.com

High-quality meats and ready to cook meals

MID AMERICA ARMS

8240 Gravois Rd.

Affton

314-631-3120

midamericaarms.com

First responders and 2nd Amendment fans and sportsmen will find a wide array of products to suit their needs

SCHAEFER'S HOBBY ARTS AND CRAFTS

11659 Gravois Rd.

Sappington

314-729-7077

schaeferhobby.com

The second generation continues a family tradition; wide selection for the consummate hobbyist

THE TEACHERS' LOUNGE

4121 Elm Park Dr.

Concord

314-894-7000

the-teachers-lounge.com

Stuffed with educational products/toys, instruments, classroom decs, and tools, plus free weekly storytime and activity popular with pre- and home-schoolers

UNCLE SAM'S MILITARY SURPLUS AND SAFARI OUTFITTERS

8380 Watson Rd.

Affton

314-823-2424

unclesams.com

Not planning a safari? No worries—Uncle Sam's has gear for the outdoorsmen, law enforcement, and paintballers

THE WOMEN'S CLOSET EXCHANGE

11575 Gravois Rd.

Sappington

314-842-8405

womensclosetexchange.net

Nationally recognized extreme upscale resale; guaranteed authentic designer labels from Dolce and Gabbana, Christian Louboutin, Prada, Chanel, Dior, and many more

{ ANIMAL FARM }

Suson County Park (6073 Wells Rd., 314-615-4386, stlouisco.com/parks/suson), located not far from the Meramec River, offers picnics and playgrounds, a stocked fishing pond, and an animal farm with petting opportunities. The farm is open daily at 10:30 a.m. year-round and closes at either 3 p.m. or 5 p.m., depending on the season. The farm is home to pigs, sheep, goats, horses, ponies, cows, ducks, and chickens and offers information about different breeds and their histories.

Grant's Farm (10501 Gravois Rd., 314-843-1700, grantsfarm.com) is the location of Ulysses S. Grant's cabin and farm, which was purchased by the Busch family in 1907. August Busch Sr. had the cabin moved and reassembled approximately one mile from its original location. Attractions include exotic animals in the wild, animal shows, hospitality center (read here: free beer for adults), and a tram ride of the 80-acre grounds. Days/hours vary depending on the time of year; closed Nov. 1–April 15.

RECREATION

ARTS & EDUCATION

LAUMEIER SCULPTURE PARK AND MUSEUM
12580 Rott Rd., **Sunset Hills**
314-615-5278
laumeiersculpturepark.org
Stroll and play in a park while surrounded by world-class scultures; the Mother's Day art fair is a big draw

WHITEHAVEN
7400 Grant Rd., **Affton**
314-842-1867
nps.gov/ulsg
The National Park Service runs this 10-acre plot that was the childhood home of Gen. Grant's wife, Julia, and the spot where the Grants planned to return after the war

FESTIVITIES

AFFTON DAYS AND FESTIVAL
Third Saturday in September
Annual parade and festival that, despite the name, is a one-day event

{ LANDMARK }

Jefferson Barracks National Cemetery (2900 Sheridan Rd., 314-845-8320, cem.va.gov/cems/nchp/jeffersonbarracks.asp) opened in 1866 after the Civil War. The 331-acre cemetery at Jefferson Barracks hosts hundreds of thousands of visitors each year. Memorial Day is quite a sight with an endless sea of white markers and American flags.

There are more than 4,400 burials each year and more than 180,000 veterans buried here from every U.S. war, including Confederate soldiers and German and Italian prisoners of war. Johnnie Johnson, Robert McFerrin Sr., and Jack Buck are a few household names who are buried at Jefferson Barracks National Cemetery.

NORTH COUNTY

BELLEFONTAINE NEIGHBORS ★ BELLERIVE ★ BEL-NOR ★ BEL-RIDGE
★ BERKELEY ★ BEVERLY HILLS ★ BLACK JACK ★ BRIDGETON
★ CHARLACK ★ DELLWOOD ★ FERGUSON ★ FLORISSANT ★
HAZELWOOD ★ JENNINGS ★ MOLINE ACRES ★ NORMANDY ★
NORTHWOODS ★ OVERLAND ★ PAGEDALE ★ PASADENA HILLS ★
PINE LAWN ★ ST. ANN ★ ST. JOHN ★ SPANISH LAKE ★ UM-ST. LOUIS

HISTORY

St. Louis County is known for its inordinate amount of small municipalities.
North County is filled with these mini-municipalities. They are quaint in some
respects, but they present governmental challenges in many others. Bel-Nor,
Bel-Ridge, Dellwood, and Charlack (well-known for their I-170 ticket-writing
ability), Pagedale, Jennings, and Black Jack are representative of dozens
of these mini-municipalities, which add to the character and uniqueness
of North County. The end of World War II created a housing shortage. Old
communities like Bridgeton and newly incorporated Bellefontaine Neighbors
experienced an unprecedented building boom lasting into the early 1950s.

FLORISSANT

Florissant is one of Missouri's first settlements. As part of the Louisiana
Territory, it saw several governmental changes between 1762 and 1804
when Spain and France passed the land back and forth, first from France to
Spain and back again to France. The U.S.'s Louisiana Purchase in 1804 was
the final transfer of governmental authority.

The French gave Florissant its name. *Fleurissant* means blossoming or
prosperous. French remained the primary language well into the nineteenth
century. Old Town is an ever-present reminder of Florissant's French
heritage.

FERGUSON

William Ferguson deeded part of his farm to the railroads in return for a regular rail stop in Ferguson. The promised "regular stop" led to the town's expansion during the streetcar era. Ferguson became a popular place for the upper middle class looking for more pastoral digs outside the city. Today, the town offers plenty of charm, along with the Ferguson Farmers' Market and annual Ferguson Streetfest.

NORMANDY

Charles Lucas named the area after the French coastal region where his father had been born. Lucas became involved in two duels with Thomas Hart Benton (later a U.S. senator), the second fatal. Lucas's land later became the first location of Bellerive Country Club, and today it includes Incarnate Word Catholic High School and the campus of the University of Missouri–St. Louis. Ironically UMSL's first building was named for Lucas's nemesis, Thomas Hart Benton.

{ PROTOSUBURBIA }

Take a spin (and in your car is the way to do it) through **Pasadena Hills** (Lucas and Hunt Rd., off I-70, pasadenahills.com/historic-district) for a look at the emergence of the auto-centric suburb, as it developed in St. Louis in the 1920s and 1930s. Among the first local communities of the automobile age, this collection of stunning private homes (and the meandering streets, driveways, and massive entrance tower) is on the National Register of Historic Places, in its entirety.

FOOD AND DRINK

Here's what you need to know as regards North County's food scene: There are serious, well staked-out camps around "best pizza." Like, to a more intense degree than anywhere else in St. Louis. So, tread lightly or better yet, try them all and choose your own favorite. (Plenty of non-pizza options abound, too.)

A BITE TO EAT

ADAMO'S
12207 Natural Bridge Rd. # A
Bridgeton
314-291-3555
adamositalian.com
Pizza, pasta, subs

ALASKA KLONDIKE COFFEE COMPANY
3200 N. US 67
Florissant
314-830-3488
rrochat.com/akcc
Micro-roaster of top-notch (and many organic/rainforest-friendly) beans from around the world

ANGELO'S PIZZERIA
4814 Parker Rd.
Florissant
314-355-3242
Family-owned pizza joint

BREAKAWAY CAFE
8418 Natural Bridge Rd.
Bel-Nor
314-381-3554
Pastas, pizzas, salads, and more in casual atmosphere

CORK
423 S. Florissant Rd.
Ferguson
314-521-9463
corkwinebarstl.com
Wine bar and tasty small plates (Match meat crab cakes recommended)

COSI DOLCE
100 S. Florissant Rd.
Ferguson
314-799-2157
cose-dolci.com
Charming bakery with cakes, cookies, biscotti, and to-die-for rugelach

CUGINO'S
1595 N. US 67
Florissant
314-831-3222
dinecuginos.com
Pizza, steak, chicken, & Italian specialties

{ WHAT'S BREWING? }

At **Ferguson Brewing Company** (418 S. Florissant Rd., 314-521-2220, hillbrewingco.com), it might be vanilla bourbon porter, or a distinctive pecan brown ale: whatever it is, it'll be innovative and fresh...and served in a glass for you to enjoy on site with a bite, or now in party-proper kegs, too.

{ COLD WAR }

You can start a fight, if you're not careful, publicly naming a favorite ice cream/frozen custard stand in these parts. Among the contenders? **Fritz's** (1055 Saint Catherine St., 314-839-4100, fritzsfrozencustard.com), **Doozle's** (717 S. New Florissant Rd., 314-921-3452, doozlesfrozencustard.com), **Velvet Freeze** (7355 West Florissant Ave., 314-381-2384; the last of a once-dominant chain), and the **Whistle Stop** (1 Carson Rd., 314-521-1600, whistlestopdepot.com, inside the historic Ferguson train depot).

DONUT DELIGHT
3605 Dunn Rd.
Florissant
314-838-4856
Cheap and oh-so-good
(special nod to the
coconut donut)

FARACI PIZZA
520 S. Florissant Rd.
Ferguson
314-524-2675
The thinnest of STL-style
crusts and provel

FREE RANGE COOKIES
425 S. Florissant Rd.
Ferguson
314-882-0163
freerangecookies.com
Gluten-free goodies
from cakes & cookies
to bread & buns

HELFER'S
PASTRIES & DELI
380 Saint Ferdinand St.
Florissant
314-837-6050
helferspastries.com
Old-fashioned bakery with
generations of birthday-
cake fans (and known for
seasonal/ethnic delights,
too, like kringles, paczki,
king cakes, etc.)

INDIA PALACE
4534 N. Lindbergh Blvd.
Bridgeton
314-731-3333
indiapalaceairport.com
Buffet lunch, menu dinner,
airport runway view...
surrounded by tiki-bar
decor

KNODEL'S BAKERY
6621 W. Florissant Ave.
Jennings
314-385-2000
knodelsbakery.com
110 years of custom cakes
& confections; if you need
a retirement-party cake that
looks like a bottle of Crown
Royal, don't mess around
with anyone else

NICK & ELENA'S
3007 Woodson Rd.
Overland
314-427-6566
Rave-worthy pizzas,
salads, Italian specialties

OMAR'S
10111 St. Charles Rock
Rd.
St. Ann
314-429-6881
Pizza joint meets
Mediterranean (shawarma, kabobs, hummus)

PIRRONE'S
1775 Washington St.
Florissant
314-839-3633
pirronespizza.com
St. Louis–style pizza &
Italian lunch buffet; perennial "best pizza" mention

**PONTICELLO'S
ITALIAN GARDEN**
12260 Bellefontaine Rd.
Spanish Lake
314-741-3637
ponticellos.com
Long family history at this
popular Italian restaurant

PUEBLO NUEVO
7401 N. Lindbergh Blvd.
Florissant
314-831-6885
Muy autentico. To wit, beef
tongue tacos

REDZ BARBEQUE
9901 West Florissant Ave.
Dellwood
314-521-1002
redzbbq.com
Ribs, brisket, fried chicken,
& mac-n-cheese

REYNOLD'S BBQ
6409 Natural Bridge Rd.
Pine Lawn
314-385-3100
Carolina-style vinegar-
based sauce for ribs,
pork steaks & more

ROBERTO'S
16 Mullanphy Garden
Shopping Ctr.
Florissant
314-837-7674
Thin-crust pizza, fried
chicken, Italian specialties

SIMPLY THAI
2470 N. US 67
Florissant
314-921-2179
stlsimplythai.com
Former Taco Bell now
shines with tom yum
soup, massaman curry,
grilled meat skewers

SWEETIE PIE'S
9841 West Florissant Ave.
Dellwood
314-521-9915
Lip-smackin' soul food

{ MODERN FOOD, HISTORIC SETTING }

At **Hendel's Market Café** (599 St. Denis St., 314-837-2304,
hendelsrestaurant.com) in Florissant you'll find a lovely, casually
elegant American restaurant housed in a historic brick building
that began its life as a grocery in the 1870s. Dine inside and you'll
enjoy a side of nostalgia (along with well-regarded seafood, steak,
and pasta dishes) in the form of historic photos of the building and
area; choose outside and while away the hours on one of the more
pleasant, breezy patios in town.

**TAM TAM AFRICAN
RESTAURANT**
35 Florissant Oaks
Shopping Center
Florissant
314-921-3805
tamtamstl.com
Culinary melting pot for
Senegalese, Morrocan,
Ivoirian cuisines, plus
weekend music/dance
events

VINCENZO'S
242 S. Florissant Rd.
Ferguson
314-524-7888
vincenzosstl.com
Italian dishes from pasta
melanzani to a meaty,
cheesy lasagna; all local
beer on tap

WHITE BARN
2457 Chambers Rd.
Moline Acres
whitebarnhamburgers.com
Burger shack also slings
meatloaf, catfish, & Polish
sausage

{ SERIOUSLY LOCAL }

Missouri Mercantile
(5555 St. Louis Mills Blvd.
#218, 314-227-5005,
missourimercantile.com),
inside the Mills mall, sells
100% Missouri-made
products, from wines, BBQ
sauce, and Dad's Cookies to
backyard washers games.

{ GOURMAND GO-TOS }

When dinner calls for something special, a trio of shops will jazz up your menu: Hit **John's Butcher Shoppee** (2608 Walton Rd., 314-423-8066, johns-butchershoppee.com) for just the cut of meat you want (or a smoked hambone), **Specialty Seafood Plus** (300 Saint Ferdinand St., 314-838-9333) for everything from catfish filets to oysters and alligator meat, and **Goeke Produce** (449 Saint Ferdinand St., 314-831-1931) for, well, everything else (veggies, eggs, local honey, and jams).

SOMETHING TO DRINK

BJ'S
184 Washington St.
Florissant
314-837-7783
bjspizza.co.cc
Yep, it's open, and a dive fave for cheap drinks, tasty pizza, & pull-tabs; rotating selection of produce for sale behind the bar

DEAVER'S SPORTS BAR
2109 Charbonier Rd.
Florissant
314-838-000
deaversrestaurant.com
Lots of screens, friendly service...and your kids are welcome, too

K.D. GRAY'S
6130 Madison Ave.
Berkeley
314-521-5309
Electronic darts, cozy tables, & surprisingly fancy drink options

MATTINGLY'S
8108 N. Lindbergh Blvd.
Florissant
314-831-9181
mattinglysportsbar.com
Casual hangout for after the little-league game or what-have-you

REDBIRDS SPORTS CAFE
9085 Dunn Rd.
Hazelwood
314-731-1234
redbirdscafe.com
Pool tables, darts, washers, and Wii, plus big screens to keep tabs on other athletes in the world

{ UMSL UNIVERSE }

As the largest university in the area, **UM-St. Louis** brings together a plethora of resources, people, and attractions that benefit far more than just its students. Among the spots worth setting foot on campus: the **Touhill Performing Arts Center** (1 University Blvd., 314-516-4949, touhill.org; though the "Tou-PAC" nickname never took off, you'll still find plenty of world-class entertainment options here, especially dance and musical performances); **Schwartz Observatory** (new location on North campus near the Fine Arts Building, 314-516-5706, umsl.edu/~physics/astro; open for free, monthly stargazing sessions, where an astronomy student can school you on constellations); **Gallery 210** (44 East Dr., 314-516-5976, umsl.edu/~gallery; a handsome, nationally renowned facility hosting a regular schedule of visual arts exhibitions, free & open to the public); and the **Mercantile Library** (314-516-7248, umsl.edu/mercantile; oldest library west of the Mississippi, rich in documents/artifacts/fine art/ephemera related to Westward Expansion, St. Louis history, river/rail transit systems, and more, plus regular exhibits from its collections, free & open to the public)

RECREATION

EXERCISE

AMF DICK WEBER LANES
4575 Washington St.
Florissant
314-838-4822
amf.com/dickweberlanes
Named for local legend Weber, a pro bowler and ambassador for the sport

COACHLITE SKATE CENTER
3754 Pennridge Dr.
Bridgeton
314-739-2057
coachlitestl.com
Open skate sessions at various times on Sa-Su, Tu, F, including weekly gospel music slots; cheap skate rental

CREST BOWL
650 New Florissant Rd. North
Florissant
314-837-0494
crest-bowl.com
Plenty to do here, from 32 lanes of bowling to a hoppin' sports bar, darts, video games, & karaoke nights

ICE ZONE
5555 St. Louis Mills Blvd. Ste. 345
Hazelwood
314-227-5288
icezoneatmills.com
Daily public sessions on the same ice used by the St. Louis Blues for practice

{ BACK TO THE LAND }

Two farms with deep roots in this neck of the woods offer food...and food for thought. At **Thies Farm** (4215 N. Hanley Rd., 314-428-9878, thiesfarm.com), a 125-year-old operation, a dedication to quality produce, flowers & plants, and edible items like local honey and jams/jellies is the core business, and fun annual activities like the popular Pumpkinland, a hay-bale/produce/petting zoo fall extravaganza. **EarthDance** (302 Thoroughman Ave., 314-521-1006, earthdancefarms.org) took up the cause a little more recently, farming 14 acres on a century-plus-old plot, and dedicated to preserving heirloom varieties, growing new farmers through its active apprenticeship programs, and engaging the community (e.g., summer camp for kids, film/music programs, and discussions).

{ KIDZONE }

Aviation buffs will find plenty of planes (both civilian and military, plus missiles & spacecraft) alongside a detailed mockup of the International Space Station and informative video clips on the history of air/space travel and technology at the source of much of it: the Boeing company's **Prologue Room** (in Building 100 at the corner of McDonnell Blvd. and Airport Rd., 314-232-6896, boeing.com/companyoffices/aboutus/tours/prologueroom/index.html) is free and open to the public from 9-4 on weekdays, June-August.

JAMES J. EAGAN CENTER
1 James J. Eagan Dr.
Florissant
314-921-4470
florissantmo.com/Parks/rink.shtml
Florissant's modern civic center includes indoor pool and ice-skating rink open to the public

**NORTH COUNTY
GOLF & SPORTS CENTER**
3555 N. US 67
Florissant
314-837-7543
ncgasc.com
Covered driving lanes, large putting green

NORTH OAKS BOWL
101 North Oaks Plaza
Northwoods
314-382-5757
northoaksbowl.com
64 (!) lanes make it the state's largest bowling facility, and you can bowl til at least midnight every night of the week; plus darts, pool, snacks, & cocktails

PLAN NINE SKATEPARK
5555 St. Louis Mills Blvd., Ste. 373
Hazelwood
314-227-5294
ciemo.com/skatepark.asp
Wheel demons, shred to your heart's content at this spiffy indoor skatepark for boards, scooters, blades, and BMX bikes

TED JONES BIKE TRAIL
Ferguson
traillink.com/trail/ted-jones-trail.aspx
2.2-mile paved path that links up with more extensive trail network and UM-St. Louis

**WHITE BIRCH BAY
AQUATIC CENTER**
1186 Teson Rd.
Hazelwood
314-731-0980
hazelwoodmo.org
Newish, fancy outdoor municipal water park in Hazelwood, with features like a bubble slide, lazy river, dumping water bucket, and more

It might be the most surprising feature of the whole North Countyplex: how unbelievably wild and natural wide swaths of the area are. With rivers wrapping around much of the area (to the west, north, and east), you're never far from some remarkable topography and flora/fauna spotting. Among the best vantage points: **Columbia Bottom Conservation Area** (Take the Riverview Drive exit from I-270, then go north on Riverview about 2.5 miles, 314-877-6014, mdc4.mdc.mo.gov/applications/moatlas/AreaSummaryPage.aspx?txtAreaID=9736; with a spectacular and informative visitor center; stop here to find out exactly where you'll find today's best birding, biking, and so on); **Sioux Passage Park** (17930 Old Jamestown Rd., 314-615-4386, bookit.stlouisco.com/cgi-bin/prp_fbk.exe?act=facInfo&facCode=SIOUX; a sprawling piece of land abutting the Mississippi, with horse trails and a lively disc golf scene); **Fort Belle Fontaine Park** (13002 Bellefontaine Rd., 314-544-5714, stlouisco.com/parks/ftbellefontaine.html; where you gain access via a somewhat off-putting guard gate, thanks to the shared land with a state-run youth facility; it's worth the trouble to get to the massive, WPA-built stone staircase); and **Little Creek Nature Area** (2295 Dunn Rd., 314-831-7386, fergflor.schoolwires.com/115810130131529260/site/default.asp; a Ferguson-Florissant school district–owned collection of easy trails and a nature center, perfect for introducing young hikers to the great outdoors; open weekdays.)

CHALLENGER LEARNING CENTER
205 Brotherton Ln.
Ferguson
314-521-6205
clcstlouis.org
Space education programs for school groups, scouts, community groups, and others, based on simulated, hands-on space missions, and experiments (periodic public sessions available, $15/person)

FRANZ GITTEMEIER HOUSE
1067 Dunn Rd.
Florissant
314-921-7055
historicflorissant.com
150-year-old home houses Florissant's historical society, local genealogical records

GENERAL DANIEL BISSELL HOUSE
10255 Bellefontaine Rd.
Bellefontaine Neighbors
314-615-4386
stlouisco.com/parks/bissell.html
Outstanding Federal-style home from early 1800s, includes many original Bissell family funishings & possessions; open by reservation only

HAWTHORNE PLAYERS
1 James J. Eagan Dr.
Florissant
314-921-5678
hawthorneplayers.com
One of the area's oldest theatre companies performs a repertoire of drama, musical revivals, and holiday favorites at the Florissant Civic Center Theatre

PAYNE-GENTRY HOUSE
4211 Fee Fee Rd.
Bridgeton
314-739-5599
bridgetonmo.com
Restored nineteenth-century home/doctor's office with many original furnishings; also perpetually reported to be haunted

ST. STANISLAUS HISTORICAL MUSEUM
3030 Charbonier Rd.
Florissant
314-837-3525
Rural farmhouse provides a setting for artifacts of the early frontier life and interactions between Jesuit priests (including Pierre De Smet) and Native American tribes who lived and traded in the area

{ KIDZONE }

Race fans! BE THERE! Make the wacky world of monster truck motorsports a little more, uh, tame with a visit to the birthplace and world HQ of **Bigfoot 4x4** (6311 N. Lindbergh Blvd., 314-731-2822, bigfoot4x4.com) in Hazelwood. Since the late 1970s, a small team of innovators (and engineers and repairmen, natch) has built up a fleet of about 17 Bigfoot monster trucks, which are now dispatched nearly every weekend to events around the country and world, including the ever-popular car crush. Your little fans can crawl under and around some of the vehicles, learn what goes into making a monster truck, and take home tons of related merch and souvenirs.

EAGLE DAYS
January
Old Chain of Rocks Bridge
mdc.mo.gov/discover-nature/programs/
eagle-daysconfluencegreenway.org/
eagledays
Cold temps bring soaring eagles back
to the corridor along the Mississippi
River, and this two-day event provides
help spotting them and learning about
their habits

FIESTA IN FLORISSANT
June
Knights of Columbus Park
(near the corner of Lindbergh and
Washington St.)
314-837-6100
florissantmo.com/Local/PressReleases/
FiestaFlor.shtml
Mexican heritage festival includes folk
dancers, music, puppets, and plenty of
delicioso food & drink

FLORISSANT VALLEY HISTORICAL SOCIETY HOUSE TOUR
Late spring
314-839-3626
Peek inside some of the city's most
interesting and storied houses during
this 50-year-old tour

ST. LOUIS STORYTELLING FESTIVAL
May
314-516-5961
stlstorytellingfestival.org
Chew the fat with locally treasured and
internationally renowned tellers of tales
for all ages, at locations throughout the
region, but based at UM-St. Louis

STREETFEST
September
fergusonstreetfest2010.com
Thousands flock to the live music festival
in Ferguson, but only a few are chosen
for the Manly Man High Heel race

VALLEY OF FLOWERS FESTIVAL
May
314-837-0033
florissantvalleyofflowers.com
Marking 50 years, the community
celebration in Florissant includes flower/
plant sales, a carnival midway, tons of
music, craft sales, kids' activities, and a
parade, plus the crowning of a Queen &
Court

SHOPPORTUNITIES

ANDREA'S BOUTIQUE
1145 N. Lafayette St.
Florissant
314-831-7500
Great jewelry, handbags, &
vintage apparel

ARCADES-N-MORE
6 Patterson Plz.
Florissant
314-838-1210
arcadesandmore.com
Been wanting a full-size Centipede
game or pinball machine?

CR FRANK POPCORN & SUPPLY
5757 N. Lindbergh Blvd.
Hazelwood
314-731-4500
crfrankpopcorn.com
Popcorn machine & supply rental/
sales...plus fresh-popped big bags,
ready to party

EL-MEL
6185 N. US 67
Florissant
314-741-2117
Old-time lawn-garden-feed store,
with tons of pet supplies, bird feeders,
garden gear, and such

THE FANTASY SHOP
8232 N. Lindbergh Blvd.
Florissant
314-831-5211
fantasyshoponline.com
Graphic novels, comics, collectibles

FRISON FLEA MARKET
7025 St. Charles Rock Rd.
Pagedale
314-727-0460
All manner of stuff ranging from bizarre
to kinda useful, conveniently located
adjacent to the Rock Road MetroLink
station

**GAGA'S VINTAGE
FURNITURE AND GIFTS**
258 S. Florissant Rd.
Ferguson
314-522-0035
raindropflowers.com/gagas.html
Found objects, restored furniture,
monogrammed giftables

GENERATIONS ANTIQUE MALL
250 Saint Catherine St.
Florissant
314-831-6070
150-year-old home, itself an antique
of sorts, houses more than 35 vendor
booths under one roof

NAGLE'S
19 Patterson Plz.
Florissant
314-838-4444
Five-and-dime hanging on to a nostalgiac
past of penny candy, toys, tchotchkes,
little gifty stuff, craft, & party supplies

ST. LOUIS MILLS MALL
5555 St. Louis Mills Blvd.
Hazelwood
314-227-5900
stlouismills.com
Massive space filled mostly with discount
retailers (outlets for Marshall's, Sears,
Gymboree, & Levi's), plus an IMAX-
equipped cinema, ice rink, & indoor
playspaces

{ MULTIPURPOSE BUILDING }

Myers Barn & Deli (180 Dunn Rd. #1, 314-838-3670; or some variant of that name, depending on who you ask) is a historic structure that's currently home to the Weaving Department and Helen's Hen House Quilt Shop (crafts cornucopia, both), as well as the popular Barn Deli, a good stop for a lunch sandwich.

{ GET FRESH IN FERG }

The **Ferguson Farmers' Market** (20 S. Florissant Rd., 314-324-4298, fergmarket.com) is the place to be on Saturday mornings during the growing season: farm-fresh produce, local handicrafts, and tempting treats abound, along with an engaging schedule of music, kids' activities and fun special events (pie contests, bike relays, etc.).

{ AFROCENTRIC }

All your African-American heritage merchandise needs can be met at **AfroWorld** (7276 Natural Bridge Rd., 314-389-5194, afroworld.com). Think prints of famed ancestors, Obama campaign memorabilia, African-American devotional books, handmade cards and jewelry, special occasion clothing, plus hair and beauty products. Super-friendly and community-minded staff. And as a bonus, if you're looking to put a little color in your Christmas, your brood can get a photo snapped with Soulful Santa around the holidays.

ALL GOD'S CREATURES
WELCOME HERE

{ PETS RIP }

Put aside any lingering Stephen King fears and instead marvel at the soul connections betwixt man and beast at the **Imperial Crown Pet Cemetery** (115 N. US 67, 314-921-1558, imperialcrownpc.com), the oldest in St. Louis. Founded by a local veterinarian in the 1920s, it's still in use today and provides a rather unlikely, but definitely tranquil, spot to remember your furry (or feathered, or finned) friend.

{ SAINTS AMONG US }

Old St. Ferdinand Shrine (#1 rue St. Francois, 314-837-2110, oldstferdinandshrine.com), the oldest Catholic church west of the Mississippi, forms the centerpiece of this well-preserved complex, also including a convent, church, and rectory. A fascinating glimpse into the French & Spanish forebears of the area's early development. Tours for any size/age group, by appointment. The convent was home to St. Philippine Rose Duchesne.

WEST AND SOUTHWEST COUNTY

BALLWIN ★ CHESTERFIELD ★ CREVE COEUR ★ DES PERES
★ ELLISVILLE ★ EUREKA ★ FENTON ★ FRONTENAC ★
MANCHESTER ★ MARYLAND HEIGHTS ★ TOWN AND
COUNTRY ★ WILDWOOD

HISTORY

West and Southwest County sit on the edges of the Ozark foothills. The tree-lined country roads, limestone bluffs along the Meramec, and richness in preserved history make this region distinct. Pro athletes, local celebrities, and other affluent residents call the area home. Olive Boulevard follows an old Indian trail, which once ran between the Missouri and Mississippi rivers. The trail became a widely used road by farmers, stagecoaches, and travelers heading into or out of St. Louis. Manchester Road, a road to market and a link between St. Louis and Jefferson City, was designated a part of Route 66 in the 1930s. Businesses sprang up along the route, which today are part of Ballwin, Manchester, and Ellisville.

Bellefontaine, Hilltown, Gumbo, Hog Hollow, Monarch, Eatherton, and Bonhomme were former towns with post offices, which today are part of **Chesterfield**. Gumbo Flats—now called Chesterfield Valley—was submerged in the Flood of 1993. Levees were built, and today one of the country's longest strip malls can be found here. Thornhill Estate, built by Missouri's second governor Frederick Bates, was later purchased by the Faust family. Wanting to preserve Thornhill's historical significance, the Fausts donated the estate and 98 acres to St. Louis County, creating Faust Park, a Chesterfield treasure. Nearby, **Wildwood** is geographically comparable to St. Louis City but maintains its country-living ambience with a population of fewer than 40,000.

Creve Coeur is French for "broken heart." Legend has it that an Indian princess was distraught over the unrequited love of a French fur trapper and jumped off the ledge overlooking Creve Coeur Lake. It was then the lake formed itself into the shape of a broken heart. Creve Coeur Lake hosted the rowing competition during the 1904 Olympics and remains a popular place for sailing. Originally a resort, Creve Coeur Lake Memorial Park in **Maryland Heights** officially became a county park in 1945. Maryland Heights also is where the Verizon Wireless Amphitheatre and Harrah's Casino are located. The Holocaust Museum and Learning Center located in Creve Coeur houses an extensive historical collection, including personal accounts of Holocaust survivors who came to St. Louis.

Town and Country residents have one of the highest median incomes in the state. Maintaining the pastoral led to a soaring deer population with collisions between cars and deer becoming a regular occurrence. A deer management program, which harvests a select number of deer annually, has led to the donation of venison to local food banks via the Missouri Department of Conservation's Share the Harvest Program. **Frontenac**'s Benjamin Wood and his wife were frequent visitors to Quebec. Enamored with the history Quebec's Chateau Frontenac, they named their Missouri property Frontenac. Today the Woods property is the central part of the town.

French Jesuit missionaries settled near the confluence Des Peres River and were responsible for giving the river and area the name **Des Peres,** or in English "Of the Fathers." The name has stood the test of time as churches, post offices, schools, and societies adopted the Des Peres name as well.

Eureka's location near wonderful state parks like Lone Elk and Route 66 brings new residents looking for country living. **Fenton** is a small village on the Meramec River, which has blossomed into a full-fledged southwestern suburb of St. Louis. Seasonal flooding near its downtown has made relocation of some residents and businesses necessary. However, the Navajo Hotel, built in 1929, offers a glimpse of the kinds of resorts that were once popular getaways in places like Valley Park, Castlewood Park, and Fenton.

{ KIDZONE }

For authentic Japanese (both food & decor) and notable fam-friendliness, look no further than the venerable **Tachibana** (12967 Olive Blvd., 314-434-3455, tachibanastl. com): gotta love a kids' menu with small portions of orange chicken, BBQ beef ribs, shrimp tempura, and California rolls, nary a nugget nor grilled cheese in sight.

FOOD AND DRINK

Take the time to explore strip malls and hidden commercial developments. Even if you can't see them from the street, some independent gems lurk there for your dining and drinking pleasure.

....

A BITE TO EAT

ADDIE'S THAI HOUSE
13441 Olive Blvd.
Chesterfield
314-469-1660
addiesthaihouse.com
White-tablecloth Thai, with fresh rolls and waterfall beef recommended

ANNA MARIE'S ICE CREAM
16497 Clayton Rd.
Wildwood
636-273-1900
annamariesicecream.com
Homemade ice cream and gourmet treats, including ice cream cakes

ANNIE GUNN'S
16806 Chesterfield Airport Rd.
Chesterfield
636-532-7684
anniegunns.com
Wood-paneled and homey while still feeling "special night out"; American cuisine and superlative wine list

BABBO'S SPAGHETTERIA
17402 Chesterfield Airport Rd.
Chesterfield
636-536-0000
babbosspaghetteria.com
Spaghetti, yes, and meatballs, chicken spiedini, risotto, and more

BARNEY'S BBQ
16011 Manchester Rd.
Ellisville
636-227-2300
barneysbbq.com
Vinegar-based sauce on ribs, chicken, pork, & beef; seasonal operation May-Sept

IL BEL LAGO
11631 Olive Blvd.
Creve Coeur
314-994-1080
ilbellagosaintlouis.com
Fine dining Italian, fountainside in strip center

BISTRO 1130
1130 Town and Country Crossing Dr.
Town and Country
636-394-1130
bistro1130.com
Haute cuisine French (sauteed sweetbreads, vol-au-vent, escargot)

LA BONNE BOUCHEE
12344 Olive Blvd.
Creve Coeur
314-576-6606
labonnebouchee.com
Cafe & patisserie features croissants, quiche, and more...to say nothing of the tempting bakery cases

BRICK TAVERN
2 McBride & Son Center Dr.
Chesterfield
636-536-6291
brickhousetavernandtap.com
Embrace your inner dude in this self-proclaimed man cave: beer, deviled eggs, meatloaf, & beer

{ BAGELS BY THE BOOK }

Mass popularity has ruined many a noble foodstuff, and such is arguably the case with bagels. Forget the toothless variety you might be accustomed to pulling from your grocer's freezer section: Go straight to the **Bagel Factory** (11256 Olive Blvd., Creve Coeur, 314-432-3583; well, hit the ATM first, 'cause they don't take plastic) and stock up on the real deal. Water-boiled before baking, these are the bagels lesser bagels dream of being when they grow up. Poppyseed, onion, strawberry, egg, and a handful of other varieties, strictly grab-and-go atmosphere.

CHARLOTTE'S RIB BBQ
15467 Clayton Rd.
Ballwin
636-394-3332
charlottesribbbq.com
Sweet, saucy ribs, pork steak, and standout sides

CLASSIC RED HOTS
41 Forum Shopping Center
Chesterfield
314-878-4687
classicredhots.com
Vienna beef dogs in many varieties, sandwiches, & hot tamales

CUISINE D'ART
701 North New Ballas Rd.
Creve Coeur
314-995-3003
cuisine-dart.com
French-inspired offshoot of catering service, with small chalkboard menu, Sunday brunch

D&H STEAKHOUSE & BISTRO
323 Westport Plaza Dr.
Maryland Heights
314-878-1801
dierdorfharts.com
Recently re-invented Dierdorf & Hart's, with burgers & small plates on bistro side, traditional steaks & chops in the dining room

DAVE & TONY'S PREMIUM BURGERS
12766 Olive Blvd.
Creve Coeur
314-439-5100
daveandtonys.com
BYOB: build your own burger, from 4 choices of bun (and 6 proteins!) on up

DREAM HOUSE & TEA ROOM
15425 Clayton Rd.
Ballwin
636-227-7640
dreamhouseandtearoom.com
Ladies, your lunch: soups, salads, quiche

EAST COAST PIZZA

17304 Chesterfield Airport Rd.

Chesterfield

636-536-7888

eastcoastpizza.net

Slices & pies (NY and Chi style), stromboli, calzones

GERARD'S

12240 Manchester Rd.

Des Peres

314-821-7977

stlgerards.com

Old-school continental dining room, with plenty of seafood, beef, and serious wine

GIANFABIO

127 Hilltown Village Ctr.

Chesterfield

636-532-6686

gianfabio.com

Flash-fried spinach, brick oven pizzas, pastas

HAPPY CHINA

12921 Olive Blvd.

Creve Coeur

314-878-6660

Stomach-pleasing buffet of potstickers, hot-and-sour-soup, sushi, crawfish, fried squid, and plenty more

ICHIBAN

12388 Olive Blvd.

Creve Coeur

314-579-6002

Japanese specialties and sushi

JOO JOO

12937 Olive Blvd.

Creve Coeur

314-469-1999

letseat.at/joojoo

Bi bim bop! Fun to say, fun to eat; Korean food and karaoke rooms

KABOB PALACE

14424 Manchester Rd.

Manchester

636-230-8800

kabob-palace.com

Afghan/Persian, including burani, sambosas, and various kabobs

LAL QILA

15222 Manchester Rd.

Ballwin

636-527-4717

lalqilastl.com

Pakistani/Indian, with weeknight dinner buffet

LAZY RIVER GRILL

631 Big Bend Rd.

Manchester

636-207-1689

lazyyellow.com

Steaks, fish, burgers in "LL Bean-rustic" atmosphere

....

{ FOR THE HEALTH OF IT }

Surprise, surprise: The burbs have one of the very few vegan/raw-centric restaurants in the region! At **VegaDeli** (177 Hilltown Village Center, Chesterfield, 636-536-6938, vegadeli. com), wraps, salads, and "burgers" provide an easy entree to the world of vegan for the nonfamiliar, while vegetarian-minded folks can expand their palates with raw tacos, zucchini Alfredo, and wheatgrass shots.

MAGGIE'S LUNCHBOX
867 Horan Dr.
Fenton
636-326-4411
maggieslunchbox.com
Great soup/sandwich/
salad cafe, plus evening
menu; many off-the-menu
faves among regulars, so
don't be afraid to ask!

MATADOR
17304-115 Chesterfield
Airport Rd.
Chesterfield
636-536-6500
Casual Mexican spot
serving fajitas, enchila-
das, tacos, and more

MILLER'S CROSSING
14156 Olive Blvd.
Chesterfield
314-439-0400
Nary a hint of gangster
noir at this burgers &
beer sports bar

MONSOON
14248 Manchester Rd.
Ballwin
636-256-8838
monsoon-stl.com
Dumplings, pho, and
extensive entree menu,
upscale

NIPPON TEI
14025 Manchester Rd.
Ballwin
636-386-8999
nippontei-stl.com
Bento boxes, sukiyaki,
and other Japanese dish-
es, but sushi is the star

PM BBQ
103 Chesterfield Towne
Ctr.
Chesterfield
636-536-1966
pmbbq.com
Memphis-style BBQ,
from ribs to pulled pork
plus wings & chicken 'n'
dumplings

PACIFIC CAFE
11921 Olive Blvd.
Creve Coeur
314-872-7272
Asian (of the "pan"
persuasion: pad Thai,
banh mi, crab rangoon)...
plus subs & gyros

PAUL MANNO'S
75 Forum Shopping Ctr.
Chesterfield
314-878-1274
Sicilian-Italian spot
that's generally packed

PICASSO'S BISTRO
138 Chesterfield Towne
Ctr.
Chesterfield
636-532-5353
picassosbistro.com
On the Mediterranean
diet? Lots to love here,
prepared with healthful
technique and ingredients

PUJOLS 5
342 Westport Pl.
Maryland Heights
314-439-0505
pujols5grill.com
Cards fans will be ecstatic
at the memorabilia &
sports theme; non-fans
will be delighted with the
pollo con arroz

PUMPERNICKLES DELI
11036 Olive Blvd.
Creve Coeur
314-567-4496
pumpernickles.com
Deli/diner classics with
added Jewish flavor, from
mishagos, homemade lox,
and bialys

SAPORE
403 Lafayette Ctr.
Manchester
636-256-3949
saporeitaliancafe.com
First-class interpretations
of Italian dishes in casually elegant ambiance

SISTERS TEA HOUSE
505 W. Main St.
Fenton
636-305-1319
sistersteahouse.com
Luncheon is served: tuna
salad, soups, croissants,
or more traditional high
tea service

ST. LOUIS
KOREAN BAKERY
13357 Olive Blvd.
Chesterfield
314-523-1332
Korean baked goods and
other treats like pat bing
soo (shaved ice)

SURF & SIRLOIN
13090 Manchester Rd.
Des Peres
314-822-3637
surfandsirloin.com
Extensive seafood menu
(red snapper, grouper,
trout, sole), steaks, and
Greek flourishes

SURF DOGS
137 Chesterfield Towne
Ctr.
Chesterfield
636-537-8799
surfdogsgrill.com
Tons o'hot dogs, plus
burgers, Polish, fish baskets, and key lime pie

TABLE THREE
16765 Main St.
Wildwood
636-458-4333
table-three.com
Smart-casual contem-
porary American spot, from
flat-screen-facing bar seats
to lush patio

THAI NIVAS
11054 Olive Blvd.
Creve Coeur
314-567-8989
thainivassushi.com
Sleek room for sushi
and Thai specialties
like tom yum soup,
Mas-a-Man curry

VILLA FAROTTO
17417 Chesterfield
Airport Rd.
Chesterfield
636-519-0048
villafarotto.com
"Multi-concept" Italian
fine-dining restaurant/
takeout/patio/shop

WHIPT CREAM
143 Chesterfield Towne
Ctr.
Chesterfield
636-532-0020
whiptcream.com
Whimsical cupcakes
and cakes, expertly
decorated but more
importantly, delicious

{ EAST MEETS WEST (COUNTY) }

Sample the wide variety of the Indian subcontinent without ever going
east of 270: recommended are **Gokul** (10633 Page Ave., 314-428-8888,
gokulrestaurant.com; 100% vegetarian), **Flavor of India** (11939 Olive Blvd.,
314-997-4224, flavorofindiastl.com; strong on Northern Indian), **Mayuri**
(12513 Olive Blvd., 314-576-7272, mayuri.com; north & south Indian dishes
represented, plus a healthy dose of Indian-Chinese), **Saffron** (2137 Barrett
Station Rd., 314-965-3822, saffronstl.net; lamb dishes are tasty), and **Taj
Palace** (92 THF Blvd., 636-728-1000; plenty of tandoori-cooked dishes).

WILD HORSE GRILL
101 Chesterfield Towne Ctr.
Chesterfield
636-532-8750
wildhorsegrill.com
Spiffy place for ambitious dishes like duck Wellington, smoked tenderloin lasagna

THE WOLF PUBLIC HOUSE
15480 Clayton Rd.
Ballwin
636-527-7027
thewolfpublichouse.com
Popular gathering spot, early morning til late evening, for coffee, breakfast, sandwiches, live music. Plus, grilled cheese du jour. Yeah.

ZOYA'S CAFE
725 N New Ballas Rd.
Creve Coeur
314-432-5050
Gyros, Greek salad, and other quick lunch/dinner bites

SOMETHING TO DRINK

BONE'S FRENCH QUARTER
14766 Manchester Rd.
Ballwin
636-391-8293
fqstl.com
Nonstop Mardi Gras atmosphere, plus bar food (and breakfast, from 7 a.m. daily)

EUREKA WINE HOUSE
107 S. Central Ave.
Eureka
636-938-5411
eurekawinehouse.com
120 wines, pet-friendly patio, & live music

HARPO'S
136 Hilltown Village Ctr.
Chesterfield
636-537-1970
harpos.com
Like you never left Mizzou, right down to the Shakespeare's pizza

THE HAUS
14815 Clayton Rd.
Chesterfield
636-386-5919
thehausstl.com
Drink specials, karaoke, occasional live music

THE HIVE
609 North New Ballas Rd.
Creve Coeur
314-569-1769
Post-office-work hangout with nice, smallish patio

ITAP
161 Long Rd.
Chesterfield
636-537-8787
internationaltaphouse.com
Beer bonanza, with brews
from around the globe.
BYO food from neighbor-
ing establishments

MORGAN LEFAY'S
14314 South Outer Forty
Rd.
Town and Country
314-317-9181
morganlefays.com
Small spot for cocktails
and tapas, live music

POOR RICHARD'S
960 Brookwood Ctr.
Fenton
636-349-3438
poorrichardsstl.com
Burgers, wings, & beer for
game day with the fam

THE SPORTS PAGE
13431 Olive Blvd.
Chesterfield
314-434-4115
thesportspage-barandgrill.
com
A renowned burger, high-
end TVs, and friendly
atmosphere

VERITAS
1722 Clarkson Rd.
Chesterfield
636-530-9505
veritasgateway.com
Weekend three-taste
wine flights, plus stellar
selection in retail tasting
shop atmosphere

{ BASTA IN THE BASEMENT }

"Nondescript" isn't the half of it:
Balducci's Winefest (12527
Bennington Pl., 314-576-5024,
balduccisstlouis.com) shares a
strip with, among other tenants,
a hair stylist and a 7-11. Descend
the steps into the basement-level
Italian restaurant, though, and you'll
find a cheery, family-run joint that's
been keeping its patrons happy for
decades, with good food (pizza &
t-ravs are tops) and homey decor
(giant wire-spool tables, stained
glass).

{ NATURE IN THE RAW }

At **Lone Elk Park** (1 Lone Elk Park Rd., Valley Park, 314-615-7275, stlouisco.com/parks/loneelk.html) yep, there are elk—and bison, wild turkeys, turtles, deer, and all manner of wildlife—roaming free and quite happy to meander up near you, your car, or your pic-a-nic. Take only pictures, leave only footprints (and perhaps a donation), then fly over to the neighboring **World Bird Sanctuary** (125 Bald Eagle Ridge Rd., Valley Park, 636-225-4390, worldbirdsanctuary.org) to see owls, hawks, bald eagles, falcons, parrots, and more, in habitat displays and in live animal encounters. And in the grandest St. Louis tradition, it's all free to visitors.

RECREATION

Perhaps it's the availability of big tracts of cheap, exurban real estate, but a cluster of indoor amusement facilities dots the West County & area landscape.

EXERCISE

AQUAPORT
2344 McKelvey Rd.
Maryland Heights
314-738-2599
marylandheights.com
Outdoor waterpark with slides, lazy river, splash playground, and more

THE CAGES
14918 Manchester Rd. Rear
Ballwin
636-391-0616
thecagesinballwin.net
Indoor batting cages & pitching mounds, with instructors for baseball and softball

{ HIT THE TRACKS }

Romance the rails at several unique whistle stops in West County. First (and free!), you can ride a large-scale model train in Eureka's Kircher Park on select dates under the auspices of the **St. Louis Live Steamers** (Kircher Park, on Williams Rd., stlouislivesteamers.org)—something like sitting atop a steam-operated footstool. Or take it up a notch and hop aboard the **Wabash Frisco and Pacific Railroad**'s (109 Grand Ave., Glencoe, 636-587-3538, wfprr.com) 12-inch gauge steam locomotive, which winds along the Meramec River near Glencoe for a 2-mile, 30-minute loop. (You'll be sitting single file on bench seats; $4/ages 4 and up). Budding engineers will be in choo-choo heaven at **Whittle Shortline Railroad** (24 Front St., Valley Park, 636-861-3334, woodentrain.com), a store/playspace selling American-made, lead-paint-free wooden trains & accessories. It's not all pushy retail, though; tons of tracks make up a free play area, there's coffee for the tall people, and upstairs in the historic building are rooms for parties and special Family Fun nights, held monthly.

CASTLEWOOD STATE PARK

1401 Kiefer Creek Rd.

Ballwin

636-227-4433

mostateparks.com/park/castlewood-state-park

Mountain-biking nirvana in these parts, plus Meramec hikes, horse trails, and playground

CHESTERFIELD SPORTS FUSION

140 Long Rd.

Chesterfield

636-536-6720

chesterfieldsportsfusion.com

Indoor funplex of laser tag, mini golf, climbing wall, dodgeball court

HIDDEN VALLEY SKI AREA

17409 Hidden Valley Dr.

Wildwood

636-938-5373

hiddenvalleyski.com

Manufactured snow covers 30 acres of terrain, from absolute beginner level to expert jumps and bowls. Plus, how fun is it to say "Ski Missouri"? Night skiing offered.

THE INFIELD

2626 Westhills Park Dr.

Ellisville

636-458-1144

theinfieldfuncenter.com

Go karts, mini golf, bumper boats, and arcade

MILLENNIUM PARK SPRAYGROUND

2 Barnes West Dr.

Creve Coeur

creve-coeur.org

Must be accessed from Barnes West Dr. just south of Olive Blvd. A hidden treasure near Barnes West, featuring two playgrounds with modern equipment and a fun sprayground

THE POINTE AT BALLWIN COMMONS

#1 Ballwin Commons Circle

Ballwin

636-227-8950

ballwin.mo.us

Indoor aquatic center features slide and water playground

SKYZONE SPORTS

17379 Edison Ave.

Chesterfield

636-530-4550

skyzonesports.com

Indoor trampoline park for all ages

SWING AROUND FUN TOWN

335 Skinker Ln.

Fenton

636-349-7077

swing-a-round.com

Go karts, bumper boats, mini golf, batting cages

{ RELAXATION HARVEST }

Breath deep at Eureka's **Winding Brook Estate** (3 Winding Brook Estate Dr., Eureka, 636-575-5572, windingbrookestate.com). You're surrounded by the state's only commercial lavender farm (don't breath too deep: they also raise and sell lambs.) Pick your own tussie-mussie when the harvest comes in, or buy their organic bath, body, and culinary products.

{ KIDZONE }

On a hot day, or a rainy day, or a day which is not quite merry enough, hightail it to the **St. Louis Carousel**, in Faust Park (15185 Olive Blvd., Chesterfield). A buck a spin on this circa-1920 merry-go-round—relocated from Forest Park Highlands Amusement Park with rousing musical accompaniment by the Stinson Band Organ, might be the best deal in town.

ARTS, ENTERTAINMENT, & EDUCATION

AKC MUSEUM OF THE DOG
1721 South Mason Rd.
Manchester
314-821-3647
museumofthedog.org
If your exposure to dog art begins and ends with them playing poker, visiting the 700-item collection of fine art here will be a treat. Handsome facility, great gift shop, and you can bring Fido along for the trip.

BACKSTREET JAZZ & BLUES
610 Westport Plaza Dr.
Maryland Heights
314-878-5800
Small jazz club in Westport Plaza draws tops from local blues scene

BUTTERFLY HOUSE
15193 Olive Blvd.
Chesterfield
636-530-0076
butterflyhouse.org
Science and beauty on the wing (plus added attractions like hissing cockroaches, spiders, & scorpions), fun annual events like "Hot! Hot! Hot!" in the dead of winter (with steel drum music, tropical theme, and beachy activities)

THE ENDANGERED WOLF CENTER
6750 Tyson Valley Rd.
Eureka
636-938-5900
endangeredwolfcenter.org
Founded by Carol and Marlin Perkins (of *Wild Kingdom* fame), offers education programs, tours of wolf enclosures (featuring African wild dogs, red wolves, swift foxes, and more)

FUNNY BONE COMEDY CLUB
614 Westport Plaza Dr.
Maryland Heights
314-469-6692
stlouisfunnybone.com
Stand-up comedy and open mic
for 18+ crowd

HOLOCAUST MUSEUM
12 Millstone Campus Dr.
Maryland Heights
314-432-0020
hmlc.org
Eye-opening detail and firsthand
accounts of the Holocaust in artifacts,
photos, letters, and exhibits dedicated to
a future free of hatred and indifference

KEMP AUTO MUSEUM
16955 Chesterfield Airport Rd.
Chesterfield
636-537-1718
kempautomuseum.org
40 stunning cars showcase the art
& history of European automobiles,
including Mercedes, Porsche, and
Rolls Royce models

{ AHOY }

If you've ever thought longingly about living
somewhere on the water, perhaps getting
a little boat and chucking it all for the coast,
head out to **Creve Coeur Lake** (2143 Creve
Coeur Mill Rd., stlouisco.com) on alternate
Sundays for most of the year and cast your
lot with the friendly folks from Creve Coeur
Sailing Association. They race small sailboats
in the afternoon, but the preparation and
rigging time is when even novice sailers can
get in on the action, volunteering to crew for
a few hours. It's great fun to participate or
even watch, and you'll need that small craft
experience if you ever trade up to the high
seas, anyway.

{ THE GREAT PUMPKIN }

Each year, when he finds the patch that's most sincere...well, you know the rest. Start a fall family tradition with an October visit (weekends offer the most activity) to **Rombachs Farm** (18639 Olive Street Rd., 636-532-7265, rombachsfarm.com; in Chesterfield, with pumpkins for sale, a pumpkin pyramid for pix and hayrides, plus a small country store) or **Stuckmeyer's** (249 Schneider Dr., 636-349-1225, stuckmeyers.com; in Fenton, offering pre- or u-pick pumpkins, hay and pony rides, corn maze, live music, and produce sales). Make sure you're prepared for a cute-photo-opp overload: think babies plunked in pumpkin patches, kids eating apples as big as their heads, and so on.

FESTIVITIES

THE ART FAIR AT QUEENY PARK
Labor Day weekend
Greensfelder Recreation Center,
Queeny Park
gslaa.org
Juried fine art and craft festival features more than 100 artists in all media

CREVE COEUR DAYS
May
Grounds of Barnes Jewish West
County Hospital
crevecoeurdays.com
Large community-planned festival that has taken place since 1967, features carnival rides, games, food, and fun, including live music and a parade

FAUST FALL FOLK & FINE ARTS FESTIVAL
September
Faust Park
Get your fine arts and folk arts fixes in one convenient location: everything from modern jewelry and paintings to rug making demos and corn husk dolls

MISSOURI WINEFEST
February
Westport Plaza
westportstl.com
Charity wine-tasting event from the state's top vintners

SHOPPORTUNITIES

FAZIO'S FRETS & FRIENDS
15440 Manchester Rd.
Ellisville
636-227-3573
faziosmusic.com
Huge music store with instruments, accessories, rentals, performances, and instruction; after-school Rock Academy program

GABI'S WINE
14433 Manchester Rd.
Ballwin
636-527-2997
Vast selection including beer, plus good staff advice

GO!SPA
11735 Manchester Rd.
Des Peres
314-822-0772
gospagirl.com
Full menu of spa services in a fun, upbeat, drop-in-and-get-pampered-in-a-flash venue; great gift selection, too

LUKAS LIQUOR
15921 Manchester Rd.
Ellisville
636-227-4543
lukasliquorstl.com
The big daddy of West County booze superstores, with raveworthy selection and service

THE NAKED VINE
1624 Clarkson Rd.
Chesterfield
636-536-0711
nakedvine.net
Avoid the Mondavis and Kendall Jacksons of the world here, and instead hone in on small-production wineries, craft beers, and handmade salumi

NEW DAY GLUTEN FREE
15622 Manchester Rd.
Ellisville
636-527-5000
newdayglutenfree.com
One meal in the cafe is great, but it's the grocery side where you'll find the dishes and ingredients to make every day in your home easier for a gluten-free lifestyle

OLD HOUSE IN HOG HOLLOW
14319 Olive Blvd.
Chesterfield
314-469-1019
oldhouseinhoghollow.com
Folk art, linens, collectible figurines, pewter, holiday decor, and plenty more

{ DECLARATION OF INDEPENDENTS }

Right there in the mall, stereotypical purveyor to the mass market, is a haven of uniquity: **Artropolis**, in the Sears wing of Chesterfield Mall (chesterfield-mall.com). It brings together seven local arts endeavors, from a black-box theatre (Dramatic License Productions, dramaticlicenseproductions.org) to a locally focused gallery (Mind Works). And if that's not enough indie-cred for you, pop into **The Foundrie** (219 Chesterfield Mall, Chesterfield, 636-465-2356, thefoundrie.com), an all-local boutique for art, apparel, jewelry, gifts, tote bags, stationery, and more from area crafters and artists.

{ SELF-REFLECTION }

While the A-B ads certainly capture...something of the spirit of St. Louis, perhaps a bit more artful entry would be preferable to commit our town's likeness for posterity. Renowned plein-air painter **Billyo** (314-229-7693, billyoart.com) fills a storefront at Chesterfield Mall with his impressionistic landscapes, street scenes, and snapshots of Missouri culture, while **John Pils** (15011 Manchester Rd., Ballwin, 636-227-1155, johnpilscities.com) captures cityscapes, street elevations, and entire communities in a few deft pencil line strokes, with watercolor accents. Both would make excellent additions to your collection.

ONE LUCKY MUTT
2414 Taylor Rd.
Wildwood
636-458-8838
oneluckymutt.com
Natural foods/treats, fancy pet fancies, and a DIY dogwash

ST. LOUIS WINE MARKET AND TASTING ROOM
164 Chesterfield Commons East
Chesterfield
636-536-6363
stlwinemarket.com
Retail space + tasting area means you can find a new favorite and take it home tonight

{ THANKS FOR YOUR SUPPORT }

Laugh if you will at the "Got Bra Problems?" billboards, but we'll bet your wife (or your mom) nods in sympathy. **Ann's Bra Shop** (13483 Olive Blvd., Chesterfield, 314-878-4144) is nationally known for fitting, selection, and especially care and products for post-mastectomy patients. Even we giggle, though, at the drive-through window.

SUMMER HOUSE
14356 Manchester Rd.
Ballwin
636-256-9264
Interior design firm also sells retail, meaning well-curated, just-so touches for your house (or gift for your next hostess)

TOBAKKO'S
17205 Chesterfield Airport Rd.
Chesterfield
636-536-0606
Cigars and other manly accoutrements

TOY TYME
146 Chesterfield Valley Dr.
Chesterfield
636-532-9696

Chesterfield Mall (lower level near Sears)
Chesterfield
636-733-0088

West County Mall (upper level near Macy's)
Des Peres
314-965-0086
toytyme.com
Every baby and kid toy or game you can imagine...and more than a few you'll wish you'd had as a kid

TREASURE ROOMS
17373 Chesterfield Airport Rd.
Chesterfield
636-728-1899
treasurerooms.com
Trick out your nursery or big-kid room with fancy furniture and all the extras

VJ COFFEE & TEA
12595 Olive Blvd.
Creve Coeur
314-542-9292
Independent coffee and tea retailer glommed onto the front of Dierbergs

. . . .

{ HANDIWORK }

For the county crafter, plenty of specialty shops can provide the supplies, instruction, and inspiration for projects in a variety of media. Beaders/Jewelry makers: **Bizzy Beads** (135 Chesterfield Towne Ctr., Chesterfield, 636-728-1515, bizzybeads.com), **B&J Rock Shop** (14744 Manchester Rd., Ballwin, 636-394-4567, bjrockshop.com). Glass/Metal fabrication: **Glasshopper Studio** (13011 Olive Blvd., St. Louis, 314-205-0220, glasshopperstudio. com). The Edible Arts: **Sallie's Cake & Candy Supplies** (14340 Manchester Rd., Manchester, 636-394-3030, salliesonline.com). Textiles: **Susie Q Quilting** (131 S. Central Ave. #B, Eureka, 636-587-2772, susieqquilting.com), **Wool Gatherings** (510 West Ave., Eureka, 636-221-2826, woolgatherings.net).

ST. CHARLES COUNTY

**COTTLEVILLE ★ DARDENNE PRAIRIE ★ LAKE ST. LOUIS ★
ST. CHARLES ★ ST. PETERS ★ WELDON SPRING**

HISTORY

The French were the first European settlers in St. Charles County, arriving late in the eighteenth century. Daniel Boone, a Spanish land grant recipient, came soon after. German immigrant Gottfried Duden, a neighbor of Boone's, spent a lot of time with the famous frontiersman exploring this area. Duden later returned to Germany and published a glowing report of life here, and his writings inspired Germans to immigrate to Missouri.

Until the arrival of the automobile, St. Charles County was largely rural. The building of the Interstate Highway System and the Blanchette Bridge linked St. Louis City and County with St. Charles. The population soon followed. By 1980, St. Charles County grew from a population of 14,000 to 50,000. The trend as one of the nation's fastest growing counties continues today, especially in St. Peters, O'Fallon, and Wentzville.

St. Charles is the county seat and the oldest city on the Missouri River. Founder Frenchman Louis Blanchette, named it *Les Petites Côtes* (the little hills), which was changed by the Spanish to *San Carlos del Misuri*, or "St. Charles of the Missouri." After the Louisiana Purchase, the name became St. Charles. The city would serve as Missouri's first state capital for six years between 1820 and 1826. Lindenwood University, established in 1827, has evolved into a highly respected educational institution. Main Street St. Charles is renowned for hosting some of the Midwest's best festivals and craft fairs.

St. Peters provides a prime example of St. Charles County's population boom over the last four decades. The 1970 Census revealed a population of 486. The 1980 Census population was 15,700. By 2010, the population was over 52,500.

O'Fallon is another one of Missouri's fastest growing cities. In 1812, Zumwalt's Fort was built to protect settlers from Native Americans who'd been armed by the British. The Spirit of 9/11 Memorial is 13 tons of twisted steel brought to Missouri from the Twin Towers in New York. Dedicated in 2003, it serves as a poignant reminder of one of the saddest days in U.S. history.

Lake St. Louis began as a private recreational lake and original planned community built in the spirit of Reston, Virginia, and Columbia, Maryland. Facing annexation to Wentzville or O'Fallon, after the developer declared bankruptcy, the residents came together and formed what today is Lake St. Louis. According to the 2010 Census, **Wentzville** is Missouri's fastest growing city. Living history aficionados can relive life in sixteenth-century France at the Greater St. Louis Renaissance Faire. Get in the spirit of it all and wear period costume! There'll be jousting, sword fighting, strolling minstrels, period craftsman, artisans, and food.

Throughout its history St. Charles County has undergone a transformation from a collection of small villages to a thriving part of the metro area. From the historical to the most modern conveniences, St. Charles has it all.

{ **HINT OF HISTORY** }

St. Charles, the final embarkation point of the Lewis & Clark Expedition, could not be more closely intertwined with that historic journey, and the **Lewis & Clark Boat House & Nature Center** (1050 Riverside Dr., St. Charles, 636-947-3199, lewisandclark.net) is a kind of one-stop interpretive shop for All Things L&C. Dioramas illustrating the mission's highlights, encounters with native peoples, animals, and habitats along the way, and more. The highlight, for many, is the Boat House, where full-scale replicas of the Corps of Discovery's vessels are displayed. A wetland marsh around the site makes for good birding, too.

FOOD AND DRINK

As in many suburban and exurban locales, chain eateries are ascendant, but independent options exist, too, even if you have to drive the strip mall to find them.

A BITE TO EAT

BC'S KITCHEN
11 Meadows Circle Dr.
Lake St. Louis
636-542-9090
billcardwell.com
Latest outing from chef-owner Bill Cardwell, upscale American food

CONCETTA'S ITALIAN RESTAURANT
600 S. 5th St.
St. Charles
636-946-2468
concettas-stcharles.com
Family-owned Italian for more than 25 years

GRAPPA GRILL
1644 Country Club Pl.
St. Charles
636-940-5400
grappagrill.com
Casually elegant Italian spot

HEAVEN SCENT BAKERY
1133 Bryan Rd.
O'Fallon
636-240-8311
heavenscentbakery.net
Donuts, gourmet desserts, frozen custard, 24-hour drive-thru

KITARO
4551 Hwy. K
O'Fallon
636-300-4422
kitarojapan.com
Sleek & contemporary Japanese cuisine

LADY DI'S DINER
630 N. Kingshighway
St. Charles
636-916-4442
ladydisdiner.com
Classic diner breakfast & lunch, including 10-egg omelet and the tornado casserole; cash/check only

LEWIS & CLARK'S
217 S. Main St.
St. Charles
636-947-3334
lewisandclarksrestaurant.com
Brick-clad, historic setting for American/Mex comfort food, Trailhead beer on tap; balcony seating is tops

LOUISIANA CAFE
2698 Technology Dr.
Dardenne Prairie
636-561-8878
louisianacafeonline.com
Gumbo, fried catfish, crawfish etoufée, and more from down N'awlins way

{ WHEEL COOL }

Is it a bike shop, a coffee bar, a restaurant, a trailhead? Yep. Get it all, from bike tires (and free air!) to breakfast wraps, at the funky **2nd St. Bike Stop Café** (1325 N. 2nd St., St. Charles, 636-724-9900, 2ndstreetbikestopcafe.webs.com), just a block off the Katy Trail in St. Charles. Hang out and talk shop, join up in the weekly rides, or just tuck into a Field Hippie salad.

MAD DOG & CAT'S
1005 Wolfrum Rd.
Weldon Spring
636-300-9171
maddogandcats.com
Pastas, sandwiches,
shrimp scampi, and steak
specials at tasteful spot

MISS AIMEE B'S
837 1st Capitol Dr.
St. Charles
636-946-4202
saucecafe.com/missaimeeb
Tearoom with hearty
breakfast and lunch
options from chicken salad
to praline French toast;
mooncake is a don't-miss

MOTHER-IN-LAW HOUSE
500 S. Main St.
St. Charles
636-946-9444
motherinlawhouse.com
Historic home fine dining,
serving salmon, sole,
chicken, and steak dishes

OLD MILLSTREAM INN
912 S. Main St.
St. Charles
636-946-3287
millstreambar.com
Lovely patio with
sandwiches at lunch,
plus smoked shrimp,
beef tips at dinner, and
famous Millfries

PAUL'S DONUTS
1289 Jungermann Rd.
St. Peters
636-447-8836
paulsdonuts.com
Hand-kneaded yeast
and cake donuts and two
words: Donut Sundae

PICASSO'S
COFFEE HOUSE
101 N. Main St.
St. Charles
636-925-2911
picassoscoffeehouse.com
Locally roasted coffees
and bakery goods in the
a.m., wine/beer/craft
cocktails at night, plus live
entertainment

PIO'S
403 First Capitol Dr.
St. Charles
636-946-2522
piosrestaurant.com
Pastas & pizza, chicken
dishes, frog legs, and, in
a nod to more than 50
years in business, a
"grandkids" menu

ROSCIGLIONE BAKERY
2265 Bluestone Dr.
St. Charles
636-947-6500
Fig cookies, date bars,
peanut biscotti, and
spice balls at authentic
Italian bakery

STONE SOUP COTTAGE
5525 Oak St.
Cottleville
636-244-2233
stonesoupcottage.com
Farmhouse setting for
by-reservation, prix-fixe
dining on local foodies'
must list

THYME OUT
CAFE & BISTRO
5212 Hwy. N
Cottleville
636-441-8496
thymeoutcafe.com
Casual, historic home
atmosphere (and pretty
patio) serving pizzas,
paninis, & pastas

{ MAMMA MIA }

What's a neighborhood hangout without a daunting food challenge? At **Cusumano's** (1120 Technology Dr., Ste. 110, O'Fallon, 636-329-8333, cusumanos.com), in addition to a tast, homemade pie (STL or NY styles available) and pasta favorites, the strong of stomach can take on the Meatball Challenge: scarf down a 24", 8-meatball sandwich with sauce & provel, plus a super-size side of fries, in 45 minutes and it's free, along with all the glory you can handle. Reservations, and adherence to some rules, required. Beware: The wall of shame is littered with the weak-willed who came before you.

SOMETHING TO DRINK

COTTLEVILLE WINE SELLER & WINE GARDEN
5314 Hwy. N
Cottleville
636-244-4453
cottlevillewineseller.com
Plenty of wine choices and light bites

DUCHESNE BAR & GRILL
1001 S. Duchesne Dr.
St. Charles
636-947-0920
Drinks, karaoke, peel 'n' eat shrimp

MCGURK'S PUBLIC HOUSE
108 South Main St.
O'Fallon
636-978-9640
Guinness, homemade chips & pub food, and nice patio

QUINTESSENTIAL
149 N. Main St.
St. Charles
636-443-2211
q-stl.com
Nightclub, live music, & dancing...which also happens to have an ambitious food menu

RENDEZVOUS CAFE & WINE BAR
217 S. Main St.
O'Fallon
636-281-2233
rendezvouscafeandwine-bar.com
Boutique wines, micro-brews, coffee drinks, and tapas

TRAILHEAD BREWING
921 S. Riverside Dr.
St. Charles
636-946-2739
trailheadbrewing.com
Craft brewer right on the Katy Trail, with people-watching patio

THE VINE
325 S. Main St.
St. Charles
636-946-8463
thevineonmain.com
Wine bar & schmancy dinner menu

WINERY OF THE LITTLE HILLS
501 S. Main St.
St. Charles
636-946-9339
littlehillswinery.com
Huge by-the-glass selection, full food menu; we recommend the warm Little Hills Alpenglow for a winter holiday treat

FESTIVITIES

FESTIVAL OF THE LITTLE HILLS
Third weekend in August
Main Street and Frontier Park,
St. Charles
636-940-0095
festivalofthelittlehills.com
Large, family-oriented festival of crafts from all over the country; live music, food, and drink

HERITAGE & FREEDOM FEST
Fourth of July weekend
O'Fallon
heritageandfreedomfest.com
Parade, carnival/midway/rides area, plus stage for national musical acts and nightly fireworks shows

MOSAICS FESTIVAL
FOR THE ARTS
September
Main Street
St. Charles
stcharlesmosaics.org
Juried fine art show, plus live entertainment and children's art village

OKTOBERFEST
September
Frontier Park
St. Charles
saintcharlesoktoberfest.com
German music, food, "wiener takes it all" dachshund races, 5K, kids' activities and bier, bier, bier

SANTA PARADE
Thanksgiving through Christmas
Main Street
St. Charles
stcharleschristmas.com
Part of the larger Christmas Traditions celebration (with costumed carolers, fife and drum corps, carriage rides, and more), the 40-Santa parade includes such characters as Frontier Santa, Civil War Santa, Pere Noel, and many more. Kids will love collecting the trading cards from each!

{ ENSHRINED }

The Modernist **Shrine of St. Rose Philippine Duchesne** (619 N. Second St., St. Charles, 636-946-6127, ash1818.org) was erected in the 1960s to honor the life and work of the pioneer educator and missionary to the Indians from the Society of the Sacred Heart. Mother Duchesne founded the first free school west of the Mississippi River and was canonized in 1988 by Pope John Paul II. Interestingly, the shrine remains unfinished according to its original plan, a fact you can see in its architecture and exterior surface.

RECREATION

EXERCISE

ADRENALINE ZONE/
DEMOLITION BALL
1875 Old Hwy. 94 South
St. Charles
636-940-7700
db-az.com
Multi-level laser tag & demolition ball
(billed as hockey + polo + football +
basketball, in bumper cars), plus arcade
games, foosball

BOSCHERTOWN
GRAND PRIX RACING
3500 N. Hwy. 94
St. Charles
636-946-4848
boschertowngokarts.com
Go karts, sprint karts and even
double-seaters for younger riders
to accompany parents

BRUNSWICK ZONE XL
8070 Veterans Memorial Pkwy.
St. Peters
636-474-2695
bowlbrunswick.com
Entertainment plex of bowling, laser tag,
arcade amusements

GREAT SKATE
130 Boone Hills Dr.
St. Peters
636-441-2530
greatskaterollerrink.com
Roller rink like you remember!

KLONDIKE PARK
4428-4506 Missouri 94
Augusta
636-949-7535
Rustic cabin and tent camping among
challenging county park hiking/biking trails

{ SHOE IN }

Do you know your ringers from your
leaners? You bet your horseshoes that
the folks at the **National Horseshoe
Pitchers Hall of Fame & Museum**
(100 Bluestem Way, Wentzville,
quailridgesales.com) do, and more
importantly, they can explain it to
you. Once you've got the intellectual
grasp of the game's finer points, pick
up some shoes and let 'em fly on the
indoor courts.

At just a hair over 600 acres, **Indian Camp Creek Park** (Dietrich Rd., one mile west of Hwy. 61, parks.sccmo.org) is the county's largest; fitting, then, that the four-foot-tall Bob Cassilly-designed frogs and a 22-foot-high aluminum windmill should be prominent features of the eco-friendly play area here. Everything's bigger in St. Charles County! (Don't tell Texas.) Beyond sheer size, your brood will delight in the sand dig, fossilized animal tracks, 10 miles of multi-use trails, slides, tire swing, and boardwalk-enclosed fishing pond.

RENAUD SPIRIT CENTER
2650 Tri-Sports Circle
O'Fallon
636-474-2732
renaudspiritcenter.com
City-owned community center includes
Alligator's Creek outdoor water park

ST. PETERS RECPLEX
5200 Mexico Rd.
St. Peters
636-939-2386
stpetersmo.net/st-peters-rec-plex.aspx
Community center features multiple ice-
skating rinks, adult drop-in ice hockey,
indoor pools, and more

WAPELHORST AQUATIC CENTER
1874 Muegge Rd.
St. Charles
636-936-8118 (in season)
stcharlesparks.com/119/aquatics/wapel-
horst-aquatic-facility.php
Outdoor waterpark offers innertube rapids,
kids' play area, underground waterslide,
and a five-story speed waterslide

WELDON SPRING SITE
& INTERPRETIVE CENTER
S7295 Hwy. 94 South
St. Charles
636-329-1438
greatriverroad.com/stcharles/weldonsite.htm
You don't necessarily want the Department of Energy running local parks, but
in this case, they've undertaken to reclaim
the former ordnance facility & Superfund
site, now home to the 150-acre Howell
Prairie grass/wildflower preserve and a
Native Plant Educational Garden, as well
as a bike/hiking trail

{ KIDZONE }

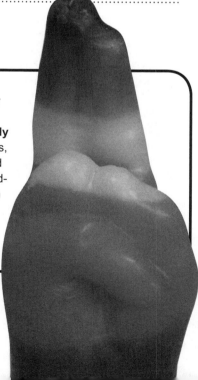

Little people put their grubby hands plenty
of places, so why not channel that natural
urge? At the literally hands-on art studio **My
Handyworks** (205 S. Main St., St. Charles,
636-724-7337, myhandyworks.com), hand
(and foot) prints, along with wax hand models, can be the basis of cool wall art, room
murals, giftable art objects, and more.
Plenty of other art and craft projects to
choose from.

ARTS, ENTERTAINMENT, & EDUCATION

BOTTLENECK BLUES BAR
One Ameristar Blvd.
St. Charles
636-949-7777
ameristar.com/St_Charles_Entertain-
ment_Bottleneck_Blues_Bar.aspx
Casino take on down-and-dirty Delta
blues club hosts occasional big-name
national acts, plus homegrown talent

DIY STYLE
7322 Village Center Dr.
O'Fallon
636-925-1829
diystyle.net
Fashion sewing classes, private
lessons & parties for the latest
wearable fashion & home decor

FOUNDRY ART CENTRE
520 N. Main Ctr.
St. Charles
636-255-0270
foundryartcentre.org
Cultural and artistic hub for fine arts
performances, exhibition, classes, and
working artists' studio spaces (many
open to the public on periodic basis)

RIVER CITY RASCALS
900 T.R. Hughes Blvd.
O'Fallon
636-240-2287
rivercityrascals.com
Get up close and personal at the
minor-league baseball games of this
Frontier League team

**J. SCHEIDEGGER
CENTER FOR THE ARTS**
2300 W. Clay St.
St. Charles
636-949-4433
lindenwood.edu/center
Exquisite new venue at Lindenwood
University houses 1,200-seat Broadway-
style theatre, flexible black box space
and art gallery, with numerous national
touring shows on the calendar

ST. ANDREWS CINEMA
2025 Golfway St.
St. Charles
636-947-1133
standrews3.com
Dollar movies, dollar hot dogs;
with five bucks, you're a king!

**ST. CHARLES COUNTY HERITAGE
MUSEUM & CENTENNIAL TRAIL**
Near the intersection of Hwy. 364 (Page
Extension) and Hwy. 94
St. Charles
636-949-7535
parks.sccmo.org
Archaeologial, agricultural, and cultural
exhibits explore the history and settlement of the area; 2.2-mile asphalt trail
links to Katy Trail

{ CHIMNEY DREAMS }

In the center of **Historic Fort Zumwalt Park** (1000 Jessup Ln., ofallon. mo.us/ParksandRec/parks_zumwalt.htm) stood a limestone chimney, lone sentinel and only remaining sign of the family fort that stood on the property and provided shelter for 10 families during the Indian raids in the War of 1812. The city of O'Fallon has begun rebuilding the fort home around it and will use the facility to display the artifacts excavated from the site and tell the story of early settlers.

SHOPPORTUNITIES

The dominant retail scene in the area is found along the cobblestones of **Main Street St. Charles**. Although its reputation as a Red Hatted "woman of a certain age" paradise is intact, interspersed you'll find shops carving out a slightly different niche. Even if it's not your cup of tea, the strolling is pleasant, the ambiance is charming, and you're never far from an ice cream stop!

CALISA HOME DECOR
3354 Mid Rivers Mall Dr.
St. Peters
636-970-0069
calisahomedecor.com
Consignment of like-new furniture & home accessory items

CANINE COOKIES & CREAM DOG BAKERY
822 S. Main St.
St. Charles
636-443-2266
All-natural gourmet goodies for your pup, including dog ice cream & cakes

DI OLIVAS OIL & VINEGARS
617 S. Main St.
St. Charles
636-724-8282
diolivas.com
Olive oils from around the world, plus vinegars, spices, gourmet gifts

DORSEY'S CORNER STORE
1328 N. 2nd St.
St. Charles
636-328-6849
Small market of fresh produce, gourmet mixes, local eggs, & vintage kitchen gear

FAST LANE CLASSIC CARS
427 Little Hills Industrial Blvd.
St. Charles
636-940-9969
fastlanecars.com
Pristine showroom of classic & muscle cars, plus collectible/gift shop

FIGUERO'S
524 S. Main St.
St. Charles
636-947-9847
figueros.com
Potential dude respite along Main Street, with a staggering 1,600 hot sauces/rubs/jerk spice mixes

FIRST CAPITOL TRADING POST
207 S. Main St.
St. Charles
636-946-2883
firstcapitoltrading.com
Disney, Swarovski, Lladro, Christopher Radko, and many other collectibles

THE FLOWER PETALER

620 S. Main St.
St. Charles
636-946-3048
flowerpetalerstcharles.com
Fresh flowers, botanical arrangements
& accents, garden decor, jewelry, artwork, and gifts

FRIPERIE

610 S. Main St.
St. Charles
636-947-7980
Accessory heaven, from scarves
to handbags

HARDWARE OF THE PAST

405 N. Main St.
St. Charles
636-724-3771
hardwareofthepast.com
Have an old house? Or want to capture
that magic? Get antique reproduction
locks, doorknobs, casters here, plus entire
drawers/furniture replacement elements

HOLIDAY HOUSE

612 S. Main St.
St. Charles
636-946-3048
Love Christmas (and others?) Dress
your house from top to bottom here

I AM WHAT I AM

107 N. Main St.
St. Charles
636-578-6923
iamwhatiamshop.com
100% locally made artisan goods,
most of the clothing/jewelry/gift stripe

J. NOTO FINE ITALIAN CONFECTIONS

336 S. Main St.
St. Charles
636-949-0800
jnoto.com
Delectable truffles, cookies, pastries,
seasonal sweets

JOHN DENGLER TOBACCONIST

700 S. Main St.
St. Charles
636-946-6899
johndenglertobacconist.com
Pipes, loose tobacco blends, cigars, &
accessories

KNIT & CABOODLE

330 S. Main St.
St. Charles
636-916-0060
knitandcaboodle.com
Thousands of yarns (including locally
spun & dyed) and classes

MAIN STREET BOOKS

307 S. Main St.
St. Charles
636-949-0105
mainstreetbooks.net
Historic building chock full of good reads
from local histories to bestselling page-
turners, plus great kids' selection

THE MEADOWS AT LAKE ST. LOUIS

20 Meadows Circle Dr., Ste. 224
Lake Saint Louis
636-695-2626
themeadowsatlsl.com
Outdoor lifestyle center includes Banana
Republic, Talbots, Clarkson Jewelers, and
state's only Von Maur department store

{ **KIDZONE** }

Watch eyes bug out at **Riverside Sweets'**
(416 S. Main St., St. Charles, 636-724-
4131) array of fresh fudge (in tons of
flavors), penny candy, peanut brittle,
popcorn caramel apples, and so much
more, all made onsite. Great stop for a
hand-dipped ice cream cone to savor as
you stroll the Main Street cobblestone.

{ BRIT BITS }

If you fancy a spot of tea, or would give your eyeteeth for a Cadbury's Curley Wurley, pop into **The English Shop** (703 S. Main St., St. Charles, 636-946-2245, theenglishshoponline.com) and get your Brit fix, pronto. Candies, English teatime accessories, Union Jack-emblazoned apparel, flags, soaps, and more, all authentically English.

MUDDPUPPIES
1120 Technology Dr., Ste. 114
O'Fallon
636-329-9940
muddpuppieswellnesscenter.com
Natural & holistic dog/cat food, treats, supplies, plus DIY dog wash

NATIVE TRADITIONS GALLERY
310 S. Main St.
St. Charles
636-947-0170
Native American art, pottery

OOH LA LA BOUTIQUES
340 S. Main St.
St. Charles
636-940-2020
Women's clothing & accessories, and down-the-block kids' store, too

PATCHES QUILT & BUTTON SHOPPE
337 S. Main St.
St. Charles
636-946-6004
patches3.com
Yep. It's just what it sounds like

PROVENANCE SOAPWORKS
523 S. Main St.
St. Charles
636-577-1972
facebook.com/ProvenanceSoaps
Handmade soaps, bath salts, bath bombs, and oils

SAGE BOOKS
1128 N. 2nd St.
St. Charles
636-352-0515
sagebooksfrenchtown.com
New & used, plus fair-trade gift items

THISTLE & CLOVER
407 S. Main St.
St. Charles
636-946-2449
thistleandclover.com
Luck of the Irish (Scottish & Welsh, too) abounds in heraldry gear, tartans, Waterford, clothing, music

METRO EAST

ALTON ★ COLLINSVILLE ★ BELLEVILLE ★ CAHOKIA ★
COLUMBIA ★ EAST ST. LOUIS ★ EDWARDSVILLE ★ ELSAH
★ FAIRMONT CITY ★ FAIRVIEW HEIGHTS ★ GLEN CARBON
★ GODFREY ★ GRAFTON ★ GRANITE CITY ★ HARTFORD ★
MARYVILLE ★ MILLSTADT ★ O'FALLON ★ SAUGET

HISTORY

Mound City is a St. Louis moniker. Mississippian Indians known as "The Mound Builders" built more than 100 mounds at Cahokia, near Collinsville, centuries ago. Archaeological digs reveal a sophisticated society of close to 100,000 people once lived here. Why Mississippian Mound Builders abandoned their city is a mystery. What is clear is that Cahokia Mounds is one of North America's largest archaeological sites, which has been designated a World Heritage Site by the cultural organization UNESCO as well as a National Historic Landmark.

Today, dozens of towns comprise the eastern portion of the metro area. Here is a sampling of the rich modern heritage of this region. **East St. Louis** earned a reputation as a jazz, blues, and rock musical melting pot, with Miles Davis and Ike and Tina Tuner leading the way. Three of Metro East's most prominent towns—**Belleville**, **Collinsville**, and **Edwardsville**—are rich in history and intact historic homes that provide a peek into nineteenth-century life. Belleville was the site of the last of the famed 1858 Lincoln-Douglas debates. Art on the Square in Bellville is perennially ranked a top U.S. art fair. Collinsville produces much of the world's horseradish and is home to the world's largest catsup bottle, a water tower built in 1949 by the now-defunct Brooks Catsup Company. Edwardsville is one of Illinois' oldest cities. Southern Illinois University–Edwardsville, a vibrant downtown, and historic homes have landed Edwardsville on small-town "best places to live" lists.

Running parallel to the mighty Mississippi River from Pere Marquette State Park to the Lewis and Clark State Historic Site is the Meeting of the Rivers Scenic Route and Sam Vadalabene Bike Trail. Along this beautiful byway are river towns that are worth a visit any time of year.

Illinois' first prison was built in **Alton** and saw Civil War duty, housing nearly 12,000 Confederate POWs. Today, Alton greets antique seekers and eagle watchers with equal enthusiasm. Enjoy a river cruise, a fall foliage drive, or from December through February, a bald eagle–watching excursion along the Mississippi's Great River Road.

The quaint village of **Elsah** is home to Principia, a private college listed on the National Register of Historic Places. **Godfrey**'s namesake and founder, Benjamin Godfrey, was rumored to have sailed with pirate Jean Lafitte. Nearby Rocky Fork was once a refuge for runaway slaves who moved on from there via the Underground Railroad. Just upriver, **Grafton** is a town that suffered extensive flood damage in 1993, but today visitors might find that difficult to believe. Grafton has re-emerged as a popular tourist destination for wine tasting, boating, bikers (both motor and non), eagle watching, and autumn foliage drives. **Hartford** is home to the Lewis and Clark State Historic Site. The Meeting of the Rivers Confluence Tower offers a spectacular view of area and the Mississippi River.

Columbia and Waterloo's immigrant heritage is Germanic. The Dreamland Palace just outside of Waterloo is one of the few remaining German eating establishments in the metro area. The Waterloo German Band, led by Harry Wolf, a former music teacher from Belleville, continues to delight fans of oompah music.

On the short list of other Metro East places to check out: Maryville, Maeystown, Millstadt, Wood River, Glen Carbon, and Fairmont City, where the highest point in the village is actually atop an Indian mound. And if the horses are running, those who like to play the ponies will enjoy Fairmount Park.

FOOD AND DRINK

A BITE TO EAT

222 ARTISAN BAKERY
222 N. Main St.
Edwardsville
618-659-1122
222bakery.com
Breads & fancy pastries

ANDRIA'S COUNTRY-SIDE RESTAURANT
7415 State Rt. 143
Edwardsville
618-656-0281
andriascountryside.com
Fine dining (steaks, pastas, seafood) in historic home setting

ANNIE'S FROZEN CUSTARD
245 S. Buchanan St.
Edwardsville
618-656-0289
anniesfrozencustard.com
Edwardsville's homegrown frozen custard stand

BELLA MILANO'S
1063 S. State Rt. 157
Edwardsville
618-659-2100
bellamilanos.com
Italian dishes like eggplant parm, homemade toasted ravioli, pasta three ways for the indecisive

BIGELO'S BISTRO
140 N. Main St.
Edwardsville
618-655-1471
bigelosbistro.com
Casual bistro with a dozen craft brews on tap

BOBBY'S FROZEN CUSTARD
2525 N. Center St.
Maryville
618-345-3002
bobbysfrozencustard.com
Weekly custard special flavor, and frequent live bands on weekends

{ KIDZONE }

Turn up the steps to the second floor of the **Collinsville Library** (408 W. Main St., 618-344-1112, collinsvillelibrary.org) and enter an enchanting children's library (complete with Arthur, the Mouse and his cookie, Alice in Wonderland, and more to lead the way) where kids can sprawl, play, read, paint, giggle, and generally be kids. Entirely separate from the hush-hush crowd, this is a hidden gem for families needing a change of scenery from their living rooms.

If your children give you a blank stare—or worse, say "the store"—when asked where peaches come from, it's time to load those city slickers up and head out to **Eckert's** (618-233-0513, eckerts.com) farms, with locations in Belleville (951 S. Green Mount Rd.), Millstadt (2719 Eckert Orchard Ln.), and Grafton (20995 Eckert Orchard Rd.). Pick-your-own orchards (apples, blackberries, peaches, pumpkins) and cut-your-own Christmas trees provide the kind of family snapshots you thought only existed in *Martha Stewart Living*, and the farms also have an assortment of animal encounters, pig races, slides, wagon rides, funnel cakes, and all the homespun fun you can imagine. Check website for location particulars and the latest ripening schedules.

BULLY'S SMOKEHOUSE
1280 Columbia Ctr.
Columbia
618-281-2880

1035 Century Dr.
Edwardsville
618-659-1802
bullyssmokehouse.com
Award-winning, hickory-smoked BBQ pork, beef, & ribs

CASTELLI'S RESTAURANT AT 255
3400 Fosterburg Rd.
Alton
618-462-4620
castellis255.com
Fried chicken all day long, plus gizzards, t-ravs, and more at this fam-friendly legend

CASTLETOWN GEOGHEGAN
104 W. Main St.
Belleville
618-233-4800
ctgpub.com
Irish pub down to its homemade Guinness brown bread

THE CUP
1057 Century Dr.
Edwardsville
618-656-2287
cravethecup.com
Cute-as-a-cupcake bakery

DON & PENNY'S
306 State St.
Alton
618-465-9823
Your basic bar/pizza/Italian/Creole joint

DUKE BAKERY
819 Henry St.
Alton
618-462-2922

5407-C Godfrey Rd.
Godfrey
618-467-2922

3202 Nameoki Rd.
Granite City
618-877-9500
dukebakeryinc.com
Old-school classics, awesome donuts, and meringue pies

FAZZI'S
1813 Vandalia St.
Collinsville
618-344-5440
fazzis.com
Greek specialties like gyros, saganaki, baklava

FIN INN
1000 W. Main St.
Grafton
618-786-2030
fininn.com
Fish & frog legs on the menu, and on the move in wall-to-wall aquariums

GENTELIN'S ON BROADWAY
122 E. Broadway
Alton
618-465-6080
gentelinsonbroadway.com
Upscale food & decor with New American bent

GRACE MANOR
1801 N. Main St.
Edwardsville
618-655-0650
gracemanorrestaurant.com
Seasonal menus done with simplicity and care, served in cozy historic home

J. FIRE'S BISTRO
725 N. Market St.
Waterloo
618-939-7233
jfires.com
Wood-fired pizzas, Cajun dishes in a historic brick farmhouse

JOSEPHINE'S TEA ROOMS
6109 Godfrey Rd.
Godfrey
618-466-7792
josephinestearooms-andgiftshops.com
Sandwiches, salads, and stuffed tomatoes for the red-hatted

KRUTA BAKERY
300 Saint Louis Rd.
Collinsville
618-344-1115
Stollen, cream puffs, and darling sugar cookies

{ MARKET DAYS }

Saturdays at the courthouse may not sound like much fun, until you realize it's **Land of Goshen Community Market** (618-307-6045, goshenmarket. org) day: 60+ vendors selling everything from farm-fresh produce and jams to fresh-baked treats and handwoven baskets. A "Market Sprouts" program gets little kids involved in the action, and live music fills the air—8 a.m. to noon, next to the Madison County courthouse, which is located at 155 N. Main St., Edwardsville.

LO-CAL CAFE
408 W. Bethalto Dr.
Bethalto
618-377-9500

138 N. Main St.
Edwardsville
618-692-0095
lo-calcafe.net
Healthful, tasty eating
from breakfast bowls
to burgers

MISSISSIPPI HALF-STEP
420 E. Main St.
Grafton
618-786-2722
mississippihalfstep.com
Comfortable riverside
room for tasty lunch,
dinner, and eagle-season
Sunday breakfast

MY JUST DESSERTS
31 E. Broadway
Alton
618-462-5881
myjustdesserts.org
Pie. Lunch if you must,
but pie. Pie above all

NERUDA
4 Club Centre Ct.
Edwardsville
618-659-9866
neruda2dine.com
Eclectic American fare,
elegant room (belies strip-
mall placement)

ORIENTAL SPOON
KOREAN CUISINE
229 Harvard Dr.
Edwardsville
618-655-9633
orientalspoon.net
Authentic Korean faves
like bulgogi, bibimbap,
and kimchi

PEEL
WOOD-FIRED PIZZA
921 S. Arbor Vitae #102
Edwardsville
618-659-8561
peelpizza.com
Crowds flock to this trendy
pizza cafe; great salads
and dessert pizza, too

PIE PANTRY
310 E. Main St. #1
Belleville
618-277-4140
marilynspiepantry.com
Comfort food, and pie

PRINCIVALLI'S CAFE
602 E. Third St.
Alton
618-465-3255
princivallis.com
Apps, pizzas, sandwiches,
& pastas, all with Italian
accents

RAMON'S EL DORADO
1711 Saint Louis Rd.
Collinsville
618-344-6435
Classic Mexican dishes,
plus stellar guac and
'ritas, mariachi music

RAVANELLI'S
3 American Village
Granite City
618-877-8000

26 Collinsport Dr.
Collinsville
618-343-9000

1214 Central Park Dr.
O'Fallon
618-589-3628
ravanellisrestaurants.com
Brick-oven-cooked pastas
& pizzas, plus steaks,
fried chicken

SACRED GROUNDS
233 N. Main St.
Edwardsville
618-692-4150
Vegetarian-friendly
coffeeshop

SEVEN
7 S. High St.
Belleville
618-277-6700
sevenrestaurantand-
lounge.com
Popular downtown spot
for drinks, dinner, and
frequent live music

TONY'S
THIRD ST. CAFE
312 Piasa St.
Alton
618-462-8384
tonysrestaurant.com
Not to be confused with
another famous Italian
Tony, this one's known
for pepperloin steak

SOMETHING TO DRINK

ARDIE & TINY'S
100 Joe St.
Collinsville
618-345-4933
Roadhouse en route to
the racetrack

BIG DADDY'S
313 E. Main St.
Belleville
618-257-0315

132 N. Main St.
618-656-9706
Edwardsville
bigdaddystl.com
Party bar for the party
crowd, surprisingly
good food

CUTTERS
239 Carlyle Ave.
Belleville
618-235-7642
Tons of space and tons
of food

ENCORE WINE BAR
253 N. Main St.
Edwardsville
618-606-3458
Wildey Theatre-
adjacent, great for
post-show libation

ERATO ON MAIN
126 Main St.
Edwardsville
618-307-3203
eratoonmain.com
Boutique wines, specialty
beers from around the
world, locavore food

FAST EDDIE'S BON-AIR
1530 E. 4th St.
Alton
618-462-5532
fasteddiesbonair.com
Coldest beer and meat on
a stick, no minors allowed

FRIDAY'S SOUTH
624 S. Illinois St.
Belleville
618-233-1724
Corner bar; live music and
bar food

Collinsville
618-223-1017
Pizza on Main Street

GLOBAL BREW
112 S. Buchanan St.
618-307-5858
Edwardsville
globalbrewtaps.com
Hundreds of brews from
all over the globe

LAURIE'S PLACE
228 N. Main St.
Edwardsville
618-656-2175
lauriesplacebar.com
Margaritaville-meets-
your-backyard decor,
frequent live music and
hoppin' patio

{ WATERWORLD }

The **Gateway Geyser** (in the Malcolm W.
Martin Memorial Park, 185 W. Trendley
Ave., 618-346-4905, meprd.org), across the
river from the Arch in East St. Louis, has the
fame-claim of being, at an Arch-mirroring
630 feet, the tallest fountain in the United
States (and second in the world only to a
Saudi Arabian behemoth).

The old **Lincoln School** (1210 N. Main St.) in Edwardsville was the city's African-American school from 1912 to 1951, and although today it sits boarded up, eye-popping murals on its exterior are a testament both to its past (with notable alums and historical themes represented) and to its hopeful future, if building owner Mannie Jackson (a star, and now owner, with the Harlem Globetrotters who attended Lincoln) can bring his renovation dreams to fruition.

PIASA WINERY
225 W. Main St.
Grafton
618-786-9463
piasawinery.com
Local producer of Norton, Chardonel, Chambourcin, served on a sizeable riverfront deck

ROPER'S REGAL BEAGLE SPORTS BAR & GRILL
3045 Godfrey Rd.
Godfrey
618-466-2112
ropersregalbeagle.com
Beer (21 taps), TVs, and gameday fun

STAGGER INN AGAIN
104 E. Vandalia St.
Edwardsville
618-656-4221
Cheap beer, live music, and local color

WINE TAP
223 E. Main St.
Belleville
618-239-9463
thewinetapbelleville.com
Copious glass & bottle offerings and light, eclectic bites to savor on the patio

{ MONUMENTAL NOTABLES }

What do abolitionist **Elijah P. Lovejoy** (Alton Cemetery at Monument Avenue, downtown Alton), World's Tallest Man **Robert Wadlow** (2800 block of College Ave., Upper Alton), and Shoshone guide **Sacagawea** (on the campus of Lewis and Clark Community College, Godfrey) have in common? All are immortalized in the Metro East in statuary form, impressive monuments, indeed, to three who left such lasting impressions.

RECREATION

The Illinois towns across the Mississippi are frequently touted as family-friendly, down-home, neighborly places, so it's not surprising to find a gaggle of community amenities, high-quality outdoor diversions, and enough fairs, festivals, and events to fill anyone's calendar.

EXERCISE

ARLINGTON GREENS
200 Arlington Dr.
Granite City
618-931-5232
arlingtongreens.com
18-hole public facility, par 72, and recently renovated

BIG MUDDY ADVENTURES
1164 Moorlands Dr.
St. Louis
314-610-4241
2muddy.com
Guided & outfitted canoe trips, including full-moon and canoe camping excursions, on the Missouri and Mississippi rivers

CENTERFIELD PARK
5620 Old Collinsville Rd.
Fairview Heights
618-624-7074
centerfieldpark.net
Mini-golf, batting cages, & bumper boats

GRAFTON CANOE & KAYAK
12 E. Water St. #2
Grafton
618-786-2192
graftoncanoeandkayak.com
They rent those, plus bikes, pontoon boats, waverunners, and a tipi

THE NATURE INSTITUTE
2213 S. Levis Ln.
Godfrey
618-466-9930
thenatureinstitute.org
Guided bird migration hikes, prairie burns, & kids' camps, all with the aim of environmental education and conservation

RAGING RIVERS WATERPARK
100 Palisades Pky.
Grafton
618-786-2345
ragingrivers.com
Big fun directly overlooking the Mississippi, with wave pools, body flumes, lazy river

{ RUSTIC ON THE RIVER }

A jewel at the northern stretch of the Great River Road, **Pere Marquette State Park** (Route 100, Grafton, 618-786-3323, greatriverroad.com/pere) serves as a worthy destination for a few hours (Sunday brunch in the historic 1930s-era lodge) or a few days (with horse stables, riding/hiking trails, and fishing). The park and its naturalists are a great resource during the overwintering bald eagle season, too, so bring binoculars and make a day of it! Finally, make sure the kids see the giant chess set at the lodge.

SAM VADALABENE BIKE TRAIL
(Piasa Park on Hwy. 100) to Pere
Marquette State Park (at Lodge
Turnout on Hwy. 100)
Alton
Hugging the Great River Road and the
mighty Mississippi for 20 miles

WATERSHED NATURE CENTER
1591 Tower Rd.
Edwardsville
618-692-7578
watershednaturecenter.com
46 acres of trails and wetlands for
hiking, birding and contemplation

SPLASH CITY
10 Gateway Dr.
Collinsville
618-346-4571
splashcity.org
Tons of waterpark features for kids, and a
popular surf/bodyboarding feature

WILD TRAK BIKES
1001 E. Broadway
Alton
618-462-2574
wildtrakbikesracing.com
Rentals & gear for treks up the
Vadalabene trail

1820 COLONEL BENJAMIN STEPHENSON HOUSE
409 S. Buchanan St.
Edwardsville
618-692-1818
stephensonhouse.org
Federal-style brick home devoted to preservation of early history of the Illinois Territory

CHILDREN'S MUSEUM OF EDWARDSVILLE
722 Holyoake Rd.
Edwardsville
618-692-2094
childrens-museum.net
Rambling old house with tons of exhibits & nooks for kids to explore

CIGAR INN JAZZ CLUB
119 W Main St., Suite A
Belleville
618-233-4000
cigarinn.net
Stogies and jazz in loungey atmosphere

KATHERINE DUNHAM CENTERS FOR ARTS AND HUMANITIES
1005 Pennsylvania Ave.
East St. Louis
618-874-8560
kdcah.org
World-renowned dancer's cultural center showcases her work (via costumes, programs, and artifacts from her anthropological studies) and her collections (African and Caribbean folk & contemporary art), by appointment only

FAIRMOUNT PARK
9301 Collinsville Rd.
Collinsville
618-345-4300
fairmountpark.com
Play the ponies (thoroughbred and harness racing)

{DID YOU SEE WHAT PIASA?}

The fearsome **Piasa bird** of lore was a man-eating, winged monster enshrined in tales of the prehistoric Illini people and first recorded in petroglyph form. Explorers Jacques Marquette and Louis Joliet wrote of seeing renderings of the bird in their 1673 travels. Today, the creature takes painted shape along the river bluffs, about a mile up the Great River Road from Alton.

HISTORIC MUSEUM OF TORTURE DEVICES
301 E. Broadway St.
Alton
618-465-3200
Gruesome collection of instruments of torture used throughout human history, not for the faint of heart

JACOBY ARTS CENTER
627 E. Broadway
Alton
618-462-5222
jacobyartscenter.org
Arts & community center hosting juried exhibitions, performances, and classes for adults and kids

LEWIS & CLARK STATE HISTORIC SITE AND CONFLUENCE TOWER
435 Confluence Tower Dr.
Hartford
618-251-9101
Immerse yourself in the departure point for the unprecedented voyage of Lewis & Clark, at their winter camp (now home to many exhibits and a full-scale keelboat model), or 150 feet above the confluence of the great rivers they explored

LINCOLN THEATRE
103 E. Main St.
Belleville
618-233-0123
lincolntheatre-belleville.com
1920s-era vaudeville house now shows first-run movies, with live organ music on weekends, plus stage shows

NATIONAL GREAT RIVERS MUSEUM AND MELVIN PRICE LOCKS & DAM
#1 Lock and Dam Way
East Alton
877-462-6979
Hands-on and interactive, presenting the full story of the Mississippi River, from cultural and historical importance to the logistics of getting all those barges through

POP'S
401 Monsanto Ave.
Sauget
618-274-6720
Well, it rocks. And you can stay all night, if you're so inclined, after an ear-ringing concert or after your other bar closes

SCHMIDT ART CENTER
2500 Carlyle Ave.
Belleville
618-222-5278
schmidtart.swic.edu
Contemporary art gallery and programs on the campus of Southwestern Illinois College

WILDEY THEATRE
252 N. Main St.
Edwardsville
618-307-2053
wildeytheatre.com
Restored Art Deco–style theatre screening classic films and hosting musical performances

WOOD RIVER REFINERY HISTORY MUSEUM
Rte. 111 and Madison St.
Roxana
618-255-3718
wrrhm.org
Esoteric, yes, and run by dedicated volunteers, so expect to be regaled with all manner of trivia on petroleum refining, Shell stations, historic vehicles, and, as the website promises, "who knows what all"

{ KIDZONE }

As the region's agricultural heritage rapidly morphs (or disappears), establishments like Collinsville's **Willoughby Farm** (631 Willoughby Ln., 618-346-7529 ext. 128, collinsvillerec.com) help keep the past alive for future generations, as well as teach timeless lessons in stewardship and natural history. Bring the family out to hike up to the lookout tower, wander the grape arbor and flower/vegetable gardens, meet the farm animals, and more.

{ FERRY TALES DO COME TRUE }

Any mode of transport besides the mundane automobile makes travel more exciting, and a trip across the river on the **Grafton Ferry** (7597 N. Highway 94, 636-899-0600) is no exception. Load your car or bike up on either side, and for $15 round-trip (cars), you'll be deposited across Big Muddy about 10 minutes later. Seasonal hours, and calling ahead is not a bad idea (many river conditions can make passage impossible).

ART ON THE SQUARE
May
Belleville
618-416-3390
artonthesquare.com
Charming and internationally lauded
fine arts festival along fountain-centered
Main Street

GREAT RIVERS TOWBOAT FESTIVAL
June
Grafton
(Historic Boat Works on Front St.)
618-786-3494
greatriverroad.com
Demystify those ubiquitous boats
plying the rivers by taking a tour and
participating in a deckhand contest, or
just kick back and enjoy the bands.
Event held only as river levels permit

THE INTERNATIONAL
HORSERADISH FESTIVAL
First weekend in June
Woodland Park
Collinsville
618-344-2884
horseradishfestival.com
Celebrates all things horseradishy,

including a Bloody Mary contest,
root toss, and food vendors

ITALIANFEST
Third weekend in September
Collinsville
618-344-2884
italianfest.net
Bocce tournament, wine garden, parade,
and grape stomp

ROUTE 66 FESTIVAL
June
Edwardsville City Park
Edwardsville
cityofedwardsville.com
Embrace the Mother Road via classic
car cruises, classic rock bands, and
historical displays

WORLD'S LARGEST
CATSUP BOTTLE FESTIVAL
July
Collinsville
catsupbottlefestival.com
Music, games, classic car cruise,
catsup taste-offs, and the crowning
of Sir Catsup and Little Princess Tomato

{ MOUND CITY }

Only the nickname is left for the St. Louis side of things, but in Collinsville, **Cahokia Mounds** (30 Ramey St., 618-346-5160, cahokiamounds.org) offers the real deal: more than 70 prehistoric earthen mounds, built and painstakingly maintained by native peoples in a settlement that was, in its time, the largest Indian site north of Mexico. Its legacy is only recently getting burnished in local minds, but the rest of the world is far ahead of us: UNESCO named it a "World Heritage Site," in company with other spots like the Taj Mahal, the Great Wall of China, and the palace of Versailles. The interpretive center's walk-through replica settlement is a great place to start your exploration.

SHOPPORTUNITIES

HOME/GARDEN/BODY/GIFTS

BEYOND TIMBUKTU
224 N. Main St.
Edwardsville
618-692-9290
beyondtimbuktu.com
Unique and handmade global goods,
including clothes, textiles, artwork,
masks, and toys

CIRCA BOUTIQUE
128 E. Main St.
Belleville
618-257-0163
ilovecirca.com
Well-edited selection of handmade
boutique lines of apparel & accessories;
look for the owner's Mellow Mountain
goods, too

THE FLOWER BASKET
317 W. Main St.
Collinsville
618-344-1117
flowerbasketcoll.com
Gracious historic home displays decor,
candles, garden goodies

JOLLY ROGER SKATEBOARDS
305 N. Illinois St.
Belleville
618-277-7113
jollyrogerskateboards.com
Skater-owned wheel shop

THE LITTLE SHOPPE OF AURAS
875 Haller St.
Wood River
618-251-9646
littleshoppeofauras.com
Native American music, instruments,
metaphysical ritual items, plus massage,
chakra cleansing, & more

{ KIDZONE }

At **K-10s Model Trains** (19 Schiber
Ct., Maryville, 618-288-9720,
k-10smodeltrains.com), kids can
ogle the locomotives, slot cars, kites,
and more for sale in the hobby shop,
but what'll really get their horns
blowing is the chance to operate the
model trains in nearly 5,000 square
feet of track layout, or watch the
remote-control car races out back
on the banked dirt track, or launch a
kit-built rocket. Times of events vary;
see website for schedules.

{ ALTON ANTIQUES }

Throughout Alton's streets is a great collection of antique shops, from the **Alton Antique Center** (401 E. Broadway, Lower Level, 618-463-0888) to stops all along Broadway, selling everything from eighteenth-century European furniture to outsider and folk artwork.

LOST ARTS & ANTIQUES
254 N. Main St.
Edwardsville
618-656-8844
lostartsandantiques.com
Refurbed finds, local fine arts & crafts

MILO'S TOBACCO ROAD/
MILO'S CIGARS & MORE
228A N. Main St.
Edwardsville
618-692-1343

2921 N. Center St.
Maryville
618-288-1343
milostr.com
Cigars, spirits, and beer

MOCKINGBIRD BOUTIQUE
100 W. 3rd St.
Alton
618-462-6772
Contemporary women's clothing
& accessories

ONCE UPON A TOY
2460 Troy Rd.
Edwardsville
618-656-9596
happyupinc.com
Independent shop for kids' toys,
games, & dolls

SOLE SURVIVOR
25 E. Main St.
Belleville
618-234-0214
solesurvivorleather.com
Leather shoes, bags, and custom-
tooled belts

WHAT TO WEAR
921 S. Arbor Vitae
Edwardsville
618-655-0222
whattowearboutique.com
Of-the-moment looks for guys and gals,
from denim to dressy

....

{ SACRED SPACE }

The **Shrine of Our Lady of the Snows** (442 S. De Mazenod Dr., 618-397-6700, snows.org), in Belleville, is a Catholic complex you could spend a weekend exploring, from the large gift shop and popular restaurant (with eight soups on the lunch buffet!) to an outdoor ampitheatre, spiritual-themed kids' playground, and events like the Christmas Way of Lights. Of course, its main purpose is worship, prayer, and spiritual edification.

ARTSY

**BEAD IT & MAIN STREET
ART GALLERY**
237/239 Main St.
Edwardsville
618-655-9999
beadit-art.com
Beading supplies for you,
ready-made wearable pieces,
and fine art in the gallery

BY DESIGN
136 Front St.
Alton
618-433-1400
lillianbydesign.com
Custom and handmade clothing,
accessories by local designers

COMMUNITY CONCRETE STATUARY
300 Shamrock St.
East Alton
618-259-8270
communityconcretestatuary.com
Thousands of made-on-site choices in
the concrete garden statuary genre

KNIT ONE WEAVE TOO
303 N. Main St.
Edwardsville
618-692-6950
k1w2.com
Yarn and knitting/weaving accessories

MISSISSIPPI MUD POTTERY
310 E. Broadway
Alton
618-462-7573
mississippimudpottery.biz
Substantial and chic tableware,
vases, & more

MOJO'S MUSIC
142 N. Main St.
Edwardsville
618-655-1600
mojosmusic.com
Guitars & amps for all levels

PATCHWORK PLUS
62 Ferguson Ave.
Wood River
618-251-9788
patchworkplus.net
Quilting supplies & classes

THE QUILTED GARDEN
1310 N. Main St.
Edwardsville
618-656-6538
quiltedgarden.com
Fabric, frames, notions, and
classes for quilters

SWING CITY MUSIC
1312 Vandalia
Collinsville
618-345-6700

244 S. Buchanan
Edwardsville
618-656-5656
swingcitymusic.com
Instruments, including band rentals,
lessons, & sheet music

COMESTIBLES

CHEF'S SHOPPE
2212 Troy Rd.
Edwardsville
618-659-9840
chefsshoppe.com
Fine cookware, knives, gadgets,
and a host of gourmet mixes, spices,
and ingredients

COLLINSVILLE FARMERS MARKET
128 Saint Louis Rd.
618-344-0222

1303 Vandalia St.
618-344-0223
Fresh local produce, seeds, plants,
dressings/spice mixes at two locations

CRUSHED GRAPES
1500 Troy Rd.
Edwardsville
618-659-3530
crushedgrapesltd.com
Wine, beer, coffee, and cheese
from all over

**DAVE'S HOMEBREW &
GOURMET TOO**
122 E. Main St.
Belleville
618-277-2550
daveshomebrewgourmet.com
Beer and wine-making supplies,
plus nonstop friendly advice and an
assortment of natural home and body
goods

GREEN EARTH GROCERY
441 S. Buchanan St.
Edwardsville
618-656-3375
greenearthgrocer.com
Health food/supplement store and deli

SPIRITO'S ITALIAN GROCERY
228 W. Main St.
Collinsville
618-344-3256
Olives and sauces, oils and cheese, for
your own cucina (takeaway sandwiches
are a hit, too)

TOWNSHIP GROCER
102 N. Main St.
Edwardsville
618-656-0414
townshipgrocer.com
Gourmet market for cheese, beer, wine,
and local meat & eggs

BOOKS/TUNES

AFTERWORDS BOOKS
231 N. Main St.
Edwardsville
618-655-0355
afterwordsbookstore.com
Used books and enthusiastic
reading recommendations

HOMETOWN COMICS
110 E. Vandalia St.
Edwardsville
618-655-0707
hometowncomics.com
Comics, graphic novels,
manga, and action figures

{ PICKIN' AND PAYIN' }

Packrats and treasure hunters, put the fourth weekend of each month from
April-October on your calendars, when the massive **Grafton Riverside Flea
Market** (next to the Loading Dock Bar and Grill, 400 Front St., 618-786-8210)
takes over the Boatworks building with antiques, crafts, food, and such.

OUTSTATE

A HANDFUL OF OUR FAVORITE DIVERSIONS
WITHIN A FEW HOURS' DRIVE OF ST. LOUIS

Although the density of urban and near-urban neighborhoods makes them rich in interesting bars, restaurants, shopping, museums, and other amenities, there are a plethora of getaways within just two or three hours' drive of St. Louis that add great character to our region and make for a drive-worthy daytrip when you need a change of scenery. Small river towns, world-class wine-producing districts, natural wonders, and more are within easy reach.

DAYTRIP DESTINATIONS

CLARKSVILLE

Home to a cornucopia of craftspeople and artisans, with shops lining Main Street in media from woodworking to weaving, this Mississippi River town also boasts spectacular winter eagle watching and an award-winning inn/farm-to-table restaurant, Overlook Farm. Approximately 75 miles northwest of St. Louis. *clarksvillemo.us*

KIMMSWICK

This compact riverside town on the Mississippi is home to all manner of shopping (think collectibles like Boyds Bears, Precious Moments, Madame Alexander; hand-made gifty items like soy candles, personalized dough ornaments, table lace; and antiques galore). Highlights include Mississippi Mud Gallery for pottery and glass art, and breakfast/lunch/most definitely dessert at The Blue Owl. Approximately 20 miles south of St. Louis. *gokimmswick.com*

NEW HAVEN

On the Missouri River and along the train tracks, you'll find one modest block of bustle, but what a block it is! Several charming B&Bs overlook the downtown, the river, and its levee-top walking trail, while the single-screen Walt Theatre offers weekend shows of first-run flicks. The nonprofit Riverfront Cultural Society brings in area bands for hoppin' live shows, in addition to hosting music and cultural events, yoga classes, and a weekly farmer's market in season. And at Astral Glass Studio the whole family can watch glass creations being born. Approximately 50 miles west of St. Louis. *newhavenmo.com*

WASHINGTON

Take the westbound Amtrak from St. Louis, and you'll find plenty within walking distance of the Washington station. Charming shops, several dining options (including the renowned American Bounty Restaurant and Cowan's for mile-high pies), and the must-see Corncob Pipe Museum. Artist Gary Lucy has a studio here, and the town's newest attraction is the Missouri Photojournalism Hall of Fame. Plenty of charming, small-town annual events, including a massive Town & Country fair held the first week of August. Approximately 50 miles west of St. Louis. *washmo.org*

AUGUSTA

The closest concentration of wineries to St. Louis makes for a full day of tasting, and that's if you keep up a decent pace. The list includes Chandler Hill Vineyards, Yellow Farmhouse Winery, Sugar Creek Winery, Montelle Winery, Mount Pleasant Estates, Augusta Winery, Louis P. Balducci Vineyards, Noboleis Vineyards & Winery, and Blumenhof Vineyards & Winery. If you can only make one, we recommend Montelle: stunning, shady patio, cozy indoor fireplace for the cooler months, free weekend entertainment, yummy food...and of course, excellent wines. Of interest to beer drinkers, the nearby Augusta Brewing Company produces a full slate of craft beers (and their own root beer!). Approximately 45 miles west of St. Louis, off Highway 94. *augusta-missouri.com*

HERMANN

The earliest German settlers of this town high above the Missouri River chose the spot, it's said, because the vistas reminded them so much of their home regions. Picturesque and friendly, the area is home to Bias Winery, Bommarito Estate Almond Tree Winery, Hermannhof Winery, OakGlenn Winery, Adam Puchta Winery, Röbller Winery, and Stone Hill Winery. Special events fill the calendar, year-round; some of our favorites avoid the high season entirely and instead give you something special to look forward to in February (Chocolate Wine Trail) or July (Berries & BBQ Wine Trail). Tin Mill Brewing Company turns out fantastic microbrews in a historic (you guessed it!) tin mill, using imported German hops, barley, and copper brewing kettles. Approximately 75 miles west of St. Louis, off Highway 100. *visithermann.com*

STE. GENEVIEVE

Winding roads through some of the earliest settled areas of the state provide charming views along the way to Cave Vineyard, Charleville Vineyard & Microbrewery, Chaumette Vineyards & Winery, Crown Valley, Sainte Genevieve Winery, Sand Creek Vineyard, and Twin Oaks & Winery. Plenty of variety here in terms of setting and wine styles. We especially love Chaumette (for its patio atop a rolling hill, farm-gourmet Grapevine Grill and luxe overnight accommodations at the villa/spa complex); the sprawling Crown Valley empire, with a winery, brewery/distillery, champagne house, numerous lodging options, and, oddly, a tiger-rescue sanctuary with tours and educational programs; and the stroll down to Saltpeter Cave from Cave Vineyard. Approximately 50 miles south of St. Louis, off Interstate 55. *ste-genevieve.com*

BLACK MADONNA SHRINE

Franciscan missionary Bronislaus Luszcz, a 1927 Polish immigrant to Missouri, venerated Mary and undertook to create representations and shrines to her in his adopted country that would echo the many homages found in his homeland. Over decades, he painstakingly hand-crafted seven devotional grottos from Missouri tiff rock, which are now scattered throughout the shrine site. Various adornments, including costume jewelry, seashells, and decorative rocks, were brought or sent to Brother Bronislaus, and he incorporated them into his scenes. Approximately 35 miles west of St. Louis. *franciscancaring.org/blackmadonnashri.html*

DANIEL BOONE HOME & BOONESFIELD VILLAGE

Homestead of the legendary Kentucky frontiersman (and much of his family) from 1803 until his death in 1820, this living history museum makes the Louisiana Purchase/early Missouri statehood period come alive with restored, furnished structures including a chapel, school house, general store, and gristmill. Frequent special events. Approximately 35 miles west of St. Louis. *lindenwood.edu/boone*

ECO ZIPLINE TOURS

Ever wanted to fly through the forest's canopy like a spider monkey (or Diego, Animal Rescuer)? Here's your chance: Two courses (one for noncommittal and faint-of-heart, the other for the hardcore) cover more than a mile of cables strung high above the ground of New Florence. Minimal walking in-between stop platforms means folks of many ages and abilities can zip together (kids as young as three can join in). Check the website for pictures of people zipping around mid-Missouri's trees if you're having a hard time envisioning yourself playing treetop adventurer! Approximately 80 miles northwest of St. Louis. *ecoziplinetours.com*

MERAMEC CAVERNS

If you went there as a kid, you may find the cheese factor has been toned down a bit in recent years, and the five-story cavern is still a spectacular sight. Guided tours run about 80 minutes long, so consider that if you have small children, you may end up carrying or distracting them if patience wanes. Explore the rest of the offerings, too, from a Meramec River cruise on a canopy-covered riverboat to the newest attraction, the Caveman Zip Line, which offers a 90-minute forest canopy tour, for ages 10 and up/between 80-270 pounds. Approximately 60 miles west of St. Louis, off Highway 44. *americascave.com*

PURINA FARMS

Your kids will be in hog (and cat and dog and goat) heaven, with free-range access to all kinds of charismatic animals (the dog agility shows are a hoot), plus a barn and hayloft play area. Grab lunch from the snack bar and, by all means, check out the gift shop if you have a true animal lover on your list. Approximately 38 miles west of St. Louis. *purina.com/purina-farms/purinafarms.aspx*

OUTDOOR ADVENTURES

ELEPHANT ROCKS/JOHNSON'S SHUT-INS

Frolic among enormous, red, 1.5-billion-year-old granite boulders, and then head 15 miles down the road to frolic in "nature's waterpark," the river-smoothed gorges and chutes carved over millenia into the hard igneous rock. These two parks provide photo opportunities like no other in the state and are bound to impress even the most jaded digital-age kid. Approximately 100 miles southwest of St. Louis.

mostateparks.com/park/elephant-rocks-state-park
mostateparks.com/park/johnsons-shut-ins-state-park

HAWN STATE PARK

Perhaps the most frequently mentioned state park by St. Louisans looking to get out of town and back to nature. Outstanding hiking trails lead to canyon-rimmed valleys, and through forests, along streams, and among striking indigenous rock formations. Birders delight in the multitude of species found and heard here, and pretty Pickle Creek is a favorite for exploration, providing cool respite on hot days. Approximately 65 miles south of St. Louis. *mostateparks.com/park/hawn-state-park*

KATY TRAIL

Named "Best Bike Trail in the Midwest" by AAA (and often designated as such by its more than 300,000 annual visitors), the rails-to-trails project, longest in the country at 240 miles (and also among the longest state parks), mostly hugs the Missouri River as it traverses landscapes from forests to farm pastures. Naturally, that means all kinds of options for cyclists and hikers. For proximity and pretty river views, we recommend the 10-mile stretch between Weldon Spring and Greens Bottom trailheads. And you'll do no better for exhaustive trip planning than the resources at *bikekatytrail.com*.

MASTODON STATE HISTORIC SITE

You've perhaps seen the sign from the highway as you hurtle past on southbound adventures, but if you haven't stopped, you're missing something nearly mammoth: remains of the American mastodon (dubbed "the Missouri Leviathan" by its earliest excavators in the 1830s), found in the hugely significant, Pleistocene-era Kimmswick bone bed of fossils. Check out the ice age in Missouri, and marvel at the human/mastodon coexistence that happened here, briefly, more than 10,000 years ago. Hiking trails and wildflowers are popular draws, too. Approximately 20 miles south of St. Louis. *mostateparks.com/park/mastodon-state-historic-site*

MERAMEC STATE PARK

It's an action-packed paean to the glory of the Meramec River, with floating, canoeing, fishing (in one of the state's most fish-packed spots), hiking, and more. Get your feet wet, literally, on a spelunking adventure into Fisher Cave, or ogle the massive aquariums inside the visitor's center. Facilities include dining lodge. Approximately 65 miles southwest of St. Louis. *mostateparks.com/park/meramec-state-park*

SHAW NATURE RESERVE

The far-flung conservation laboratory owned by the Missouri Botanical Garden offers more than 14 miles of scenic hiking trails overlooking the Meramec River, plus diverse acreage that's home to everything from a conifer forest to a boardwalk-traversed wetland. Approximately 35 miles southwest of St. Louis. *shawnature.org*

RIVER FLOATS

The tradition of floating (canoeing for the athletic, rafting for the adventurous, and innertubing for the true lazy river rat) is a time-honored and tradition-imbued one in Missourah. Some folks have been floating in the same spots, with the same gear/stupid jokes/canned beer they've been enjoying for decades...but don't let that intimidate you if you're a novice. Outfitters along some amazingly beautiful streams and rivers can rent or sell you everything you need, and then they'll throw you on a school bus, haul you, your gear, and your cooler upstream, and drop you in! Bear in mind, these are large areas that draw the mass of humanity, so it's entirely possible you'll see nudity, drunken behavior, or other offensive acts, though avoiding the summer holiday weekends can cut your risk. [Side note: If you want to engage in said offensive behaviors, holiday weekends are your time to shine!] On our short list of sweet spots: **Akers Ferry** (573-858-3224, currentrivercanoe.com, Current & Jacks Fork rivers); **Bass Resort** (573-786-8517, bassresort, Courtois, Huzzah, & Meramec rivers); **Twin Rivers Canoe Rentals** (314-226-7369, floateureka.com, Meramec River, and the closest float to St. Louis); **Forest 44 Canoe Rental** (314-255-7091, forest44canoerental, Meramec River); **Cherokee Landing** (573-358-2805, cherokeelanding.com, Big River); Bearcat Getaway (573-637-2264, bearcatgetaway.com, Black River).